S

SKY TRAIN

TIBETAN WOMEN ON THE EDGE OF HISTORY

CANYON SAM

Foreword by His Holiness the 14th Dalai Lama

UNIVERSITY OF WASHINGTON PRESS

Seattle and London

Published simultaneously in the United States by the University of Washington Press and in Southeast Asia by Silkworm Books.

University of Washington Press
P.O. Box 50096, Seattle, WA 98145 U.S.A.
www.washington.edu/uwpress

Library of Congress Cataloging-in-Publication Data

Sam, Canyon.
Sky train : Tibetan women on the edge of history / Canyon Sam.
p. cm.
Includes bibliographical references.
ISBN 978-0-295-98953-2 (pbk. : alk. paper)
1. Women, Tibetan--China--Tibet. 2. Women's rights--China--Tibet. 3. Railroads--China--Tibet. I. Title.

HQ1769.T55S35 2009

305.420951'5--dc22   2009018555

A people are never defeated
until the hearts of its women
are on the ground.
—Pablo Neruda

It is harder to kill something
that is spiritually
alive
than it is to bring the dead
back to life.
—Hermann Hesse

CONTENTS

FOREWORD

THE DALAI LAMA

THE LAST SIX decades have been one of the most difficult periods Tibetans have ever had to face. We lost our freedom and so much else we hold dear in the face of both direct attacks and stealthier undermining of our very identity. At the present time, what we crucially need to do is hold fast to our language, culture, and values, the essence of our traditions. Women have made an important contribution to this effort in the past, and I hope they will continue to do so now and in the future.

This book recounts Tibet's recent past through the lives of four Tibetan women. Their stories recall our society up to the middle of the twentieth century, when life may have been hard but we were largely content. They describe the experiences of those who lived through the nightmare of the imposition of Chinese rule, with the death, imprisonment, and destruction it brought, and narrate the struggles of those who have created new lives in foreign lands, preserving the values they treasure.

The author also paints a striking picture of Tibet as it has absorbed the impact of the new railway line from Beijing—sometimes referred to as the Sky Train—an event fraught with drawbacks as well as potential benefits. Ms. Sam first spent time in Tibet in 1986, when it first opened to foreign visitors. She returned there in early 2007, seven months after the train began operation. In light of the widespread protests across Tibet this past spring, her critical and compassionate observations offer a much needed, first-hand account of the circumstances that gave rise to the unrest.

In paying tribute to the courage and resilience of Tibetan women and observing conditions in Lhasa, this book also acts as a valuable inspiration to others, neither to give up nor to give in to destructive emotions like anger and hatred.

I first met the author, who is a Chinese American herself, in 1986, after she had traveled through Tibet, and I am touched to see how she has sustained interest in and friendship for our country over the intervening years. I take this as a harbinger of greater mutual understanding and sympathy between the Tibetan and Chinese people in years to come.

I have no doubt that many readers will be moved by these powerful tales.

February 5, 2009

PREFACE

THIS BOOK GREW out of an oral history project I began in 1990. In 1986, I had visited China for the first time. As a third-generation Chinese American, born and raised in San Francisco, it had been one of my goals since youth to spend significant time in China. This was my first trip to Asia, and I planned to stay for at least a year. Instead, through a series of meetings and circumstances, my year turned to revolve around Tibet, and when I came back to the States, I became actively engaged in support of the cause of Tibetan independence. Three years later, I returned to Dharamsala, the Tibetan capital-in-exile in northern India, where I had lived during my first trip, after deciding to leave China for India after five months. It was on this second visit to Dharamsala, in spring 1990, that I began gathering the oral histories of Tibetan women. I spent the next several years fund-raising and conducting, transcribing, editing, and writing the interviews.

After many years of work on the project, I began to worry that the information was getting stale. In the process of revising different versions, I'd whittled down the thirty-six interviews to the best sixteen, then twelve, then nine. Finally, I chose the oral histories of just four older women whose powerful and moving stories addressed the period spanning pre-1950 Tibet to the present day.

A friend gave me the idea of going back to Asia and reinterviewing the women to bring their stories up to date. I returned to Tibet in the spring of 2007 at Losar, or New Year, at a critical juncture in time—a few months after the opening of the controversial railway connecting China and Tibet. The local inhabitants were still reeling from the changes wrought by the train and from the colossal transformations of the previous dozen years—a massive influx of non-Tibetans, vast construction that completely changed the face of the city, new policies pushing Tibetans out of their homes and livelihoods, and still, as ever, severe suppression of dissent. In this book, I describe these conditions from my own perspective and from the point of view of people there. A year after my visit, in March 2008, widespread protests broke out across all of ethnic Tibet against Chinese rule—a total of ninety-six different incidents involving thirty thousand Tibetans, the largest protests since the 1960s. Hundreds of Tibetans were killed and thousands detained. *Sky Train* offers some perspective on the conditions that led to these dramatic public protests.

Throughout the book, some identifying details have been changed to protect individuals in Tibet from possible political persecution. For this reason, certain events are presented vaguely or place-names are omitted. Photographs of certain people are not included, even though their stories are central to the book.

I often use the word "Chinese" in reference to the Chinese leaders or leadership and not the citizens of the People's Republic of China. When "Chinese" does refer to the people of China, this is clear from the context. I do not want to contribute to racial prejudice against the Chinese as an ethnic group, although I know this has been a temptation in the Tibetan and Tibet-support communities, as well as generally in the West. The Chinese people are not able to elect their leaders, or to depose or impeach them. Nor do they have access to wide-ranging, uncensored information about political situations, especially information their government perceives as critical of or threatening to its rule.

As a student of Buddhism, I often asked the women I interviewed how Buddhism or spiritual faith had helped them through brutal historical circumstances. In some cases, their sense of acceptance and view of karma perhaps influenced them to offer a positive interpretation of events in their lives. Mrs. Namseling, for example, enjoying a dharma practice in exile that she had never had in Lhasa, portrayed her former life as a government official's wife as rather frivolous and her current modest lifestyle as freer. This is in no way meant to diminish the tragedy of the Chinese takeover. Indeed, Mrs. Namseling says her one unfulfilled wish, remaining from three fervently held prayers in the decade she was imprisoned, is that her country regain its freedom.

I send forth this book with prayers that it bring understanding, peace, and perhaps inspiration to others to offer courageous support to Tibetans and to other indigenous peoples, for our own sake as well as theirs.

Canyon Sam
San Francisco, Losar, February 27, 2009

Annual march in commemoration of Tibetan Women's Uprising Day, March 12, 1959,
when Tibetan women in Lhasa rose up to protest the occupation of their country
by China. 1994, Dharamsala, India

SKY TRAIN

INTRODUCTION

CHINA INVADED TIBET in 1950, attacking Kham, its northeastern province, by surprise from eight directions. Eventually, in spring 1959, China launched a full-scale military invasion of the holy city of Lhasa, the seat of the national government. The stories presented in *Sky Train* start during this period, when forty thousand People's Liberation Army (PLA) troops marched into Lhasa and bombed and shelled the city in what Mao had ordered as a decisive and violent invasion. The Dalai Lama, Tibet's national government, and thousands of Tibetans escaped into neighboring India. In the crackdown that followed, forty thousand Tibetans were detained, seven thousand fled, and, by the Chinese government's own admission, eighty-seven thousand Tibetans were "eliminated."

In the next seventeen years, more than eighty thousand Tibetans left the country, over six thousand monasteries were destroyed, hundreds of thousands died as a result of Chinese policies, and 1,500 years of the history and culture of Tibetan Buddhist civilization were largely destroyed.

What is not often realized about March 1959, and certainly not emphasized or studied, is that Lhasa at the time was predominantly a city of women. Large numbers of men had left the capital to join the resistance movement in the countryside. Others had been expelled in a series of purges that had begun the previous April to ensure that the Chinese military would not meet the opposition it had encountered in eastern Tibet. Throughout the mid- to late 1950s, the Chinese met fierce resistance in Kham and in Amdo, Tibet's eastern province, in the form of guerrilla attacks and pitched battles. In March 1959, the majority female population of Lhasa, about twenty thousand people, swelled with an additional five thousand Khampas and Amdowas, refugees who arrived that winter fleeing the slaughter in eastern Tibet carried out by PLA troops bent on beating a clear, unobstructed path to Lhasa.

On March 10, a spontaneous revolt started around the Norbulingka Palace, where the Dalai Lama resided. The local people had heard that the Chinese military were plotting to capture Tibet's spiritual and temporal leader, the heart of their government and society. They rushed to his palace, terrified, outraged, and prepared to act to save him. The crackdown that followed became known as National Uprising Day.

Before 1950, Tibet was a monastic-dominated society, with a quarter of the population being monks and nuns. In earlier centuries, some 1,300 years ago, Tibet had been an aggressive, fearsome civilization whose empire extended as far east as present-day Xi'an, then China's capital. But as Buddhism flowered, starting in the seventh century, Tibet demilitarized, and in the early 1800s it began adopting an isolationist policy.

Tibetan monasteries were both wealthy and powerful, especially the three large Lhasa-based monasteries. These institutions owned large tracts of land and huge accumulations of money and grain, which they had gathered over centuries through offerings from the community. The government and the aristocracy were the other powerful forces in the society. The life of Mrs. Namseling, the first woman portrayed in this book, gives a glimpse of what members of the former group experienced—both in the influence her husband wielded to gain her hand in marriage and in her lifestyle as a high government official's wife. Their country estate, for example, actually appears on maps of Tibet.

Tibet had been a preindustrial society without roads, the use of the wheel, electricity, or telephones. Most Tibetans lived as nomadic herders or pastoralists. Women worked in the fields, out on the range, in small trading, and of course in the home. Men handled the long-distance trading that required lengthy travel. Some Tibetans practiced polyandry and polygamy. A man would marry into a wealthy family that had no sons and marry all the sisters, making him the sole inheritor of the family business and property holdings. Sometimes two or three brothers would marry one woman, which also had the effect of keeping the family's property holdings intact and the number of progeny low.

Mrs. Paljorkhyimsar and her sister, born into a tenant farmer's family, were chosen as wives by Mr. Paljorkhyimsar, a wealthy landowner. Since the Tibetan class structure was extremely rigid, people could change their standing only through marriage. Mrs. Paljorkhyimsar's fortunes improved considerably with her marriage into the landowning class. However, when the Communists came, this put her in the category of people targeted for persecution.

The 1960s and 1970s brought tremendous suffering to the Tibetans during which many were imprisoned, "disappeared," humiliated and beaten in *thamzig* (or "struggle sessions," featuring violent political denunciations), put into slave labor and concentration camps, and starved. In a campaign the Chinese government called the Big Destruction, nearly all of Tibet's temples and monasteries were demolished. Holy statues and books were desecrated, and monks and nuns killed. Valuable religious objects were looted, and Buddhism was outlawed. Subjected to harrowing campaigns like the Great Leap Forward (1958–62), an attempt to collectivize farms and enter the industrial age "overnight," and a few years later the Cultural Revolution, in which hordes of doctrine-crazed Red Guards rampaged, burned, and destroyed everything Tibetan, or, by their definition, reactionary, Tibetans lost hundreds of thousands of their people and suffered for long bitter years. The labor camps, modeled on Soviet gulags, were where Mrs. Paljorkhyimsar spent many years during these decades.

Most of the literature in Tibet had been religious. Since the written word was considered sacred, few nonreligious books existed. Also, there was no tradition of public education, so few people were literate except monks, wealthy merchants, and government officials. Mrs. Taring, born to an aristocratic family, attended school in India as a young girl, where the medium of instruction was English. Hence she became the first Tibetan woman to speak and write English. At the time of the invasion, Tibet had no Chinese residents except for a few traders and butchers and only six Westerners (although China claimed it was invading Tibet to throw off the imperialist yoke). Because Mrs. Taring spoke English, she socialized with these few Westerners. Moreover, when the Chinese government invited the Dalai Lama to China in the 1950s—three separate trips, each several months to a year in length—Mrs. Taring was part of his entourage. Her ease in moving between different societies served her well later in life when the Tibetan government called her into service to develop the Tibetan Homes Foundation. She became, in her own words, a kind of bridge.

Those who managed to flee Tibet for India arrived exhausted, traumatized, bewildered, and dispossessed of all they had owned. They were forced to accommodate to a new culture, climate, and language. Living at lower altitudes, they were exposed to unfamiliar illnesses. Age-old practices, like drinking from rivers and drying fresh meat in the open air, caused them to succumb in droves to illnesses caused by bacteria that did not exist at high altitude. The Indian government put many into work crews, mostly building roads by hand in remote locations. The tracts of land they were given to farm were nearly impossible to cultivate. Anyone over the age of eight worked on the crews, leaving younger children without care all day. This experience inspired the establishment of the Homes Foundation, the basis of Mrs. Taring's work in India.

In the 1950s, Chinese authorities sent Tibetan children to China for education and political indoctrination. Sonam Choedron grew up in Lhasa in this era but managed to hide and avoid going to China. In Lhasa, she was taught Chinese and learned to speak it fluently. She was recruited into a Chinese-formed Tibetan Opera group and blossomed into a young opera star. Her experience of performing in public laid the foundation for her eloquence and fearlessness in speaking to Chinese authorities, which she was able to do in their own language.

Mao's death in 1979 and the relaxation of policies in 1984—due to the reforms of Hu Yaobang, then Chinese Communist Party (CCP) general secretary—brought a period of liberalization to Tibet. The government supported the rebuilding of monasteries, people were allowed to engage in limited Buddhist practice, which had been forbidden for thirty years, and the region opened to tourism for the first time since the takeover in 1950. When I first visited Tibet in 1986, people fingered their prayer beads and walked around temples doing circumambulations. A couple of the monasteries were being rebuilt. This brief respite lasted only a few years.

Demonstrations in 1987–89, sparked by the renewed hope for independence that Tibetans saw in the reception of the Dalai Lama in the West—his address to the U.S. Congress in 1987, for instance, and his Nobel Peace Prize in 1989—were brutally repressed by the Chinese Communist Party in the Strike Hard campaign. More than two hundred protests took place between 1987 and 1996, most of them involving only a dozen to two dozen people. Sonam Choedron became politically active in this era. When I met her in Dharamsala in 1994, she had spent two years in prison for her underground pro-independence work.

In the 1990s, China's economic engine began to warm up, the prelude to its current turbo-driven state. In 1994, at the Third Tibet Work Forum, Chinese authorities charted a new course for Tibet, accelerating modernization and economic development, and outlining sixty-two infrastructure construction projects. Due to its former isolationist policy and its embrace of the Buddhist belief in the transient nature of reality, Tibetan society had never emphasized material development. China's plans included two key components: drawing millions of non-Tibetans into Tibet as laborers for the construction projects, thereby also populating Tibet with loyalists, and identifying Tibetan nationalists, in order to eliminate those who, it was felt, might cause instability. A critical project for facilitating these goals was the construction of a railway system linking Beijing with Tibet, which began in 1999.

In the mid-1970s, China sent geological expeditions to Tibet in search of mineral, oil, and geothermal wealth. They found coal, copper, iron, chromium, lithium, tungsten, gold, silver, oil, and more—amounting to nearly half of China's mineral reserves at the time. But owing to the difficulty of shipment, this wealth went largely untapped, and the CCP leadership became aware that exploitation of the great resources of the so-called Western Treasure House eluded them for lack of a more efficient method of transportation. Construction of the train line made the transport of both minerals and millions of Chinese emigrants possible. The Sky Train thus symbolizes the second invasion of Tibet.

The 1959 Uprising in Lhasa marks the historical line between medieval and modern-day Tibet. When Tibet's government, its supreme spiritual leader, and part of its population fled, this ushered in a new era of exile and diaspora. The trajectory of the women's stories from the late 1980s and early 1990s until now shows something of the direction and nature of that diaspora and what it means for our world civilization. With the fiftieth anniversary of the 1959 takeover, the symbolic relationship between these two countries sharpens into greater focus. This indigenous society, once the last major preindustrial sacred civilization, considered one of the most devout cultures in the world, faces a mammoth superpower that is the apotheosis of consumerist industrialization. And it is a power that seems to pursue growth at a hypercompetitive rate, cranking out products bigger, cheaper, and faster than the developed world. One society's ancient philosophies hold a key to saving our world, and the other is destroying it more quickly than any other power in history, cramming into two decades all the mistakes the West made in 150 years.

This book preserves some of the history of Tibet, viewed through the lives and insights of its older women, but is also written for the future. It is offered with the hope that we may be watchful of our own trajectory as we navigate through the twenty-first century and learn something from the model of grace, dignity, civility, and wisdom—so evident under the pressure of the last fifty years—that traditional Tibetan society so compellingly lends us.

1

SKY TRAIN

I WALKED ACROSS the huge, dimly lit concrete platform. There wasn't a soul around except a conductor in cap and uniform standing at attention, stone-faced, by one door of the sleek train. The loneliness of the scene, the hiss of the engine, the eerie lighting, and the echoing, hangarlike space in the dark night gave me chills. A scene from World War II Europe flashed to mind. At night it happened, I thought. A scene like this. The clandestine evacuation, the disappearance of a whole people. I pushed the thought from my mind and steeled myself to move forward.

A long distance away, to my left at the other end of the platform, I saw probably a hundred people thronged at a single door, trying to board, like a swarm of buzzing insects. Oh, I get it, I thought, they were elbowing to get in at the boarding gate to try for a "hard seat"—the alternative to sitting on the floor. I was the wealthy foreigner now. Not everyone could afford a soft sleeper like the one I had. From my previous trip, I remembered that not everyone got a seat; people slept all over the filthy floors, under bench seats, in aisles.

I looked for my car, number 6. The side of the train, marked with the destination points, read "Beijing," then the train logo, and then "Lasa." They had misspelled Lhasa. Rather than spelling it the Tibetan way, with an aspirated sound, the Chinese had spelled it as if it were a Chinese word. The meaning in Tibetan combines *lha* (gods) and *sa* (abode, home). Refuge of the gods. Heavenly home.

Inside the train, new brick-red carpeting ran down the aisles, and a clean modern bathroom with a trio of sinks stood at the end of each car. Signs displayed three languages: Tibetan, Chinese, and English. The reek of cigarette smoke in the cabins made my stomach turn, which the sight of fresh bed linens in my berth could hardly assuage. Oh yes, I thought, my body remembering: Here we are in China again.

Years ago I had vowed never to return to China. Never to return to Tibet. Never to return to Dharamsala. Now I was going to all of them.

"I can't take the train," I had said to my neighbor, a children's book author, on a winter night two months before, when she suggested I take the controversial Beijing-to-Lhasa train. I needed to revive my book project on oral histories of Tibetan women—shake it up, begin again, give it new life. "Go back and revisit the women in the book," she had urged. "Take that new train."

The train was China's Final Solution, I thought. It signaled the death knell for Tibet. An NGO (nongovernmental organization) staffer I'd talked to in Asia two years before, who'd seen it under construction, had said that once the train was built, there'd be no hope of ever getting the Chinese out of Tibet. I couldn't even bring myself to read the splashy travel articles that appeared when the train began operating a few months earlier in the summer.

I had said in the 1980s that I'd never visit China again. I didn't want to extend the country credibility or tourist dollars. I'd even been invited to the UN's huge Fourth World Conference on Women in Beijing in 1995, all expenses paid, but declined. You couldn't pay me to go to China.

I can't take the train, I had thought. The train would forever bind Tibet to China, just as the completion of the transcontinental railroad to California had bound the American West to the Eastern Establishment in the 1880s. The Western press of empire. The technological expression of Manifest Destiny. The rail line had forever changed the lives of all who'd lived in the West. Native American cultures became extinct. Trains imported goods and people but also ideas, culture, and value systems. On top of that, more than 80 percent of the workforce, who had been cruelly exploited, were Cantonese from southern China, my ancestral home.

I was soon joined by my cabinmates—a couple in their late twenties, a tall, strapping young man and his sweet-faced woman companion wearing Western-style outdoor clothing. He spoke some English. They began pulling things out of their spanking-new tricolored backpacks, setting up their thermos cups and foodstuffs on the window table, changing out of hiking boots into slippers, communicating in short cooing phrases.

After ranting and rejecting my neighbor's idea in that late-night phone call in San Francisco, I had toyed with the idea: I could just take the train with Tashi, I thought. That'd be easy. Tashi, my Tibetan friend, whom I'd met twenty-one years ago in Lhasa, whose family I'd lived with that summer in Tibet, now lived in Canada. She had spent the better part of the previous year lining up oncologists to treat her father's stomach cancer and waiting for approval of his visa application. He finally told her he'd rather not come, declined Western medical treatment, and asked that she just return home for Losar, New Year, the most joyous occasion in the Tibetan year. She had told me a month ago that she would be taking the new train line home.

In 1986, I had gone to China for a year, thinking I would travel for a time, then settle and teach English somewhere. Quite momentously, China had opened to the world a few years earlier, after thirty years behind the Bamboo Curtain. My first day in Lhasa, in early May, when I wandered away from the alley beside the Potala Palace where the bus from the airstrip had dropped me off—Lhasa had no airport then—I met the only English-speaking woman in town, twenty-three-year-old Tashi. On my second day in town, I was invited to live with her family in their cozy, three-room warren in a ninth-century monastery converted to family housing, with its three-foot-thick mud and straw walls.

If I took the trip back to Tibet for Losar with Tashi, I could complete my book *and* see my Tibetan family, I had thought—the father perhaps for the last time. The opportunity had loomed so large that my iron-clad resolve about never visiting China had started to melt.

"Tashi," I said one night by phone shortly thereafter, "what do you think of the idea of me joining you on the train to see your folks for Losar?"

"I think it's a great idea, Canyon," she said directly. "They would love to see you."

What compelled my first trip to China in the mid-'80s I can't exactly say. Unease, restlessness, curiosity? My life wasn't working for me. I can't say that I consciously embarked looking for answers to the meaning of life, but I knew that I'd reached the edge of a forest, the edge of the known world for me, and that now I had to enter into the unknown. In order to go forward, I had to go beyond anything I knew.

I had never set foot in Asia in my twenty-nine years. When I was growing up in the 1960s, I never heard a word about China; China then had cut ties to the outside world—diplomatic, trade, cultural. I thought China was some ancient place that no longer existed, like a land in the Bible. No one mentioned it—not my parents, my grandparents, the newspapers, the schoolbooks. True, sometimes a few dry goods sneaked through, imported from the Mainland and carrying a pungent smell of mothballs, a sour smell like something they put over your nose to revive you after you've fainted. When I was nine, my father and mother tried to tutor us in Chinese language after dinner, and the little primer books they brought home reeked of that unmistakable odor. The children on the covers and between the pages looked like red-cheeked, smiling cherubs from a bygone era, not like the Chinese American kids in our neighborhood and at my school in San Francisco, along the clean, straight streets of stucco houses edging Golden Gate Park. Did people even really exist there anymore? Was the whole place steeped in that foreign scent?

As an adolescent in the early '70s, I had a distant uncle who kept a pile of *China Reconstructs* magazines by his recliner. During one of our visits, he leaned back, flipped open the pages of an issue—all glossy color photographs of thick golden crops, spotless factories, and happy workers in lab coats—and told me with pride that China was becoming a great land, a powerful modern country, advancing on every front.

As I prepared for my trip, I read books about modern Chinese history, accounts of the devastating damage to society and to people during the Cultural Revolution. It was so overwhelming in scale and degree, so thoroughly and pointedly destructive, that I became suspicious: This was written by a Red baiter. This was biased because the writer was a white man in a capitalist country looking at Chinese in a Communist country. But to be truthful, I didn't want it to be right, didn't want to believe it had been that bad. I would just have to see for myself, I decided.

I found reassurance in the thought that the Chinese, in a major campaign at the time, were ardently inviting those they called Overseas Chinese to return home to the "warm embrace of the motherland." I saw the poster on the cork bulletin board at the tiny U.S.-China Friendship Association office on Oak Street in San Francisco. I wasn't an Overseas Chinese; I was an American, I thought. But clearly the government meant people like me. And the part about the warm embrace seemed friendly, if a bit sentimental.

The only thing I knew was that my grandparents had come from China; I might come to understand them better by living there, I thought.

By the time I left, I still hadn't secured a position teaching English, and my Mandarin comprehension was rudimentary, though my speaking was passable. What was I going to do for a year, I thought. No one spoke English. How would I survive?

After five weeks of traveling in China, starting in Hong Kong and crossing southern China to Yunnan Province, I felt bitterly disillusioned. I had thought the accounts of the Cultural Revolution must be exaggerated but being there quickly changed my mind. I saw no caring government in the gaggles of begging blind people shuffling up the street gripping one another's shirttails. I observed no free, quality health care in the sick people I saw, like the miserable man with a purple ulcer the size of an ice pack on his cheek. I saw no egalitarianism in the army trucks with sirens screaming, parading men through city streets, handcuffed, heads bowed, denounced in sidewalk photo displays as "criminals." I saw coal-burning smokestacks belching in the middle of cities, fouling the air so badly that I one time couldn't see the lamppost on the other side of the boulevard I was crossing. Instead of a model socialist society, I found Orwell mixed with Dickens in the largest nation on earth.

Far from being warmly embracing, I found the Chinese rude and unhelpful. They treated me as though I were invisible; some seemed contemptuous and envious.

At the beginning of my fifth week, I flew from Chengdu in western China to Lhasa, the capital of Tibet, a three-hour flight over the ice-blue Himalayas, into what seemed like one of the most inaccessible corners of the earth. Before the Chinese takeover, Tibetans had long shut themselves off from the outside world. In the twentieth century, only a couple thousand foreigners had ever set eyes on the holy city of Lhasa: seven hundred of them British troops who invaded in 1904, a few intrepid explorers, a handful of officials, and a dribble of Westerners in the early 1980s who came in expensive, organized tour groups.

Then, six months before my visit, in the fall of 1985, Tibet opened to anyone holding a Chinese tourist visa. Extreme weather conditions effectively closed it for the winter, but with the spring thaw, travelers trickled in—mostly independent travelers, backpackers like me, of whom I was the sole representative on the small sixty-six-passenger plane, among the silver-haired Chinese bureaucrats in drab, post-Mao fashions.

From the moment I arrived in Lhasa, I could sense something different. Even the air was different, pure and dry. The small plane landed on a vast barren plateau—I had never seen such long, clean horizon lines and such intense, indigo-blue skies. There wasn't anything around—no buildings, no airport personnel, no electric lines, no signs, no indications of civilization. After a two-hour bus ride, we arrived in Lhasa, where a few bicyclists leisurely pedaled along the wide, sunny main street; this was nothing like the jammed freeways of riders I'd seen in other cities in China. Snowcapped mountains ringed the valley, towering behind soft-sloped, brown moraine hills. Old ladies sitting on the sun-blanched street curb fingering their prayer beads tracked me as I walked down the main street and grinned as I passed, sticking out their tongues in the traditional greeting. I was struck by the bright white quality of the sunlight, the deep saturated blue of the massive sky, the air so clean and crisp it almost singed my lungs going down. I liked the relaxed atmosphere, the sense of space. Unlike everywhere else in China, Tibet was uncrowded, and one rarely saw a motor vehicle.

Over the next two months, particularly while trekking in the countryside, I had extraordinary experiences in the pristine mountains, rivers, and plains of Tibet's high desert plateau—which, I learned later, is the highest and largest landmass on earth. I was welcomed warmly wherever I went—so completely different from my experience in China. I developed an affectionate relationship with Tashi's mother, Amala. I found the people devoted to their faith, with a rare quality of equanimity and acceptance. I loved their easy humor and openness, their warmth and generosity.

Kanchenchunga Mountain, 1986.

Yarlong Tsangpo River, central Tibet, near Valley of the Kings, 1986.
This river becomes the Brahmaputra in India.

Potala Palace, 1986, from Chokpori Hill.

Later that summer, I was floating up the Yangzi River. I'd reluctantly left Tibet to resume my travels: I am Chinese, I should like China, I told myself. I had gotten the last bunk available in a twelve-passenger cabin, the upper bunk by the door. The first morning I discovered why.

From a speaker mounted in the hall, one foot from my head, a voice screamed garrulous government directives and martial music blasted at eardrum-splitting volumes at six o'clock. This was the same broadcast that railed at people everywhere in China; speakers hung from buildings and telephone poles, in cities, in the countryside. They were even wired into train compartments. Plugging my ears or covering my head with a pillow couldn't block out the shrill directives and political slogans, which blared for a solid twenty minutes.

From the traveler's co-op in Lhasa I had borrowed John Avedon's award-winning book, *In Exile from the Land of Snows*, about the modern political history of Tibet since the Chinese takeover in the 1950s. For the first time I learned in depth of the brutal destruction of the culture and people. More than 95 percent of Tibet's monasteries—equivalent to a Western church, university, and library combined—had been demolished, thousands of them. Tibetans claimed that more than a million people were killed. Religious art and literature was looted or burned. Over the next twenty-five years, the Chinese attempted to brainwash these devout people, to break them and strike Buddhism out of their hearts and replace it with fervent Maoism.

At six o'clock every morning on the ship, and several times throughout the day, the public address system blasted the state harangue. I took refuge in the dog-eared text, in the vivid handful of profiles of Tibetans— fascinating, each one of them. But by the end of nearly four hundred pages, I realized that not one of the profiles had been of a woman. Were we to assume that women's experiences were the same as men's? I doubted that was possible. It was as if women didn't exist. Or, if their experiences were different, they didn't matter. Yet my richest experiences of Tibet had often been with women.

What were women's lives like during this tumultuous period? Why weren't they portrayed?

In late summer, in eastern China, I finally gave up my long-held dream of living in China for a year and left for India—to the Himalayas where Tibetans had settled, the seat of the Tibetan government-in-exile and home of the Dalai Lama. There I became intrigued by Buddhism through reading about political history, and I got to know Tibetan nuns as I helped with an international conference on Buddhist nuns. When I got back to the States a year later, I became aware that for the first time in many years, probably the first time in my adult life, I had stopped searching. I didn't look right, I didn't look left; I was only interested in continuing to cleave close to this culture, this land, this philosophy. A woman I met at the Himalayan Fair in Berkeley asked me what my interest was in Tibet, and I thought a long moment. Was it Buddhism? Politics? The land? The people? Finally, I simply answered: "Total."

I worked as an activist for Tibetan independence. Most of the U.S. public didn't know where Tibet even was, let alone what had happened to it. The State Department under George H. W. Bush and Henry Kissinger took the hardline position that Tibet was part of China. I published articles, helped organize demonstrations, raised money for what eventually became the Tibetan Nuns Project, and gave educational slide lectures using the best photographs from my yearlong trip. A group of us started a cable television show on Tibet, for which I was on-air host and sometimes coproducer. Not a negative word about China appeared in the press, if anything appeared at all. We found out later that China had threatened to expel from Beijing any Western news bureau that printed anything critical of the country, a precursor of the censorship they would impose on the Internet twenty years later.

We worked hard, but we prayed for a miracle. We had a glimmer of a chance, we thought, to galvanize public and political support to save Tibet from China's so-called development plans. In the summer of 1989, our prayers were answered when Tiananmen Square ignited in protest. The international media picked up the story. I wrote an opinion piece that was widely published and even translated for a Chinese-language publication. As a result, I was invited to testify before a congressional subcommittee on the Chinese government's violent suppression of demonstrators in Tiananmen Square, to link human rights in Tibet with human rights in China. That autumn, though he'd been short-listed for years, the Dalai Lama won the Nobel Peace Prize. We were ecstatic, flush with new hope.

A few months later, I traveled to Dharamsala to work with the exile government. Living in the government compound, I quickly observed that virtually no women worked in the eight or nine government offices housing the various departments. I lived a stone's throw from the central Tibetan library; in the English-language section—an entire room, probably the most substantial collection of Tibet-related titles anywhere in the world—I searched for books about women, or by women, or with significant reference to women. There was next to nothing: 2 percent. Religious literature made up 60 percent of the total, and of the rest, most were autobiographies, all, except for *Daughter of Tibet*, by Rinchen Dolma Taring, penned by men. I found nothing substantive about the Dalai Lama's mother, a formidable, widely admired woman who was considered an exemplar of Buddhist ideals.

Women were invisible in the literature and the government, but I had seen in Tibet that they took a primary role in society, especially in the family and in religion. Since Buddhism had been outlawed for forty years and monasteries obliterated, women kept religious practice alive. They were out doing *kora* every day and dusting and polishing the altars every night. They visited temples and burned juniper incense and made offerings. They preserved the traditional dress and language, wearing *chubas* instead of Mao suits or Chinese fashions and keeping the traditional hairstyle of long braids woven with colorful ribbons piled atop the head, even though their conspicuous appearance sometimes made them targets for discrimination. Their courage in continuing to speak the lilting language and refusing to learn Chinese cleaved them to their culture as the PRC actively worked to destroy it. They carried traditional values and culture from one generation to the next, living and modeling compassion, equanimity, and joy. But I knew that one of the words for "woman" in Tibetan meant "lower birth." And in the traditional Tibetan community, it was widely believed that men could achieve Enlightenment much more easily than women, so women prayed to be reborn as men.

I remember vividly the first time I did a particular meditation, during a fifteen-day retreat at the Tibetan Buddhist meditation center in the hills above Dharamsala, during my 1986 stay. We undertook a guided visualization in which we imagined in graphic detail a disgusting heap of bile, bone, and guts. After a very long time conjuring and contemplating this image, we were told that this was the true nature of women! The exercise assumed that practitioners were male and wrestling with their desire for the opposite sex. Women not only were rarely mentioned in the teachings, but were debased when they were.

Midway through the same retreat, it came to light that a European woman participant claimed she had been sexually harassed by a Tibetan staff member. When it was brought to the group for discussion, the lead instructor commented merely that oppression of women was harmful for men's karma. I was dumbfounded at the disconnect between the professed tenets of the faith and the mores of Tibetan society.

On that first trip, I'd picked up a pamphlet at the Office of Religious and Cultural Affairs Office—a slim booklet maybe eight pages in length, with a line drawing of a monk on the white front cover—aimed at securing sponsors for Tibetan Buddhist monks in India. There was no mention anywhere of nuns, that they needed sponsorship or that they existed at all. I was flabbergasted. How could the government organ responsible for religion produce a publication about monastics that didn't acknowledge the existence of its female members? The nuns and nunneries were in even worse financial straits than monasteries, which received more generous support from the Tibetan community.

I combed the pamphlet line by line and page by page, adding in neat letters, written with a fine-point pen, the words "or she" everywhere it said "he," "or her" where it said "him," and "and nuns" where it said "monks." I sent it to the Religious and Cultural Affairs with a carefully and respectfully worded letter, and three months later received a copy of the identical booklet, except with every change incorporated.

From my work on behalf of the nuns—I raised the major portion of the budget for the Tibetan Nuns Project in those years through my slide show—I knew that nuns could not receive full monastic ordination, as could monks. A nun had to bow to a monk when they crossed paths, even if she had been a nun for thirty years and he a monk for only a month. Nuns didn't routinely receive a religious education in Tibet, as monks did; their training consisted of rote memorization of prayers.

A friend and neighbor in the government compound, a British woman who taught Tibetan Buddhism in England, methodically surveyed the Jataka tales, Buddhist folktales about enlightenment, with a monk friend. She found paupers, murderers, dimwits, birds and forest animals that attained enlightenment, but no women who gained spiritual realization in more than three hundred stories.

As a dharma student, I'd long ago ceased to notice that all pronouns in the Tibetan teachings were masculine. Even Western activists and scholars around Dharamsala didn't think twice about the fact that their studies, books, or projects were populated exclusively by men.

What were women's experiences? How were they different than those of men? What had their lives been like before the Chinese takeover? Tibet, before the invasion, had been called the most devout civilization on earth, the largest intact Buddhist society left in the world, free from Western influence. How had that faith been held in the women? How had it helped keep them alive during this most tumultuous period in Tibet's history? Kept them from becoming bitter or going mad?

In a few years the women who held this history would be gone, passed away, their experiences never recorded, their wisdom and insight lost. What could we learn from them? What did we need to learn from them? I realized that if I wanted to know, I would have to undertake the task to go out and talk to women myself. That spring of 1990, I decided to start collecting oral histories.

I spent years raising money to travel, then several more years collecting the interviews—thirty-six in all. I read the new literature on gender differences in oral histories, which suggested that the emphasis for women was not so much on heroic actions as on the meaning of events and experiences in the context of their lives. The male "hero" archetype of personal agency mattered less than the understanding and integration of the events in one's life. Studies in the 1990s disproved the "fight or flight" theory of survival. Men fought or fled, but women did something different: women offered and sought support, re-created family groups, built community. Gender studies showed how women resisted the Holocaust very differently than men. How was this difference manifested in Tibetan society, I wondered.

I interviewed Tibetan women across a range of ages, classes, and geographical origins, in Asia, Europe, and North America. What started out as a straightforward oral history project, over the course of more than a decade, morphed into a dharma book, a monograph, dramatic monologues. I had two near-publications. I went through three editors and three literary agents. I strained my resources many times. Publishing professionals kept pressing for more of me in the book, but I resisted. I got dejected, discouraged, disheartened, and depressed, put down the project for months at a time, once for a whole year. Every time I was reminded how amazing and important the material was, I'd pick myself up, dust myself off, and start anew. I cut the number of women's stories in the book. One of my most important interviewees, Rinchen Dolma Taring, died. Time marched on. I worried that the world would never get to see this material, and that I myself was losing touch with it.

It was years before I realized something else was driving me, that the project answered a deeper thirst. I wanted to know how these hardy, down-to-earth, open-hearted people had survived the brutality they'd suffered. One author aptly wrote that the Chinese treated the Tibetans "like ene-mies." What was it that gave them the resilience, the forbearance, not just to survive and endure, but to emerge with clean hearts? Having grown up atheist in a Christian-dominated culture, I had no sense of faith. As a per-son of color growing up in a white-dominated country, I had no trust in the benevolence of larger society.

I'd graduated from a nationally ranked, college-preparatory high school and attended a top university; I'd studied American and English literature, but I was nearly twenty-one before I picked up a book that reflected my own life experience—*The Woman Warrior* by Maxine Hong Kingston—in 1976. I was so floored just from reading the back cover and the inside jacket flaps that I put it down and couldn't pick it up again for a week. When I was growing up in the '60s and '70s in San Francisco, I never saw images in my textbooks, or on television, or in the daily newspaper or magazines of normal Asian people—not house servants, not villagers fleeing napalm, not "foreigners" or kung fu masters, but just regular people.

I thought the Tibetan women might give me a sense of my own history as an Asian woman. They had belonged to a medieval-like Buddhist society that had not been influenced by capitalism or Christianity. Not skewed by modernization or industrialization or Western culture. What could I learn from their lives? What spiritual historical legacy might they offer?

After I talked to Tashi, I went full bore planning the trip. I finally read the travel articles I'd saved about the train. Swiss and Japanese train engineers had advised the Chinese against building it. Four hundred miles crossed unstable permafrost. The constant freezing and thawing would eventually cause the support towers to buckle and crack. The Chinese prided them-selves on having built it anyway, surmounting all technical obstacles. It had taken seven years to build and cost more than $4 billion, the costliest project ever undertaken in Tibet. The route ascended to seventeen thousand feet and then back down to Lhasa's twelve thousand feet in forty-eight hours, a much faster ascent than was prudent to prevent altitude sickness, but they claimed they'd made provisions for extra oxygen.

The section from Golmud to Lhasa, from northeastern to central Tibet, they'd dubbed the Shangrila Express, marketing it to Westerners as an exotic, luxury vacation. The Sky Train, they called it. The world's highest railroad. More hype, I thought—now it seems they are spotlighting tourism with their propaganda. The name conjured an image of traveling so high that one flew across the skies, but it wasn't long ago that the Chinese had claimed that Tibet's thin oxygen, at its high elevation, was the cause behind Tibetans being stupid and backward. What this government said and what its true motivations were, especially regarding Tibet, always wildly diverged.

Golmud to Lhasa crossed over the Changtang, or Northern Plain, one of the most desolate, uninhabited expanses in Asia, inaccessible by road until the 1950s. The largest and highest plateau in the world, it was a bleak wasteland a thousand miles in length, scoured by wind and cracked by frost. High, cold, and treeless.

Apparently one needed a special permit to travel in Tibet. I wrote to one of the travel agencies listed in an article. The e-mail reply hinted at the political sensitivity of a visit, despite the tourism the Chinese government was trying to promote: "We have to have 5,000 RMB deposit for the promise that you will only stay in Lhasa and you will not do any other things which are relate to the Political. Hope you will understand our point. We will refund if you stay in Lhasa only in a smooth way."

Then, from Lhasa, I would have to get to Nepal and thence to northern India in early March, where two of the women in my book were going to be attending the Dalai Lama's teachings in Dharamsala. Getting from Tibet out to Nepal over the Himalayas might be tricky in midwinter. The overland route across the high-altitude peaks and passes was subject to landslides, washouts, heavy snowfall, and blizzards. A once-a-week airline flight was often canceled due to inclement weather.

I decided to concentrate in the book on the stories of just four of the women—all older women who had known Tibetan society before the Chinese took over and whose lives spoke to different aspects of history: the invasion, the occupation, the resistance, and life in exile. One woman had already passed away, but I would try to find the other three, whom I had not seen in about fifteen years.

A month before our departure, Tashi told me she was incredibly anxious about the possibility of snow on the train tracks at high elevation, especially since the rail line was untested in winter. Airlines had dropped fares to compete with the train, and she wanted to save time and get home. She had decided to fly. Tashi had anxiety disorder, so I understood; I tried not to take it personally. But I felt abandoned, bereft. I would be alone on a train that I didn't even want to be on, in a country I detest.

I decided to stay the course, but I took on her fears after that: What provisions had the Chinese engineers made for snow removal? What if there were an unusually heavy snowfall and road crews sent to help couldn't get through? I wrote to the authorities, but no one wrote back. I had visions of twenty-foot-high snowdrifts frozen into towers of ice on the tracks, and the train stopped dead behind them. According to reports, one passenger had died and the support towers in some places had already cracked. Apparently, the engineers had failed to factor global warming into their calculations about freezing the permafrost on which the towers had been built.

The last time I was in the Himalayas, I had experienced miserable symptoms of high altitude sickness, which I still remembered vividly: nightmares, brain freeze, breathlessness. I knew the Chinese were terrible at systems maintenance. I figured I could handle three days stuck at high altitude, but after that the toilets would reek, the heat would fail, food and water would run out, and anarchy would ensue. I'd freeze to death with a bad headache, swollen digits, and the unfinished book locked inside my scrambled brain.

After two weeks, I tired of worrying. I stocked up with twenty-four Luna™ bars, three Nalgene™ water bottles, extra rolls of toilet tissue, eight layers of clothing, and a prescription for Valium™. My hard-won Buddhist patience could carry me only so far. A doctor friend convinced me to bring Diamox™ for the altitude, although in all the times I'd been at high altitude in more than twenty years, I'd never taken it before. I was a purist in my youth as a backpack traveler, I thought, but now here I was insisting on luggage that rolled and squirreling away prescription drugs.

I lay down in my narrow train berth that night. The rank smell of cigarettes produced in me the urge to go to the bathroom, and I already had diarrhea from the bowl of noodles I'd eaten at the Beijing train station. I had thought it would be safe because the restaurant, with its big, modern, lighted yellow sign, was called California Beef Noodle. Accessing my upper berth in the middle of the night after a trip to the toilet might be tricky, I worried, because the steps looked like they'd been designed for Magic Johnson, the first one waist high.

As the train hummed along the tracks, I lay in the dark and saw images of Lhasa from the last time I'd been there, a brief touchdown in 1994. It was the only time I'd been there since 1986; I was in nearby Nepal doing interviews and crossed in. In the Barkhor, the religious heart of Lhasa, the Chinese repelled Tibetans from the Jokhang, the holiest of all the temples in Tibet, with ear-splitting soundtracks—in the vein of tactics the FBI had used in Waco, Texas, shortly before to flush people out of a compound. The soundtracks blared at sunrise and at sundown, precisely the times when custom prescribed that Tibetans circumambulate—that is, circle the temple in a kind of walking prayer. Red-and-white Marlboro™ cigarette café table umbrellas dotted the Jokhang plaza. Chest-high metal barricades along the main street installed to prevent demonstrations choked pedestrians into narrow arteries. I watched shrunken Tibetan grannies spinning large prayer wheels on their *lingkor* walk inexplicably stop on the sidewalk in front of a towering blue glass skyscraper and pay homage; I later learned that the new building along the ancient holy walk had been built right in the line of sight of sacred Sera Monastery. The award of the Nobel Peace Prize to the Dalai Lama a few years earlier had inspired heightened political activity among Tibetans, which drew a ruthless backlash from the Chinese government. The official line on Tibet, "The iron fist of repression will smash down mercilessly [on dissidents]," had resulted in arrest, imprisonment, and torture for scores of people, including many nuns and monks. Martial law clamped down for the first time since the 1950s, lasting more than a year.

Now, thirteen years later, I felt both fear and excitement to see Lhasa again. In the last few years, the Chinese had gone even further in tearing down all the traditional mud-and-straw buildings. I knew that they'd erected a futuristic city and moved in hundreds of thousands of Chinese, and I dreaded seeing the changes. Yet I was excited to be visiting Tibet again, site of such transformation in my life, a place of breathtaking, sublime beauty.

The next morning, I awoke to soft Chinese pop music, instrumental pieces with flutes, like music you hear while getting a massage in a spa, wafting over the train's public address system. A woman's mellifluous voice came on, speaking Chinese. What a change this was from the shrill, martial barking of the past! After twenty minutes, a pleasant male voice spoke in nearly perfect, unaccented English.

"Dear Passenger," he began, "the completion of the Qinghai–Tibet Railway is one of the greatest railroad projects in the new century, the fulfillment of the dream of the Chinese people for over a hundred years. It is a construction feat recognized by the whole world, and a proud moment for all Chinese people."

He told us the Golmud-to-Lhasa section, 709 miles, had begun construction in 2001 and began operating in July 2006, seven months ago. The high point, at 16,640 feet, was at a higher elevation than the railroads in Peru. The Qinghai–Tibet Railway was "sure to bring development in a more rapid, scientific, and harmonious way to Tibet." Five tons of goods, he said, will flow daily over the track in both directions when the train is fully operational—eight trains a day. The train "will improve the social development of Tibetans and improve tourism." After all, they expect several million tourists a year to visit Tibet.

In Tibet, he continued, one "can fully enjoy scenes of big mountains and big rivers. A person can touch the bright and blue sky, the fresh air, and feel the mysterious, holy culture. Tibet is one of the few pure lands left on earth. And everyone wants a piece of pure land." This is interesting, I thought: the allusion to the Buddhist concept of Pure Land. The Chinese Communists used to think of religion as poison for the mind, the crutch of the superstitious. Now they are selling Tibet as a holy land.

The Tibetan people are "a hardworking and hospitable minority group," he informed us, good at singing and dancing. He went on to talk about their melodious music and graceful dancers. In Tibet we should "do as the Romans do," he told us. He quoted a traditional saying: "Ru xiang sui su, ru jing wen jin" (When entering a village, obey its customs; when entering a new country, inquire after its laws).

Washing up at the bathroom sink, I noticed a small gurgle of water leaking from the base of the cold tap. In China, there were always problems with plumbing, I remembered, recalling hotel bathrooms of years ago. You practically needed galoshes to wade to the commode. I could see the décor now that it was daylight: a Tibetan theme, chocolate brown with a brick-red stripe across the top, covered by a line of white dots. In Tibet, those colors and pattern signified a religious institution, a temple or monastery. The design carried through to the train's signage, carpeting, and doors. Some-

Signs on the Beijing-to-Lhasa train use a traditional Tibetan design—a row of white dots across a brick-red band above a field of dark brown—which in pre-1950 Tibet was used only on temples and other holy buildings.

one had put some thought into this, I reflected. Interesting. The Chinese government was appropriating the culture it had spent decades trying to obliterate.

My cabinmates and I chatted a bit. I explained that I was Chinese, but from America. I didn't speak Mandarin. They didn't blink an eye. In 1986, people had been incredulous that I was from the West; I could spend half an hour trying to convince them I was American. They always thought I was pulling their leg, pressed me to tell them where I was *really* from. Hong Kong, maybe? Japan?

Once, on an overnight train, about forty people crammed into my sleeper cabin the first night—packed into all three berth levels, like tiered theater balconies, crouched on every inch of floor space, spilling out into the hall, staring at me saucer-eyed. Only white-skinned people were American, they believed. But once they were convinced that I, who looked Asian, was in fact a Westerner, that I spoke a foreign tongue and no Chinese, they were spellbound. They watched my every move for hours, until they dropped off to sleep. All over China, I drew crowds six deep.

The tall, well-built fellow worked for an American company called Hyvac based in Ohio. He was in human resources. The company made industrial vacuums for cleaning up construction sites. The third roommate, a slight young man with acne, fingering a Buddhist prayer bracelet, stared out the window.

"Buddhist? You?" I asked, pointing to his prayer beads.

He spoke only a few words of English, so Hyvac translated: "He doesn't go to temple, but he likes the practice." I asked what he did in Beijing, and he pulled out a business card, printed in Chinese on one side, in English on the other. He worked as a sales rep at a winter spa in Beijing.

I asked Hyvac what drew him to Tibet. He told me he'd heard about the snowy mountains, the lama temples, the different religion. He had dreams, he said, for a big trip someday to K2 Mountain near the Pakistan border, then back through Tibet and out through southwestern China to Kunming, renting jeeps and taking treks along the way.

This is Western-style freedom of movement, I thought. Twenty years before, Chinese citizens couldn't budge without permission from the government, could barely travel to the next town, couldn't relocate. They had been stupefied that I'd traveled from so far away on my own. Now they were wholly unimpressed because now *they* had the freedom to travel.

Winter Spa asked me why I was going to Tibet—he was staying only three days and then rejoining his girlfriend, whose image he showed me on his cell phone. I answered simply that I was going for New Year's to see friends. I told him that my friend's father was sick, so it would be a reunion, and that I had visited Tibet twenty years ago. "Why did you go then?" he wanted to know. It was difficult, sitting in clean new accommodations and after all these years, to say exactly why I went—just like they were going now, I supposed, because I was curious.

Hyvac's girlfriend, who I learned was his wife, leafed through fashion magazines. She smiled and handed me one. It was filled with Louis Vuitton, Estée Lauder, and Calvin Klein ads hawking Swiss watches, diamonds, and expensive perfume.

"Can ordinary people in China afford these things?" I asked, astonished.

"In Beijing," Hyvac answered, "there are a million people who make more than US$100,000 a year. *They* buy these things."

I found the Chinese much more friendly, relaxed, and social than twenty years before. More people, almost all people, now wore Western fashions and hairstyles. The restroom sanitation was not exactly clean, but it was *cleaner.* And not just middle-aged people were increasingly middle class, but also the young, like my cabinmates; they were prosperous, ambitious, mobile. Hyvac had earned a B.A. in Chinese language and with some friends supported a movement to simplify the written language. The Chinese now had freedom of movement, but more importantly they had the freedom to hold dreams for their lives—something they didn't have before, when the government prescribed where to live and what job to do.

"What did you learn in school about Tibet?" I asked.

They looked blank, shrugged. "Nothing really," they responded. "Just, in geography, that it is the highest steppe. China has three steppes or geographical zones. First the coastal zone, then the intermediate zone, and then the high mountain zone of Qinghai and Tibet."

"That's all?" I asked.

They nodded.

All day we passed through gray bleak cityscapes. Tenements, a dredged river, industrial sites, slag heaps. I thought about the conversation with my cabinmates. I could recall why I first went to Tibet, but what I couldn't explain so simply was why I stayed, why I gave my life to it, why it held me. The Himalayas—especially the culturally Tibetan part—had a special call for me, a connection beyond rational explanation, something in the memory of my cells. I felt at home in the pristine, clean-lined beauty, the crisp air and vast horizon lines, the remote, desolate quiet.

That's why all those years I'd been heartsick and angered by the Chinese government's destructive and genocidal policies. Why secretly, at one time, I was ashamed that I was related to the people who had done such harm to the people and culture I loved so much. It was why I couldn't write the end of the book. I couldn't face it. Face the fact of the end. Face the fact that Tibet was going down, experiencing death by a thousand ignoble cuts. In full view of the civilized world.

Finally, I felt I wanted to face it. Had to, in fact. Seeing it, I thought, would free me.

2

MORNING ON THE CHANGTANG

THE NEXT MORNING I awoke to views of another world: a mountain range of golden brown, soft-sloped mountains against an indigo sky, the saturated blue I'd only ever seen in Tibet. I shot up from bed and got out my camera. Tiny patches of snow appeared, but few people or settlements. A half hour later, the mountains became dusted in snow, their surfaces craggy and wind-beaten, and the skies a blur of clouds like a picture out of focus. One of the toilet stalls was flooded in an inch of water. The entire tiled floor of the washbasin area was slippery and sloppy; I suspected the small leak at the basin had never been fixed. The bathroom-area window, obscured by a thick crust of ice on the outside, apparently did not have the same double-paned, UV-protected features of the passenger-car windows. I took my second Diamox™ pill, as today we would climb from nine thousand to seventeen thousand feet.

I had breakfast in the dining car, where all the serious photographers were pressed against the oversize windows wielding cameras half a yard long. How funny that I had worried about my point-and-shoot getting stolen on the train. That might have been likely years ago, but not in this era of China; the cameras these enthusiasts were using looked like they'd cost a worker's annual salary. After eating, I hung out with them for a couple of hours. They told me they were on a Chinese National Geographic tour traveling through Tibet and into Nepal. They came equipped with all manner of state-of-the-art electronic gadgets: little screens that swiveled 360 degrees and took dictation and translated Chinese words they wrote on the screen into English, and spouted names of birds and wildlife. The leader said he'd been on this route three times before, all by jeep. The train, he gushed, was much more convenient.

Back in my cabin later, an announcement began. It was the male English speaker.

"Dear Passengers, while you're surprised by the great achievement of the Qinghai–Tibet Railway . . . " he started off, then proceeded to inform us that the natural environment here was "original, unique, sensitive, and vulnerable."

"Here, let me brief you" he intoned. He detailed the considerations the Chinese government had made and the money—¥1.54 billion—it had spent for protection of wildlife and vegetation, including thirty-three corridors for animals to pass from east to west, the clean-energy sources used, the fact that "neither the water quality of the rivers nor the natural landscape" was affected by the railroad construction, and about its consultation with "herdsmen far and wide" on how the train would affect their flocks. In fact, he boasted, China's great construction feat "was recognized by *the whole world* as an example of the harmonious collaboration between nature and man."

He explained that the construction workers had been equipped with oxygen tanks on their backs, given that oxygen is reduced by half at the altitude of the plateau, that the government had set up seventeen oxygen centers where workers could "replenish themselves" and installed electric heaters in the their tents since "it was easy for them to catch cold while going to the bathroom at night" in temperatures of minus twenty-two degrees Celsius.

As for the four hundred miles of permafrost the tracks crossed, piers were driven a hundred feet into the ground so that "thawing and expansion would not affect the stability of the support towers."

As he droned on at length, I observed the defensive tone, as if he were answering critics in a number of possible arenas—human rights, labor law, the environment, engineering technology.

The scenery became snow-filled, three layers of white like a modernist painting, from the band of sky to the midbelt of mountains to the broad plain before us, the mountains now more conical and sharp peaked. Icy streams twisted over the landscape. At one point, snow completely blanketed the ground, creating a vast white ocean between the train and the distant mountains. Gradually the auburn-colored, gently rolling hills returned, and herds of woolly black yaks grazed. Then the black turned black and white as herds of sheep mixed in.

I kept longing for the pure vistas of the Tibetan plateau I had seen years ago. After hours of looking, I gave up trying to get an unobstructed photograph and instead deliberately took pictures of the Chinese footprint: transmission towers, endless lines of electric poles, makeshift work camps, clusters of gigantic metal storage tanks, and bridges straddling curving concrete pillars. Then there was the matter of fencing. All types of fencing were everywhere—green metal fencing, masonry form fencing, stone pillar fencing, a gridlike fencing. The scenery was always marred. A Swiss train this was not.

"To our right," the voice narrated, calling our attention to such-and-such-named bridge, ". . . built in the shape of a dragon at rest." The dragon was more than at rest, I thought; he was flat-lined: the bridge structure had completely collapsed.

View from the train window showing raised train track and line of electrical transmission poles amid traditional grazing land.

Fencing to keep out grazing animals mars the pristine landscape beside the train tracks.

Mini-lectures were played throughout the day—one about the tourist sights in Tibet ("You haven't been to Tibet unless you've been to the Potala Palace. . . . A tribute to both Tibetan and Chinese architecture"), one about precautions for being at high altitude (each berth had a hookup for an oxygen mask, and extra oxygen would be pumped into the cars), one about China's minority groups, and one about Tibetology ("Ladies and gentlemen, have you heard of the word 'Ti-be-to-logy'?").

One announcement informed us that the part of Tibet where the railroad ran was part of a Natural National Protection Zone. Therefore, it was "our common responsibility to treasure every blade of grass and every grain of wood."

I gagged at the flowery language. "Treasure every blade of grass and every grain of wood"? Sentimental poetry with a dash of Buddhist reverence for life. It was part of the new soft-pedal approach, to go with the soft sleepers and soft music and soft-voiced announcers. No longer was it "The iron fist of repression will slam down mercilessly on Tibet," which Chinese officials had thundered every time they mentioned Tibet a few years before. Now they made it sound as if they were delicately attuned to the cultural sensitivities of the Tibetan people and their land. The voice enumerated what he called Tibetan taboos: eating donkey meat, hunting eagles, smoking in temples.

I had interviewed a nun who described how Chinese troops picked apart her Lhasa nunnery with handtools, something like a spear crossed with a crow bar, based on her description. Troops marched in with Chinese women soldiers leading the charge because it was rumored that the blessing pills Tibetans wore to shield them from harm were ineffective against women.

In the summer of 1986, I had hiked to Rongbuk Monastery, just before Everest Base Camp, at nearly seventeen thousand feet. The Chinese had blasted the roofs off the beautiful hillside monastery, once home to three thousand clergy. A person could barely breathe up there, let alone drag around cannons. I remember thinking that the Chinese who had done this must have been real zealots. They left nothing except animal pens with ceilings too low for human habitation.

Every blade of grass and every grain of wood. The line reminded me of many of the women I had interviewed.

They'd say something along the lines of ". . . and then they took the house."

"What exactly?" I'd ask, thinking the PLA had taken valuable *thangka* paintings or cash or jewelry or horses.

"Everything," the woman would inevitably answer, "they took everything."

"Dzomo . . . chu gu," Mrs. Paljorkhyimsar said.

"Plowing cows . . . nineteen," Dorje translated.

"Ba mo . . . droog."

"Milk cows . . . six."

"Kam ra . . . nye shu tsa sum," Mrs. Paljorkhyimsar said, her bright pink polo shirt glowing from the couch—the only Western thing about her appearance, given that we were in Switzerland, in a postwar brick apartment block. Her husband, in a crisply pressed white dress shirt and gray dress slacks, nodded in agreement with his wife's recollection. I noticed a woven black-and-white *rangzen* bracelet on his wrist, symbolizing the Tibet freedom movement. *Rangzen* meant independence.

"Cattle . . . twenty-three head," Dorje said.

I had met Mrs. Paljorkhyimsar a few days earlier at the Dalai Lama's birthday party near Zurich, home of the largest population of Tibetans outside Asia, more than three thousand. I'd started the women's oral history project the year before, in spring 1990. I was going to be in Europe, courtesy of my frequent flier mileage, so I thought I'd try and get a couple of interviews. A close friend from Dharamsala, a Swiss Tibetan, suggested I talk to Mrs. Paljorkhyimsar. My friend said that Mrs. Paljorkhyimsar had spent twenty years in Tibet, separated from her husband, and then a few years ago had been reunited with him and moved to Switzerland, where he'd been living for some twenty years.

At the packed celebration, I was introduced briefly to Mrs. Paljorkhyimsar, a stout woman in her sixties or seventies, with a large, fleshy face. She was sitting at a long table of people in the noisy hall, both Tibetan and German languages clucking and clanging from a hundred simultaneous conversations. I told Mrs. Paljorkhyimsar about my oral history project, and she said she'd be willing to meet with me a few days hence.

On the morning of the interview, Dorje, a ponytailed acquaintance from Dharamsala who was helping translate, and I took an hour-long train ride out of Zurich to Mrs. Paljorkhyimsar's home. Walking through the sterile suburb of high-rise apartment blocks, I thought, *This is about as far away from Tibet as a Tibetan can get.* Mrs. Paljorkhyimsar had acted oddly at the door—barely looked at me, mumbled something, and withdrew back into the building. I stepped tentatively inside, unsure of whether we were supposed to follow.

In a few moments, I spotted her at the end of a hallway talking to someone out of view. A wiry man with thick, black-rimmed glasses soon bounced in from a sun porch and pumped our hands in welcome. Mr. Paljorkhyimsar, Dorje explained. After a few pleasantries, the man swept his arm toward the couch, inviting us to sit down.

Mr. and Mrs. Paljorkhyimsar both sat down after us, attentive, waiting for me to initiate the interview. Why had Mr. Paljorkhyimsar greeted us with such animation and formality while Mrs. Paljorkhyimsar had stayed in the background? Was he going to sit through her entire interview? Her appearance—wholly traditional, right down to the coral and turquoise pendant earrings and jade bracelet—displayed few clues of her living in the West: the fluorescent pink polo shirt with the Lacoste™ alligator insignia under her *chuba*, instead of the traditional silk blouse, and a Swiss watch.

Was he going to talk for her? I thought about a discreet way to say, "I'd like to talk to your wife alone," but couldn't think of one. Dorje reminded them, at my prompting, that this project was about Tibetan women; they simply nodded. My stomach tightened. We were due back on the last train to Zurich in a few hours, Dorje had only this one day to help translate, and this was my only chance to get Mrs. Paljorkhyimsar's story.

When I asked how I should address them, they said to call them Mola and Bola—Grandmother and Grandfather. Her name, however, was Jophar, and his, Norbu.

They had lived in an area an hour's horseback ride northwest of Lhasa. She had been born into a tenant farmer's family and married her husband, a landowner, a few years after her sister, Kelsang, became his wife. Kelsang bore two babies, who did not live, so Bola married Mola in the hope of producing a male child to inherit his considerable landholdings. In due time, Mola gave birth to a son, Tenpa. Fourteen years later, to everyone's surprise, Kelsang had a boy, Karma.

I asked Mola if she had been in town in March 1959, that critical month when the PLA invaded Lhasa and the Dalai Lama fled into exile. She nodded.

The Chinese had been there for many years, she said. They gave interest-free loans to the needy, built roads, and said they were there to help develop the area. She spoke in a low mumble. She was nothing like Tibetan women I knew, lighthearted and easy to laugh. She didn't smile or meet the eye. Maybe she was shy. So in 1959, she said, when the townspeople realized the Chinese were seriously taking control, they rejoiced.

"They were jubilant." Bola nodded in agreement.

"Why?" I asked, shocked and surprised. "What were they happy about?"

She explained that the Chinese had promised for years that under their governance, taxes would be abolished and debts forgiven. The local population was mostly tenant farmers, as she and her family had been, and many carried crushing debt. I knew that taxes due landowners sometimes amounted to as much as a quarter of a family's yield; if a crop failed one year, taxes were transferred to the next, compounding the debt. The Chinese, she said, had also promised that land and wealth would be redistributed fairly and equally.

Bola interjected, "I had ridden to Lhasa that week on business. I saw the troops. Thousands of Chinese troops. Marching in formation through town. I saw machine guns and tanks and jeeps. I remember it was a full moon. I thought, It is really happening, the Chinese are taking our country. I heard in town that once they took Lhasa, they planned to use it . . ." he raised his hand and drew a circle in the air, "like the hub of a wheel.

"They planned to push out in every direction . . . to take the whole country," he said. "I rode back home to get my family. We had to leave. We could only hope to escape with our lives. We didn't have time to take anything. But first I stopped at the *rinpoche*'s house. I thought I'd take him with us."

"Who's the *rinpoche*?" I interrupted. Dorje exchanged some words with Bola.

As the family had large landholdings, they knew they'd be prime targets for the Communists. Dorje explained, "His best friend was the *rinpoche* of the local monastery. He knew the *rinpoche* would also be targeted by the Communists because the monastery owned a lot of land."

"He asked me to come in for tea. I had tea with the *rinpoche*," Bola continued. "He was talking . . . talking a lot. . . " Bola shook his head, puzzled. "I didn't know what he was talking about. It went on such a long time. Finally I rode home."

Tea was often a very formal occasion in Tibet. Highly placed monastics such as *rinpoches* had so much clout that one could hardly decline an invitation to tea; everyone deferred to them. On his horse racing home, Bola explained, it suddenly struck him what the *rinpoche* had been saying: He would not travel with women.

"He said that?" I asked.

"Not exactly."

I knew Tibetans in polite society never directly refused or made imposing requests. Everything was indirect. This saved face for all.

"Why was that? Was it against his vows?"

Bola shrugged. Mola looked on silently.

"His ordination vows?"

He shrugged again.

"Was it just personal preference? Or did he not get along with your wives? Was it some practical reason?"

He shook his head.

"I don't know," Bola murmured.

"You never found out?"

"No. But it was clear."

"You mean . . . that's why he kept you for tea?"

He nodded slowly. The *rinpoche* had made his views firmly known by holding forth at formal tea. The full implication of this started to dawn on me.

"So you had to decide between saving your wives and saving the *rinpoche*?"

He shook his head, lips pulled tight, gazing into space. A chill crept up my spine. Not to aid a high incarnation such as a *rinpoche* would draw tremendous negative merit, or karmic consequences, in Tibetan Buddhist thinking, for many lifetimes. He could not abandon a *rinpoche* to what would be certain suffering, and maybe death, at the hands of people who considered religion poison. He could not save both his wives and the *rinpoche*.

"What did you do?" I asked.

Mola was doing something with her apron. She tamped down the cloth in her lap, holding an object in her hand. This decision, I thought, had altered the course of her life.

"We rode to the border," he answered.

"Who?"

Mola opened a small container and shook it onto the top of her left hand, which she held arched in midair. I watched her while Bola spoke to Dorje. Mola dipped her head, sniffed, paused, then pinched her nose. She inhaled twice more. It appeared that she was sniffing tobacco. I noticed a bluish gray stain on her hand.

"Myself, my older son, the *rinpoche*, and another lama, another *rinpoche*."

Bola said he was friendly with some monks at Lokhar Monastery, near the border. He thought it would be safe there, and if anything happened, they could easily cross into India. He kneaded his palms into his thighs, his trousers hanging loosely over bony legs. Mola closed the tobacco container and put it down on the coffee table.

He had planned, he said, to deliver the two monks to safety at the monastery near the border, then he and Tenpa, who was twenty-two at the time, would head into the countryside to find the resistance movement. He'd come back later for his wives and younger son, eight-year-old Karma. But, he continued, "after I left with the *rinpoche*, everything went wrong."

A knot tightened in my stomach. Mola sniffed dryly. She smoothed her apron flat. Bola extended his arm overhead.

"At the border, bombs fell from the sky. They flew over our heads. All around us. We'd never seen anything like it. We feared for our lives. We drove straight to India."

He and Tenpa settled in Dharamsala, a refugee settlement at the time.

Did he really believe, I wondered, that the Tibetan resistance guerillas would fight off the powerful PLA troops and that he'd be able to go back for his wives?

"Mola, what happened to you after Bola left?"

"First thing they called a meeting of all the landowners," she recalled. "They wanted a male head of each family to attend. We had no Bola, no Tenpa. I said I would go, but they insisted it be a man. I offered many times, but they said no. My sister and I finally found a distant cousin to go represent the family." She paused.

"We never saw him again."

"What do you mean?"

"He went to the meeting and never came back."

They inquired after him for months but got no answers and no cooperation, she said. He'd been "disappeared." The PLA troops sealed off their house and made her, Kelsang, and Karma live in an upstairs kitchen. Later they were moved to a basement room. Then she and Kelsang were brought to a meeting and forced to confess the crimes they had committed.

"What crimes?" I asked. Had I missed something in translation? Had she inadvertently committed crimes?

She spoke at length to Dorje. I was a step behind, preoccupied with wondering if the so-called meeting of male heads of families had been simply a ploy to round up more men and reduce the chances of the Tibetans fighting the occupiers.

Dorje explained, "The crimes were helping their husband escape. Employing workers on their farm. 'Forced labor.' That's what the Chinese called 'crimes.' She and her sister were beaten and tortured."

I looked at Dorje. He met my gaze, scratched his mustache.

"How?" I asked.

"They gathered the poor Tibetans to beat us," Mola said.

"Poor?"

"Landless workers," she answered.

She described how the Chinese even made their own workers beat them. The workers had to form a long line and then step up in turn to deliver blows to her and Kelsang. She leaned forward in her seat, spreading her hands on her thighs.

"We had to stand like this. Bow our heads. Then our workers moved along past us and knocked our hands out. Socked us. Pinched our arms. Kicked our shins."

She tucked her chin to her chest like in a somersault. "You had to keep your head like this, or the soldiers struck you." She stood up and propelled her arm forcefully from the shoulder, as if swinging a golf club, to show us, her movements heavy, slow, but strong. If their former servants didn't strike them as instructed, they were pulled out of line to receive beatings themselves.

These, I knew, were *thamzig*: tightly orchestrated political spectacles disguised as frank, ideological confrontations between "the masses" (tenant farmers, field workers, and household staff) and those whom the Maoists termed "criminals" (landowners, members of the aristocracy, and monks). Criticism/self-criticism.

The criminal charges against Kelsang and her, Mola said, were for being members of a traitorous family—traitors because her husband and son had fled—and a landholding family, which they had married into. They were never allowed to refute or speak to the charges, only to confess to them.

But it was Bola who had fled, and he had been the wealthy land baron, I thought. They had been penniless before they'd married him. How ironic that after he left them behind, they were punished for his leaving.

Mola sat slack-jawed, open-mouthed, but her eyes were alive, intelligent, as if the train of memories was slowly pulling in and she was watching it arrive. Bola, lips pressed together, braced his arm on the armrest.

"Then they took everything," she said. When I asked what exactly she meant, she and Bola slowly unpacked the memory, the inventory of their former life: *dzomo* . . . nineteen plowing cows, *dzo* . . . six milk cows, twenty-three head of cattle, more than three hundred sheep and goats, a stable of thirteen riding horses, a small poultry farm with fifteen hens. . .

She did most of the recalling, the speaking; he just nodded in agreement. She had a good head for numbers, I thought, even after forty-something years.

An eighteen-room house, household staff, and also farmhands, fourteen in number, but in a good year as many as a hundred helped with the harvest. Religious statues, scripture books, jewelry, a year's store of grain. All the furniture, a bicycle, a phonograph (the only one in town), cookware "down to the last ladle."

Everything was taken as part of a redistribution-of-wealth program. The soldiers claimed everything would be allocated equally among the people, that the wealthy, who owned so many fine things, now had to live as the poor people had. They took the religious objects, saying, "These will not feed you or give you clothes."

For three years, Mola and Kelsang did forced manual labor during the day and attended mandatory *thamzig* every night. Months later, the Chinese concluded the redistribution-of-wealth program, Mola said, handing out single shoes, chipped plates, outdated calendars, rusty washbasins. This was the much-touted program that was a cornerstone of socialism, I thought.

"It didn't surprise me," Mola said, "because from the beginning women did not trust the Chinese."

"What do you mean?" I asked. I was curious: Why just women?

She explained that, before 1959, the Chinese had paid the local men handsome wages in newly minted silver coins for doing road construction. In the fourth month of the Tibetan calendar—May or June 1959—they rounded up all able-bodied men and took them to outlying areas to plow land and build roads. Women had always worked side by side in the field with men, she said. Now the Chinese insisted that women stay back, remain at home and care for the children, not be exposed to harsh conditions. Men trusted the Chinese and were excited to be part of the new socialist experiment. They believed the promises about the Chinese coming to liberate the Tibetans.

"But women knew differently."

They knew this because women had lived in town alone with Chinese troops for weeks, months at a time, she explained. With the men away, the so-called liberators stole from women in the market, committed rape, and treated the women with contempt.

"We learned quickly," she said "that those promises about liberating and benefiting us were hollow."

After three years under house arrest, Mola and Kelsang were transferred to Tsogtu Rukha, or Building Workers Group, where they were made to haul stones, carry soil, split boulders, and dig trenches. They worked every day for long hours in sixty-person teams. When, every three or four months, they finished a project—an irrigation site, power plant, army barrack, hospital, or prison—they were shifted to another site without a break. The Chinese called them "yaks," the Tibetan beast of burden. They were forced to work very, very hard, Mola said, and were forbidden to talk to one another. They slept in communal tents at night.

"I came to think that our house arrest in Penpo had been quite civilized."

She and Kelsang, branded with an unfavorable political status, were assigned extra duties—hauling tools to the work site for the crews early in the morning and carrying them back at night. During lunch break, they had extra chores, and at the end of the day, when others had a few minutes to rest before *thamzig*, she and Kelsang had to collect firewood and haul water. Guards watched them closely.

"If guards thought we had walked too slowly, we were criticized, beaten, and shamed that night. If you didn't speed up the next day, you were tortured at the meeting. If guards thought we excused ourselves too often to relieve ourselves, our tea rations were cut. They'd come and check the spot in the field where you relieved yourself to make sure you weren't just avoiding work.

"People died every day. You'd wake up in the tent in the morning, and two or three people lay dead. They passed in the night."

It sounded like a slave labor camp, I thought. They were literally worked to death—like in a Soviet gulag.

"Everyone's skin was drawn, our eyes pale. But we were still forced to work."

The soldiers even arranged competitions with prizes to make them work faster. The slowest teams were punished. On rare occasions, they were given a day off to launder their clothes. Pretty soon, Mola said, "I had no strength even to lift an axe."

At one point in the early '60s, their food rations dropped to one tablespoon of *tsampa,* roasted barley flour, a day. They discovered that their rations stretched further if they combined everyone's tiny portion and cooked a pot of gruel. In the summer, they picked wild nettles to add protein.

"Whenever we had a minute to sit," she said, "we thought about food. That's all we thought about. What we could find to eat."

She fell silent a long moment, eyes full of thought. I knew this had been the period when the effort to collectivize farms in China was failing and food production had plummeted. Crops grown in Tibet were shipped to China to feed the people there.

Mr. Paljorkhyimsar spoke. He said that he and their older son, Tenpa, searched for any sign of Mola's whereabouts. They scoured the Tibetan newspapers. No one had information. In 1966, they were given the opportunity to emigrate to Switzerland, which had accepted Tibetan refugees beginning in 1963. Bola and Tenpa were part of the second wave of immigrants and settled in Wadensil.

Mola leaned forward to pick up her snuffbox from the coffee table. She smoothed her apron, popped the leather stay, and shook a tiny mound of aromatic tobacco onto the saddle of her hand. She went through her sniffing ritual as Bola talked about how he and Tenpa had gotten jobs in spinning factories. I saw that the bluish gray stain on her hand was a hand-painted tattoo, a backward swastika, symbol of good luck in Bon, the animist religion that predated Buddhism in Tibet.

Bola was talking about how Tenpa had met his wife in the factory. As he spoke at length, Mola got up and left.

After twenty minutes, she was still gone. Where was she? I felt anxious. She'd up and left her own interview. It was longer than a bathroom break. She was nowhere in sight. She'd just disappeared. Bola was telling Dorje how he'd gotten a job as a storekeeper . . . it was 1968 . . . no, maybe . . .

I left the two men talking and got up to look for her. I peered down a dark corridor toward what I guessed must be the bedrooms and bathroom.

No sign of her. I didn't know the layout of the apartment, but since the hall was dark, I went in the other direction. In the living room, I saw Tibetan *thangkas* on the walls and a cabinet of Buddha figures illuminated by a glowing prayer wheel. Its letters, spelling the mantra "Om mani padme hum," spun around, glowing from within. We could have been anywhere in the Tibetan world, I thought, with that altar.

I crossed to a small dining room and stopped to look at a collection of family photos on a wall, framed eight-by-ten-inch color portraits of Mola and Bola with Tenpa and his wife and children. Photo by photo, year by year, the grandchildren, two girls and two boys, matured incrementally from children to adolescents to young adults—both with the thin nose and thin face of their grandfather. One passport-sized black-and-white snapshot, like the ones people take in a booth in an arcade, showed a granddaughter, about nineteen, grinning toothily at the camera, cheek to cheek with a wild-eyed Mediterranean-looking youth. I pushed open another door.

I saw Mola standing over a huge boiling pot on the stove, clouds of steam rising like fog around her head and shoulders. She pinched noodle dough into the roiling water. She acknowledged me with a nod.

Was this meal for us, I wondered? Dorje and I had eaten right before we came, so we weren't hungry. Did her husband expect a meal in the middle of the afternoon? Was she nervous talking about the past? I became even more panicked that there wouldn't be enough time to complete the interview. Patience, I told myself.

I made small talk with the few words of Tibetan I remembered, standing by the window, out of her way. She stirred something in a small saucepan on another burner. The kitchen was immaculate but bare—yellow chintz curtains, bone-colored tiles, and '60s-era wood cabinets. She stirred the big pot with a long-handled stainless steel spoon. Her movements were heavy, unrushed. The spoon reminded me of what she had said earlier: "The Chinese took everything . . . down to the last ladle."

Mola turned all the way around, walked over to me, and motioned for me to put out my hand. I raised my fingers. She dropped a small boiled red potato into my palm. Still warm, the size of a large egg. She nodded. Then she checked me with a knowing glance, as if to say, "A little something for you," and sidled back to the stove.

What was this? I thought. Why was she acting so secretive when it was just the two of us in the room? What did that mean? She stirred the saucepan; I heard the spoon scraping against the sides of the pan. All of their farmland, their house, their livestock, their possessions had been reduced down to the contents of this modest apartment halfway around the world from Tibet. Reduced down like the sauce she was stirring.

She filled a few bowls and carried them out of the kitchen on a tray, still steaming, placing them on TV tables. We sat down, and Bola enjoined us in a commanding, spirited voice to eat up. Mola asked if we wanted more salt or broth. After eating a few spoonfuls, I noticed she had no bowl; she was not eating. She sat on the loveseat, hands in her lap, looking at nothing in particular. Only when we had nearly drained our bowls did she speak, to offer us a second helping. I was flabbergasted. The husband and guests eat, and she just cooks and serves? When did she eat? Later? Alone? Out of view? These were old-world manners, her treating us like honored guests.

After lunch, I asked her why the workers in the camp hadn't tried to escape.

She said there wasn't a chance. Armed guards were everywhere. If you were caught, you were brought back, put in chains, and savagely beaten. The prisoners were terrified of the authorities and too weak physically any-

Mrs. Paljorkhysimsar at her home outside Zurich, 1991.

way. There was no hope for an end, and no rest. Old people just collapsed in place, with a shovel in their hand. Guards said they were "taken to the hospital," but they were never seen again.

"I never believed I'd see an end to it. With every shovelful of dirt, I asked to die, to be free of my suffering," Mola recalled.

I asked what had happened to Kelsang, whom Mola had stopped mentioning.

"She died in the camp."

"From what?"

Mola stared into space for a moment. Deep furrows crossed the entire width of her forehead in parallel, like in a dry riverbed. She spoke a few words to Dorje.

"From injuries sustained during *thamzig*," Dorje translated.

"I see."

A long moment passed. After Kelsang's death, she had been alone in that hell.

How many people were in this camp?"

"About five hundred."

"How many would you say died?"

She answered that it was hard to say because people were continually dying and being replaced in the tent by new people. The Chinese guards never moved so fast as when they evacuated dead bodies.

"About half," she said.

"How many men and how many women were in the camp?" I asked.

"All women," she said.

"What?!"

"It was all women."

"But . . . where were the men?"

She whisked the air with the back of her hand and a flick of the wrist.

"They ran."

I was incredulous. I asked Dorje to confirm. They spoke at some length.

"All the men ran away," he said.

"Ran away . . . You mean . . . escaped . . . or fled the country?"

"Right," Dorje said. "She said only a handful of teenage boys and some monks were in the camp. Many younger children had been taken to China for schooling; older children were left back. Otherwise the camp consisted of women and old people. She said most of those tortured were women."

"In *thamzig?*"

They both nodded.

I suppose I had just assumed that the camp would be roughly equal with the two sexes, a reflection of the general population. I was flabbergasted. I remembered from her inventory of the farm that she had a keen head for numbers.

"About what percentage was women?"

"About 70 percent women," she answered.

The information hit me like a blow. I realized that I had never thought about the Tibetan occupation splitting along gender lines before.

After Kelsang's death in summer 1966, Mola said, she decided to try and get transferred out of the work group and asked the guard to reassign her. She wanted lighter work duty and transfer to a farm. She cited poor health, talking to the guard every day.

After several months, Mola got her wish and was moved to a collective farm, which, ironically, sat on land formerly owned by her husband's family. Her job was to collect cow manure patties and dry them for use as cooking fuel and fertilizer.

I asked about her Buddhist practice: What did her faith lend her?

"I had an altar hidden in my cupboard. Whenever I could get hold of an extra dab of yak butter, I made an offering."

I had seen the cupboard in a photo she had showed me—it was tiny, the size of a small medicine cabinet, the only furnishing other than her bed that fit in her cell.

"The Chinese were livid when they heard you say prayers. They yelled, 'Religion is poison for your mind! The gods will not feed you! Stop the religion!' So I learned to say mantras silently . . . to myself . . . inside. They gave me strength."

She said that when she was growing up, people prayed to be reborn as men. Men had better lives, and they didn't suffer childbirth.

After a few years, in 1973, Mola developed a painful, mysterious digestive ailment and obtained permission to go to Lhasa for treatment at the Tibetan Medical College. There she bumped into an old family friend, a woman who could move freely between Tibet and Nepal because she was half Nepali. From her, Mola heard news of Bola and Tenpa for the first time in fourteen years.

In 1980, after China liberalized its policies and allowed for family reunification, Bola and Tenpa entered Tibet to retrieve Mola. She recognized her son right away, she said, as soon as he got off the bus, but Tenpa kept craning his neck looking for her, not able to recognize her after twenty-one years. She'd lost fifty pounds and nearly all her teeth.

She was in shock when they first stood face-to-face, she told me, couldn't sense or feel anything. For many days they could hardly speak; when they were together, they just wept.

Mola had survived five years of slave labor, thirteen years on the collective farm, three years of house arrest, and countless *thamzig* sessions. She arrived in Europe at the age of sixty-four in the early days of 1981.

I had to wrap up the session. I had already learned from missing a train a few days earlier that Swiss train schedules were ironclad. I asked to see old photographs, and Mola showed me one of Tenpa and herself when Tenpa and Bola arrived in Tibet to retrieve her. It's a heart-wrenching image: Mola is emaciated, with tiny, hunched shoulders and blackened hands as dark as her *chuba*. Her gaze draws back as if she feels threatened, her eyes full of bone-weary sadness. Tenpa, sitting beside her on her bed with a protective arm on her back, wears a shell-shocked expression on his face. The ugly wall of her cell behind them is blotched with stains. "My bed was made of twigs and a threadbare rug," she recalls, gazing at the photo.

She tries to forget the painful memories of her past and to say a lot of prayers, she said, but she is anxious about what's going on in Tibet, about what the future has in store there. She would like to see her nephew, Karma, who is like a son to her, whom she hasn't seen in eight years. Her greatest joy living in the West was living near Tenpa and the grandchildren, but otherwise, she said, "In Tibet, we had so much work to do and nothing to eat. Here, I have lots to eat but nothing to do."

Mrs. Paljorkhyimsar with her son in a Chinese labor camp in 1981, when her husband and son returned to Tibet after twenty-one years to retrieve her. Her son did not recognize her because her appearance had changed so drastically due to years of torture, starvation, and forced labor. A large percentage of Tibetans in the Chinese gulags died. Photo courtesy of the Paljorkhyimsar family.

I shook their hands, thanked them for their time, for sharing their memories, for the meal. I didn't know what else to say; I was still new at interviewing. As an afterthought, I asked about her tobacco-sniffing habit. I'd never seen a Tibetan woman with the habit. She had taken it up in the camps, she said, because if she sat down for a sniff, a long, five-minute ritual, guards looked the other way. They had the habit themselves. It had bought her time. I sensed that she had become more at ease with me. Bola stayed in the apartment while Mola walked us to the front door. "Kali pe" (Slowly go), she said. "Kali shu" (Slowly stay), I answered.

Taking the train home that evening, I pondered what could have been the *rinpoche*'s reason for not wanting to travel with women. How powerful, I marveled, was the religious hierarchy's grip over the people! Did Mr. Paljorkhyimsar really believe he could come back for his wives? Mola had noted so matter-of-factly that the majority of prisoners in the camp were women. The whole time, I had assumed a mixed population. She said that, before, women and men had always worked side by side in the fields, so I just had the image in my mind. Her reply to my question about the whereabouts of the men rang in my ears: "All the men ran away."

Mola wasn't anything like the usually cheerful Tibetan women I'd met before. She had little affect in her voice or her facial expressions. She wore a bland mask, a concept I heard about years later, used by sociologists to describe the blank, neutral expression people adopt when forced into conformity over a long period of time, such as in the case of an indentured worker. It presents to superiors or captors no information that can be used against you, that would make you stand out. It was in this loss of affect that I saw the price she'd paid for her years between the 1959 invasion and her arrival in Switzerland twenty-two years later, for the fact that she couldn't protest the charges for which she was punished, couldn't talk or bond with the other women, couldn't right the injustice of being left behind by her husband because of the whims of a monk. Starvation, torture, forced labor, the murder of her sister—there were no bounds to her misery.

And what was the strange behavior in the kitchen about? What did the potato mean? She had slipped it to me clandestinely, with a wink and a nod, even though it was only the two of us in the room. As we pulled into Zurich, I recalled her saying that, during the years of starvation, all that she and the other women did when they had a free moment was dream about food. I pictured a dozen emaciated women sitting around a meager campfire in the barren landscape. Perhaps the potato was a clandestine gift, a way women communicated when talking was impossible. In an inhumane environment, with brutal guards driving you to perform, starving and humiliating you, with people dropping dead every day, such an act, slipped past the guard's eye, kept not just the body but a sense of humanity alive. A small private generosity translated to an act of solidarity with another woman. And an act of resistance against the will of one's captors.

I felt I had known modern Tibetan history. I had studied. I had been an activist. I kept my ear to the ground. But I was starting to unpeel an invisible layer of history. All Tibetan historians, I now realized, were male.

In Tibet, they had a saying that men were the pillars outside the home and women the pillars inside the home. This translated to men handling trading and business, while women took care of family and hearth. Men had wide freedom of movement all over the region; they practically lived on the trail. Some had left, like Mr. Paljorkhyimsar, to join the resistance. The privileged who knew they would suffer under a Communist system—landowners, high-ranking lamas, and aristocrats—fled.

Years later, as I worked on this book in America, after the catastrophe of Hurricane Katrina, people posed a similar question: Who got to leave and who got left behind? I suddenly saw the occupation in a new light. Who, I asked, really suffered in Tibet? The face was changing.

The train climbed steadily in elevation. The ground became marshy and glassy with ice. Tall, needle-nosed, snow-covered peaks loomed behind the closer mountain range. Only occasionally did we pass a walled Tibetan hamlet or a lone *chorten*, a stupa. A transport truck on the parallel road, a few horses. A couple stood by a wooden cart loading overstuffed bags, she in a red coat and pink wool scarf, the frozen plain on which they stood broken in pieces like a gigantic cracked mirror. Otherwise the terrain looked desolate, wind-whipped, inhospitable.

The Changtang was prone to drastic changes in temperature, earthquakes, and low barometric pressure; at one time it was the least populated area in Central Asia, with only about two people per square mile. I remembered one of my interviewees, a first cousin of the Dalai Lama—his father and her father, brothers, had homes side by side. The children were all raised together. When she was nine, she often took care of her three-year-old cousin. "No one comes over that pass," she recalled her aunt saying to her toddler son, the future Dalai Lama. The child had insisted that some men from Lhasa were headed toward their home in search of him. They'd crossed the pass and would be arriving soon, he declared, anxious that his mother ready the stable for the party's horses.

"There's nothing up there," his mother explained. "People can't survive that crossing—it's too high and remote and cold. Lhasa is very, very far away."

Back then no one ever came over the Changtang, except the tax collector once a year. The toddler finally compelled his mother to fill the water troughs and hay bins in the stable, insisting they be ready for the horses, which he said were exhausted, thirsty, and hungry. The next morning, the search party from Lhasa arrived.

When I was in Lhasa in 1986, I'd heard of a passenger dying on the bus from Golmud—not just from lack of oxygen, but from exposure, because the buses then were old Soviet rejects. Door and windows didn't close, and engines struggled. One bus I rode for three days and nights through the countryside had a first gear so weak it could only crawl, snail-like, on uphill sections with its load of passengers; the driver made us get out and climb all the mountain passes on foot so he'd be able to get the bus to the top.

The announcer stated that no workers had died from work-related illnesses building the railroad. He was mum on the subject of the 14,500 who had been hospitalized during construction for potentially fatal swelling of the lungs and brain due to extreme altitude, as a railroad official had told a Hong Kong newspaper reporter the previous year. I had recently learned that the Karakoram Highway from China to Pakistan, on which I'd traveled in summer 1986, had also been funded by the Chinese government, which wanted access to a seaport in the region. I remembered well the experience of crossing the more than 650-mile length and being keenly aware of the fact that the death toll averaged one worker per half mile or so. It was very hard to believe that no workers had died building this railroad. I couldn't begin to imagine what the truth might be about the construction—the number of lives lost, the environmental damage, the hardship for the families whose land was seized, the long-term health effects for the building crews. There's another story here they're not telling, I thought, as the voice prattled on about "the proud moment" and "prodigious achievement."

The peaks in the distance grew steeper and more dramatic, like the so-called storybook formation I'd seen around the Annapurna range years before. I saw one or two tunnels, which the train voice had mentioned, that I hoped were not for the caribou herds, because they looked barely big enough for a couple of large dogs to pass through.

Near sundown, dark gray rain clouds pushed across the white billowy ones, the sun illuminating their edges and casting the landscape in shadow.

So far, no one had fainted away in a berth or experienced difficulty breathing, unlike in the photos I'd seen accompanying articles about people sucking from oxygen masks, pale and lifeless on their bunks. Either my Diamox™ had worked or they really did pump extra oxygen into the ventilation system.

It was easy to be lulled, I thought, resting on my tiny bunk, letting myself be pulled along with the train's chugging vibrations across the track.

Every blade of grass. Every blade of grass. I thought about a line that had rung in my ears from years before: Every day was a Sunday, Mrs. Namseling had said.

I had long wanted to talk to an eyewitness to the March 1959 events in Lhasa. What I knew was that thousands of women had lain down like human cobblestones on the road outside the Dalai Lama's Norbulingka Palace in a spontaneous mass civil action to prevent him from departing for what was believed to be a thinly disguised kidnapping ruse. The Chinese had used the same ploy—an invitation to dinner and a theater show at PLA headquarters—in Kham with other high-ranking Tibetans whose influence they wanted to eliminate. The lamas were never seen again.

I wanted to know how the events had unfolded, what it was like being there, and what the impact had been on the situation and on the women, both the Norbulingka action and the event of March 12, known as Tibetan Women's Uprising Day. I hoped to learn from Mrs. Namseling, who had been in Lhasa that fateful month. She not only had been at ground zero but, as a Cabinet minister's wife, was privy to an insider's view.

A 1955 *National Geographic* article on Tibet by the Austrian climber Heinrich Harrer, who'd lived in Tibet for seven years, featured a vivid color photograph of a lovely maiden with elaborately braided hair, wearing a long, ornate dress and coral, turquoise, amber, and pearl jewelry. Harrer commented, "A woman has no voice in Tibet's public affairs, but jewels denote her husband's rank in government. A Cabinet minister's wife may display gems worth $20,000. A wealthy woman spends hours making her toilet. She dotes on cosmetics." The article quoted a Tibetan folk saying: "A person's beauty lies in her clothes; the tree's, in its leaves."

The Tibetan women I had known were nothing like that. On the other hand, my experience there began thirty-five years after Communist rule took hold. What had it been like for women before Chinese takeover?

Mrs. Namseling and I met in her third-floor walk-up studio apartment on the main street in McLeod Ganj, in the spring of 1994. I was accompanied by the daughter of the younger brother of the Dalai Lama, Choedzom, a recent high school graduate, who served as translator.

Sixty-four-year-old Mrs. Namseling, silver haired, diminutive, with clear, sparkling eyes and still-smooth skin, had a lovely presence about her. I noted this in the directness of her gaze and the graceful, unhurried movements with which she fixed us tea in the kitchenette adjoining her one-room studio. Clad in a pressed, light-gray *chuba* and tan blouse, she had a style as tasteful and calm as her home, the clean yellow walls adorned with only a 1940s black-and-white family photo and two religious scrolls. "I don't put everything up," she said. "I don't like a lot of clutter." Outside the windows was a view of treetops, rooftops, and a few satellite dishes—an oasis from the noise and bustle of town.

A yellow plastic case the size of a school lunchbox lay atop Mrs. Namseling's bed, spread wide to hold an open prayer book within, next to a sheepskin-lined maroon cape spread out in a half circle, as if someone had been sitting in the spot reading. Mrs. Namseling said she woke every morning at 5:30 to the Tibetan-language version of Voice of America, then did her prayers. Her six grown children all lived in the West, except for a daughter in Gangtok. Over three or four visits, of about two and a half hours each, I gathered Mrs. Namseling's story.

Born in 1930 in a town called Tromo, with the given name Choekyi, she passed a carefree childhood, with little formal education, as was typical for girls in those days. She'd lost her father when she was a young child. When Choekyi was fourteen, living in Shigatse, central Tibet's second-largest city, a local official approached her mother via an intermediary, asking for Choekyi's hand in marriage. The official, the provincial governor, had recently become a widower and had three children, all older than Choekyi. Choekyi's mother refused repeatedly, citing the youth of her daughter and the large age difference between the two—the man was thirty-seven—until the intermediary warned that the governor "could make life hard for her."

I saw pictures of her husband, Namseling, an unusually tall, unusually stern-looking Tibetan with a dark mustache, dressed in elegant magisterial robes. He looked to be over six feet tall; she was under five feet. Mrs. Namseling, pretty when I met her at sixty-four, must have been adorable at fourteen. She was terrified, she said, of the complete stranger and pleaded with her mother, but to no avail.

"I had to go with him. My mother was afraid to refuse him. We didn't even have a proper wedding, because his wife had just died. It would have looked bad."

Luckily, she said, her husband turned out to be a nice man. The couple moved to Lhasa in the late 1940s with their family—three daughters, all born before Mrs. Namseling turned twenty-one.

"The first childbirth was extremely difficult. I was in labor for three days. No doctor, no nurse. My mother and a maidservant gave me dried tripe from a sacred lake to eat and rubbed a poultice on my belly. It was very painful. I was very scared."

Her husband became one of the four finance ministers of the Kashag, the Tibetan Cabinet. They had a fourth child, a long-awaited boy, on whom the overjoyed couple doted. When he was three, he was recognized as the reincarnation of a close associate of the Reting Rinpoche, a prominent figure in Tibet's religious hierarchy, and, sadly for his parents, was taken off to live at a monastery outside Lhasa.

In the early 1950s, the Chinese came.

"The Chinese were cunning. In the beginning they were friendly—helping old people fetch water, helping farmers plow their fields. Then after a while, they started telling people that Tibetan officials were corrupt, would bring down the society, all kinds of disparaging things. I had trouble keeping my daughters in school in Lhasa. My daughters would attend one school, and when the Chinese authorities discovered they were 'children of aristocrats,' they were thrown out. Then I'd find another school for them, and after a year or so the same thing would happen. I finally took them to India in 1956 and enrolled them in a convent school in Kalimpong.

"Eventually the Chinese took over people's houses and carried away all the contents. They became very brutal. They punished people for doing anything Buddhist. People fled to the countryside. Some headed to India. They gave their valuables to monasteries for safekeeping before they escaped.

"The Chinese army arrived in Lhasa with all their weapons. Tens of thousands of Chinese soldiers. We had never seen such weapons—machine guns, tanks, cannons. They were just loaded. They completely surrounded Lhasa and aimed their cannons toward town. Everyone was terrified. People ran all over the city, rushing here and there, upset and agitated.

"I remember one day a group of monks surrounded this army tank. Nobody had ever seen a tank, we didn't have any idea what it was. The monks started chopping it with axes, whacking it like it was a live creature." She laughed, recalling their naïveté. She had a delightfully infectious laugh. "It remained still for some minutes, then it started rolling backward. We all just stood and watched; nobody knew anything about what it was. Nobody knew to run.

"Then it stopped. And then . . . *dada da da da,*" she imitated the rapid rhythm of automatic fire. She burst into laughter again, remembering how startled they were. "It started firing."

"It shot all the monks?" I exclaimed.

"Yes."

"Shot them dead?"

She nodded, her laughter subsiding.

We call this cold-blooded murder in my part of the world, I thought. The juxtaposition of the army's heartlessness with the Tibetan people's complete and total ignorance of what they were up against was heartbreaking and mind-boggling at the same time. A foreshadowing of the events in Tiananmen Square thirty years hence. These tanks, she said, drove in procession through Lhasa, shooting, when the PLA launched its attack a few days later.

Due to her husband's official position, they had known beforehand of the nature of the imminent invasion: "Khampas who'd fled Kham visited our house. Since my husband was a Cabinet minister, they came to tell him. They told us: The Chinese slaughtered the Tibetans in Kham. Looted every place. Destroyed everything. They were absolutely ruthless."

She was somber again. Her earlier merriment might have helped to lighten the memory of her own terror at the time, which must have been significant as an eyewitness. Kham lay four days by horse east of Lhasa, between central Tibet and China. The Khampas were known as tough, proud people, excellent horsemen and warriors. Even other Tibetans feared them. Khampas, it was felt, wouldn't let anyone take their province without a fierce battle and would fight to the bitter end. The Khampa front was the only thing that stood in the way of the Chinese advancing on Lhasa and thereby taking the entire nation.

"A colleague of my husband's in government service telephoned Chamdo, in Kham, one day. He'd been in regular contact with them for several weeks. This time when he called, he heard a Chinese voice pick up the other end. He said, Can I speak to this man? He named someone. Can I speak to that man? He kept asking for this fellow and that fellow, until he'd named all his contacts there. But the only people who ever picked up the phone were Chinese. He heard lots of men yelling in the background. All in Chinese. No Tibetan ever came to the phone.

"That's when he knew Chamdo had fallen. That meant the Chinese had completely overpowered Kham, taken even the command posts. Once we heard this, we were terrified. It meant the Chinese army was on its way."

I asked about the women's action at the Norbulingka, the summer palace of the Dalai Lama, whom the Tibetans simply called The Presence, or Kundun in Tibetan. My understanding was that the women had lain down in the road in a spontaneous mass action.

"Shortly after the army arrived, the Chinese invited His Holiness to dinner and a theater show at their army base near the river. They insisted he come alone. We were very suspicious—they'd done this in Kham. Everyone in town ran to the palace to guard him one morning. I was very pregnant at the time. I and a relative who was also pregnant walked together, but by the time we got there, the road by the Norbulingka was starting to empty.

"Townspeople had packed the road from the palace to the river, where the Chinese army headquarters stood. They'd pledged to lie down to prevent Kundun from leaving his palace and getting in harm's way. Everyone was in an extreme state of agitation, worried about Kundun's safety, and furious at the Chinese. They were ready to lie down. Then word spread that a representative of the palace had appeared at the gate and told everyone Kundun would not be going to the PLA camp, to disperse and go home.

"People in the crowd yelled, 'If anyone helps the Chinese, we'll kill him! Even a Tibetan!' Some of the Tibetan officials were collaborating with the Chinese. One man, a known collaborator, whose brother was a religious leader in Kham, came out of the palace dressed in a monk's robe. He had sneaked in on a bike through an unguarded gate earlier in the morning. The crowd beat him with sticks and stones."

I asked Mrs. Namseling to back up a bit, to before the invasion. "What was your daily life like?"

She thought a moment. "Well, we'd get up in the morning and go over to each other's houses."

"Oh. And what did you do there?"

"Play cards mostly."

"And?"

"Drink *chang*." *Chang* was their alcoholic drink.

"Anything else?" I meant, did she do anything other than visit friends? Maybe something for the war effort? Something in response to the situation Tibet was in?

"We sang songs. Near sunset, we'd take some drums and musical instruments and go to the Jokhang and do *kora*." She swung her hands in front of her body as if beating a big bass drum. "*Tum-dee-dum*." She sang part of a tune, then her voice spilled into delighted laughter again.

"But what about a regular day?" I asked after a moment. "A workday?"

"That *was* a regular day."

"What about people with jobs?"

"If you had a job, you went to your office. If you didn't have a job, you just went to a friend's house."

I nodded slowly. I didn't know what I was expecting, but I wasn't expecting what I was hearing.

"Who were your friends?"

"Other government officials and their wives."

"Most of them didn't have work to do? Or a job?"

"No."

Maybe I was missing something, I thought. I decided I would probe a bit more.

"How else did you spend your time?"

"That's all, really. I had no responsibilities at home. My only responsibility was to look after my husband's wardrobe. I took a little *tsampa* dough, wet it, and wiped away lint. Easy."

"And other people you knew didn't have to work?"

Choedzom and I sat in rapt attention, hanging on her words. Crows squawked in the trees, taxi horns blared, and crash sounds from the Hollywood soundtrack at the video parlor next door drifted up to us.

She nodded.

"Most people didn't work. If you didn't have to go to a job, you just went around to this person's home or that person's home. Played mah-jong."

"That's all?"

"Laughed and joked."

I waited.

"Sang songs . . . In the summer we had picnics outside. One after another." She chuckled, recalling them fondly.

I knew that picnics were, as one author put it, practically a national sport in old Tibet. The clean mountain air and beautiful riversides were conducive to being outdoors.

"That's it? That's all you did?"

She nodded.

"Every day was a Sunday."

Choedzom and I walked home that afternoon along a gravel road. The time Mrs. Namseling had been talking about had been a tense time politically in Tibet. Mao Zedong had been dragging the Dalai Lama around China extolling the virtues of socialism. The Chinese authorities tried to hold Tibetans to a document called the Seventeen-Point Agreement, which they had forced them to sign, ceding wide-ranging powers to China. The Dalai Lama had also been approaching Jawaharlal Nehru to see if India might be able to lend help against China's aggression.

From the look on her face during the interview, I could tell that Choedzom was as astonished as I was that during this critical time, when the future of their country hung in the balance, officials were idling frivolously. I don't know what I expected them to be doing, but I thought they'd have been doing *something*. Rome was burning, and government officials were fiddling. Mrs. Namseling's account seemed to indicate that Tibetans had been completely unaware of the magnitude of the threat before them. Unaware? Unprepared? Resigned? Ignorant? I wasn't sure.

I guess if they hadn't even known what an armored tank was, they couldn't have known what the new leadership in some other country was capable of doing. They'd lived in isolation for centuries. Even so, the description alluded to a decadent bourgeoisie.

Choedzom had been raised with a strong sense of pride as a Tibetan and had received the best Tibetan education available anywhere. I knew her parents. She was the niece of the Dalai Lama, the daughter of a former *rinpoche*. Head bowed, she scuffed at stones as we walked home that day, keeping her distance from me, absorbed in thought. I'd never seen her so despondent. Usually, given that her family had recently acquired one of the few VCRs in town, when we got together she was giddy about the latest Richard Gere movie she'd seen.

"No wonder we lost our country," she murmured sadly.

My interviews with Mrs. Namseling continued over several days.

"Women felt they had to do something. Most husbands were out of town with the resistance; women were left in Lhasa. Wherever there were lots of people gathered, they organized rallies and protests. Women said, We must do something!

"A call went out for women of all classes of society to attend meetings. A neighbor in my building went in my place because I was in the late stages of pregnancy. Women gathered in front of the Potala, in Shur village. They discussed sending out appeals internationally, writing letters or petitions. The women vowed: Even if just one woman is left and the whole rest of the city is Chinese, we will fight on.

"I didn't stay in Lhasa much longer after that. I was about to have my baby, my sixth. My husband was gone. It felt too dangerous in town. I needed a quiet place to rest and give birth."

Her husband, being a respected official, had been sent to Kham by the Chinese to try and influence the Tibetan resistance forces to put down their arms. Instead he had joined them. She decided to take the family—her mother and small daughter, accompanied by three male servants—to the hermitage of her son's monastery in the mountains southwest of Lhasa. Her son was on retreat there.

"We climbed up to the hermitage on the outskirts of town. After a long time, we came upon two men lying in the road outside a brick factory, in a stream of fresh blood. We had walked about fifty feet past them when about twenty soldiers rushed up and surrounded us. They leveled their rifles and machine guns in our faces.

"Three or four officers stepped forward. 'Where are you going? What are you doing way out here? Where do you live in town? Do you have any guns or knives with you?' They tried to sound friendly. I had a feeling it was they who had shot the brick workers. We could still see the dead bodies down the path. They could just as easily shoot us, I thought. I was terrified because our servants had insisted that we bring two rifles, and they were rolled up in our bedding. The soldiers patted our belongings, checking for weapons. They felt all our bags. Tapped our radio."

The soldiers let her party go. Mrs. Namseling could see the entire city from the mountaintop house, she said. The Norbulingka, the river, the Potala.

"One morning the earth shook with tremendous explosions. I rushed to the window. *Boom! Boom! Boom!* Bombs, rockets, all manner of weapons exploded. The sounds of bombs and shooting filled the air. It was like a war. The city was clouded with smoke and ash. I couldn't stop watching. We'd never seen anything like it.

"After a time, I got so upset. I told myself: I won't look anymore. It's not good for the baby. I'll get away from the window. I'd go inside and sit down. But I could still hear everything. After a while I would want to go see what was happening. I felt sick. I felt I was about to faint. Being pregnant, I was already nervous and edgy. The bombing made me terrified. I couldn't help it. I had to go see what was happening. I'd get up and go back to the window. It went on day and night. Just when ashes started to settle and the skies to clear, bombing would start again. Back and forth I went. To the window. Away from the window. I had to watch. I couldn't watch.

"Day and night, I worried about Kundun. They continuously bombed and shelled his palace. Struck it again and again. Our hearts sank, thinking, All is lost. He's finished. He can't possibly survive this. I prayed ceaselessly for his safety."

Mrs. Namseling said the bombing lasted two and a half days. On the third day, the attacks lightened. Then for several more days, they continued intermittently.

Mrs. Namseling gave birth to her youngest daughter. Two days later, soldiers came to the house.

"They didn't come through the proper entrance; they came around the back and encircled the house. One yelled, 'Whoever's inside, come out!' I was still weak and bedridden. My mother and servants told the men I wasn't able to move, I'd just given birth. The soldiers insisted we come outside to their vehicle. My mother and servants told them I couldn't move. They said, 'Have your servant carry you on a chair on his back.' I pleaded with them to let me stay a week to recover. We were almost on our knees begging. Finally they said we could stay three days, then we had to move down to Lhasa.

"One day, my husband's oldest servant climbed up the mountain to bring me the news that Kundun had escaped to India, had fled before the bombing. It was a miracle. My prayers had been answered. I felt so relieved."

After three days, soldiers collected them and forced them to return to Lhasa, she said. Five of them—Mrs. Namseling, her mother, her young daughter, her newborn, and a young babysitter—were assigned a bare squatter's shack to live in, with no furniture, no household supplies, no cookware, no bedding. The soldiers released her servants from duty. The army confiscated the Namselings' family home north of Lhasa in Rampoche and took everything in the house—furniture, clothing, jewelry, livestock, statuary, and several years' store of *tsampa*. They converted the house into officers' housing.

Mrs. Namseling remarked that the construction of the houses in Lhasa was solid and strong, with walls over two feet thick, not like the buildings they construct in Lhasa today. She learned that her husband had escaped with the Dalai Lama's entourage, bringing up the rear guard.

I asked whether, if her husband had been in Lhasa, she would have left with him when he escaped.

"No!" she replied.

"Why?"

"It just wasn't done. Wives did not go. As a Kashag member, it was my husband's duty to follow His Holiness wherever he went. But wives didn't go along."

What were women supposed to do? I wondered. Were they just supposed to figure out how to escape themselves, with the children?

"Well, what would happen if a wife went with the entourage?" I asked.

"Mindu, mindu," she shook her head. "It wouldn't happen, it wasn't done."

"But let's say a wife did go," I pressed. "What would happen?"

"If she insisted, she would travel at the very end of the group. And camp by herself."

I was horrified. The women and children were left alone to fend for themselves. I wasn't sure if this was just tradition, or because His Holiness was a monk, or what. Even if families couldn't go with the entourage, I was dismayed that no one made provisions for them. That there was no contingency plan. Of course it was a very unusual situation, but in more normal times, would the wives and children of these men have been considered?

Mrs. Namseling said she was assigned to hard physical labor. Women hauled heavy stones up mountains for hydroelectric dams, dug ditches, worked on farms, planted trees.

"You were forced to work no matter how sick or tired you were. One lady was hauling stones one day and blood started gushing out between her legs. She died right on the spot."

The work was very, very hard, and usually unpaid. Only occasionally would the Chinese pay them a pittance.

Under the strict rationing program—the meat ration, for instance, was a pound of meat per person per year—her family starved. She sold the rings off her fingers and pawned her earrings to buy more food. In the winter, the children froze without warm clothes. When she approached the building where the townspeople's confiscated clothing was stored, the Chinese official slammed the door in her face.

In the early '60s, the PLA evacuated the remaining Tibetan men to prison or labor camps, she told us. Everything related to Buddhism was destroyed. Soldiers wearing red armbands that read "Protectors of Communist Rule" went door-to-door with a young translator, searching for Buddhist objects. If they found something, Mrs. Namseling told us, "they'd just step on it and smash it right there. They destroyed Buddha statues, prayer lamps, *thangkas*, anything.

"They paraded wives of high government officials around the streets. They'd make them walk around wearing full makeup, carrying a large tray with all their toiletries and powders, behind a soldier beating a drum to get people's attention."

The soldiers punished anyone who'd had wealth or privilege in Tibetan society, she said, made them trot around wearing the symbol of their status while being taunted with slogans. They'd shout threats like "Now we'll kill those who lived off the fat of other people's labor."

"They hauled them off to prison for some reason or another and killed them," she continued. She shook her head. "The world turned upside down. Before, we had three classes of people: those who worked, those in the middle, and those who employed workers. Now we—who used to have people work for us—worked. And the people who had worked before had privilege."

People "disappeared"—went missing—and public torture became commonplace: "I saw them torture one man so long his tongue hung out. They hung him from his arms, which were tied behind him, and then tortured him; his face grew bloated and grotesque. It went on so long I thought, I wish somebody would just kill him, so he didn't have to suffer. It was done in public, in front of everybody. They'd force the wife and family to attend and watch. And the Chinese ordered that they couldn't cry or show emotion."

Once, Mrs. Namseling said, she even saw youth paraded around in a military truck, a group of about nine teenagers who'd organized to resist the Chinese. They had taken a blood oath to continue the fight. They were found out, rounded up, and killed.

"I had a really tough time, everyone did. I had no time to spend with my young daughters. I was gone all day, working long hours. Sometimes I wished a plane would fly over and drop a bomb and end it all."

Around 1971, her son was arrested and imprisoned; seven months later, she was arrested. Chinese officials kept forcing her to confess her crime, to guess why she had been arrested. They asked her the same questions every few days for two years—about her husband's activities as an official, about their trip to India in 1956. If she didn't answer properly, they threatened her life. They brought in former servants and gave them permission to beat her if they had any score to settle with her. None did.

Apparently her name had been mentioned when two of her son's disciples were arrested as part of the resistance, she finally learned. Under interrogation, they disclosed that they'd obtained from her some precious pills, made of herbs thought to have spiritual protection properties, when her son was in prison. The Chinese accused her of creating division and revolt against their rule. At the age of forty, she was handed a ten-year prison sentence.

In prison, she said, her whole body swelled up. She could press her finger into her flesh and it would leave a depression. She spent a year in solitary confinement. "I worried about my son, that they'd kill him. I used to say, 'Punish me, but don't harm him.'"

Her second year, they put other women in her cell, and at the end of that year she was moved to a larger prison, with twelve women per cell. She was put to hard labor. After two years of inactivity, her muscles had atrophied, and it was painful to carry loads of brick and plant apple trees twelve hours a day. Soldiers drove the prisoners along back roads, so they couldn't be seen. At night, they had to attend *thamzig*.

"We were always hungry. The food was like slop you'd feed a pig, and there was never enough. We had strict orders not to talk to each other, so we could never make friends. We were forbidden to do religious practice. One or two people in the cell were always spies, so you had to be careful.

"One lady was in prison for twelve years because she had swung her spade at a poster of Mao on the wall. Before she consumed food or drink, she offered it to His Holiness and said prayers. Guards beat her. She kept doing it and kept getting beaten. She used to say, 'Whether I live or die, I always keep Kundun in my mind.' They eventually killed her, saying her thinking was not correct.

"Guards brought in newspapers with articles touting China's accomplishments. The theme was that China was the top country in the world. China was the powerful, honorable nation. America was a paper tiger. Japan and European countries were headed for ruin. They'd make us read the articles out loud, then they'd ask each person her opinion."

Despite the harsh existence, Mrs. Namseling said she'd been optimistic: "I always held the hope deep down that we'd get our country back and all this would soon be over. All of us felt that way."

The Chinese tried to demoralize them, to convince them the situation was hopeless. "You're dreaming. You're counting on the Dalai Lama to save you, but he's going around with a staff in one hand, a sack in the other, begging," they told her. "The Tibetans who escaped with him are dropping dead from the heat and brutal work conditions in India. Give up your false hopes."

In her ninth year, prison officials starting coming around a lot, interrogating her, asking questions about her children—what each did, where they lived.

"My cellmates said that when the Chinese suddenly became interested in you, it meant either they were about to kill you or about to release you."

They released her six months shy of her ten-year sentence, citing her record as a good worker.

"That wasn't the real reason. There were women who were much better workers. Model prisoners. My daughter was coming to visit me, and they found out that she was married to the prince of Gangtok. They didn't want to get into any trouble with higher-ups for having locked up the mother-in-law of the prince of Gangtok. When she came, they put on a big banquet and made speeches about how Gangtok was a free country, with its own monarch, yet under India's political rule. It was a similar situation, they said, to Tibet and its relationship to China.

"My daughter spoke back: 'It's not the same. Here you have taken everything the Tibetans had and left them not a shred of freedom or autonomy. This is not so in Gangtok.'"

Mrs. Namseling happily rejoined her children in Lhasa. She never saw her husband again after 1958, although she had received a letter from him in 1962 from India. He passed away in Sikkim two years before she gained her freedom. She learned that many of her friends and acquaintances had suffered a fate similar to hers.

"When I left for prison, you couldn't move freely, even across town; you couldn't visit other people's homes; there was no food for sale. Attending *thamzing* every night was compulsory. When I got out of prison, things were more relaxed. People could come and go, and food was for sale again in the market. There was no forced labor, and you were not punished for not attending struggle meetings."

In 1981, she traveled to India, via Nepal, and moved to Dharamsala the next year.

"In prison all those years, I had three prayers: to see His Holiness again, to see my children again, and that Tibet be free again. The first two have been fulfilled," she said. In exile, she had developed a religious practice, took teachings, read scripture, and said daily prayers. Her adult children, in Switzerland, the United States, and Gangtok, gave her financial support. "Everything has worked out."

In Mrs. Namseling's account, Lhasa was a city of women. In Mrs. Paljorkhyimsar's story, slave gulags were made up predominantly of women. Both took for granted that women's participation in government affairs was something that "just wasn't done." Neither government nor religious officials would tolerate having them around. Women were left to take care of themselves.

Mrs. Namseling with five of her six children, Kalimpong, 1957. Her older children were schooled in India because of the difficulty of keeping them in schools in Tibet in the 1950s. Photo courtesy of the Namseling family.

As we drew within a half a day of Lhasa, I grew excited at the thought of seeing Amala and Pala soon. I had such vivid memories of living with the family in their snug, warrenlike monastery home twenty-one years before: the sociability and gentility of the family, the warmth and laughter, the sense of peace and order. The simplicity, yet richness of their life.

Tashi and I had met within hours of my arriving in town in late spring 1986, when she, the only English-speaking postal clerk in Lhasa, helped me retrieve my mail from the United States, which had been forwarded there. This was not a small task, because her higher-ups routinely stole mail, either for the valuable goods inside packages or for the foreign stamps, which people collected. My second day in town, I bumped into her again in my guesthouse. She was visiting the friendly British couple, long-term residents in Lhasa, one of whom was her English tutor, who lived in the room next to mine.

Tashi was in her early twenties and warmly attractive, with large, lively brown eyes and a short, Western-style haircut, wearing blue jeans and a down parka. She beamed a megawatt smile at me, the likes of which I hadn't seen in a month in China, where people generally ignored me and one another. We chatted. She had been born and raised in Lhasa; her father was a traditional woodcarver. We connected instantly. Tashi took me home for tea that afternoon.

I followed her across the street and through a narrow space between two shops. We took several quick turns through a labyrinth of close-packed buildings until we suddenly arrived at a pair of gigantic, medieval wooden doors. Stepping over the high threshold, a foot high and six inches deep, we emerged into a sunlit courtyard inside a two-story, traditional Tibetan building complex. It looked centuries old. Tashi said the place was a former monastery.

We climbed a steep, ancient wooden staircase—half ladder, half stairs—the banister silky smooth from the oil of hands touching it over countless years. Upstairs at the corner of the balcony, she pushed open a short door. We stepped over another high threshold. As Tashi shut the door behind us, we were plunged into complete darkness and cold. It felt like a walk-in cooler.

"This way," I heard her say a few paces ahead. Her voice always seemed to carry a hint of a laugh. She pushed aside a heavy cloth door-hanging and climbed over another high threshold. We entered a snug room with low ceilings and hand-plastered walls. A plate of butter cookies sat on a gleaming black lacquer table, bathed in a pool of light from a single bulb hanging above.

"Please sit," Tashi waved. I sat down on the center part of a U-shaped arrangement of couches around the low table. Thick, navy blue carpets bearing colorful traditional designs covered each couch. She left again.

Across the room stood a cabinet, shoulder high, its eight panel doors decorated with paintings of bouquets. A long row of bronze water bowls sat in front of a Buddha draped in a gauzy white scarf on the cabinet top. A peacock feather brushed the low ceiling. Something about the scene of the cookies so carefully arranged on the blue-and-white china plate in the pool of light, the immaculate care and sense of expectancy it showed, moved me.

Tashi returned after a while with a woman dressed in a traditional Tibetan long black jumper dress. Each carried an oversize red thermos.

"You like Tibetan tea or milk tea?" Tashi asked.

I'd read that Tibetan tea was made from rancid yak butter and rock salt churned with black tea. Nomads drank up to sixty cups a day in the winter; the fat kept them warm.

"Oh, gee . . . I don't know. I guess I'll try Tibetan tea," I said. When in Rome . . .

The woman, in her thirties maybe, poured a frothy, steaming yellowish brown brew into a cup. As she did this, she bowed her head, and I saw that pink and pale blue tassels had been woven into long, thick, black braids coiled atop her head. She picked up the saucer and offered it to me with two hands, in an extraordinarily gracious manner.

"Please drink," Tashi urged. The tea tasted savory and oily like soup broth, but not as flavorful. "A biscuit?" she asked, lifting the plate of cookies.

"My father has painted all . . . " Tashi said, sweeping her hand toward the polished gold-leaf lacquer table before us and then over to the cabinet. "He is teaching himself. From fourteen years old. Schools not teaching."

"Maybe try milk tea—it is sweet," she said, noting that I hadn't touched the Tibetan tea after my first sip.

The woman filled another cup with a steaming brown beverage from the other thermos and placed it before me in the same almost ritual-like manner. The hot, sweet tea, the color of coffee with cream, melted down my throat.

"Tibetan people like Tibetan tea. Foreigners like milk tea," Tashi giggled. The woman beamed now, displaying an impish, laughter-lined face. She had a lump the size of a lemon on her neck. Goiter, I thought.

"Tashi, who is this woman?" I asked. She seemed too young to be her mother. Was she a family friend . . . or the cook?

"This is my mother," Tashi said.

"Oh!" I exclaimed.

Her mother acknowledged me with a shy nod and a broad, endearing smile.

"Does she speak Chinese?" I asked.

"No, only Tibetan."

"Tashi delek!" I said, addressing her with the traditional greeting. I mimed my thanks. Tashi said I should call her mother "Amala."

Amala had an ineffable quality about her, something completely present, and serenely lovely. It shone through even though I couldn't speak to her. Amala did tailoring, according to Tashi; she could sew anything—*chubas*, blouses, suits. The *chuba* was the traditional dress, ankle-length for women, thigh-length and long-sleeved for men.

Tashi explained that when she had returned from India a couple of months earlier, her multilingual skills caught the attention of the Chinese government, which had launched a new tourism campaign in Lhasa. They assigned her to work at the main post office where we'd met, in the center of town. After graduating from high school, she had begged her parents to let her go to India to learn English and to pay respects to the Dalai Lama.

"You like the Dalai Lama?"

"Oh yes," she gushed. "All Tibetans very much like him."

"But you weren't born when he left."

"No."

"Did you get to see him?"

"Yes, I saw," she nodded, smiling broadly. "I saw him New Year's." She touched the top of her head lightly and briefly with her fingers, dipping her forehead. She didn't know the word in English. He had blessed her, I guessed.

She spoke to her mother, filling her in on our exchange.

"Uhhhh. La, la," Amala nodded approvingly. "Dalai Lama." She bowed her head reverently.

"Canyon Sam, do you speak Chinese?" Tashi asked, calling me by my full name.

"My family speaks Cantonese, but I can only speak a bit. And I studied Mandarin before I came, but I know only enough to travel." I told her my family had been in California for more than a hundred years.

"America is very nice, yes? Very nice things there, yes? Many cah-sits?"

"Many what?"

"Cah-sits."

I drew a blank.

"Like Michael Jackson . . . "

"Oh, *cassettes*! Music tapes!"

She nodded and told me she'd discovered music tapes in India, but none were available in Tibet. "But A-mer-i-ca . . . " She chatted excitedly about her vision of America, a veritable bonanza of pop music, hip fashion, and fun discotheques, as if Americans spent all their time there.

"Would you like to go to America?"

"Yes, very much," she answered enthusiastically.

Gold Mountain, I thought. It was no different from what my forebears had believed when they dreamed of going to America. Gold dust glittered in the streets and dollar bills grew on trees. How could I explain the reality? How could I characterize in rudimentary English the contradictions of an industrialized Western capitalist society to someone from this preindustrial, Eastern, Communist society?

Tashi's face dropped. "But not possible. No money. No visa."

Her mother plucked the cork out of the thermos again.

"No, please," I begged, covering my cup. She had already topped off my teacup several times, every time I took two sips. I had been raised to finish whatever was placed before me; the Tibetans, I learned later, kept a guest's cup full at all times, clear up to the brim. I kept trying to finish, and she kept filling, which kept me drinking, which kept her filling.

"La, la, la," she urged me to move my hand, holding the thermos spout an inch above it. That was where Tashi got her gleeful smile, I thought. I turned to Tashi for help. She just laughed.

"No. Really . . . please." I flattened my hand.

"La . . . la," Amala urged with a mock frown, nudging the thermos over my knuckles.

I shook my head no. Firm, but polite.

Amala nodded even more insistently. We were in a standoff. She grunted, nodding yes. I grunted, nodding no. She had such a sense of lightness and fun about her.

Yes.

No.

I gave up, moved my hand. We all burst out laughing.

"How long you stay Lhasa?" Tashi asked.

I hadn't liked any place in China well enough to stay longer than a few days, but from my first moments in Tibet the day before, I had sensed something wholly different.

Where China was overcrowded, impersonal, and frenzied, Lhasa was laid back, sparsely populated, friendly, and slow paced. Everyone walked everywhere. Only a few people had bikes—identical black, three-speed, Pigeon models. In China, vendors and shopowners clamored and clanged, hollered and banged from before sunup until after sundown in the so-called special economic zones, areas where the government was experimenting with free enterprise. In Tibet, vendors would mosey out about ten in the morning and start to set up their cots and awnings, lay out their merchandise, taking their sweet time.

"Maybe a month," I answered.

Tashi and Amala invited me to stay with them, live with the family, in that very room. The daybeds on which we sat converted to three single beds at night—one for Tashi, one for her youngest sister, and one for me. The spare belonged to the middle sister who was away at a job posting.

I stayed seven weeks in central Tibet, taking forays of a week or two out of Lhasa to see the surrounding countryside. Tashi and I, the British couple, and a couple of others all became good friends, enjoying picnics by the riverside, hanging out on the large veranda at the guesthouse, and having dinner out occasionally. We few backpackers in town roamed around, exploring the town and the culture on our own, since there was no tourist infrastructure. So few Westerners had ever stepped foot in Tibet that locals in the countryside were mesmerized by the zipper on my backpack and startled by the digital watch pulsing out the seconds on my wrist. They stared curiously at the flip-up shades attached to my eyeglasses and gingerly rubbed the nylon material of my backpack between their fingers. They had never before seen such things.

Tashi got up early, before anyone else in the family, to sweep the floors and haul water from the courtyard well, build a fire in the woodstove, and make Tibetan tea in a wooden churn, plunging the handle up and down to mix the yak butter, rock salt, and black tea into a steaming brew. Amala spoke Tibetan to me very naturally, but with a lot of gesturing, always wanting to communicate. She told me her worries about Tashi and made jokes. She left me alone in the house one day and shortly afterward had a neighbor knock on the door and grill me about everyone's whereabouts, then burst out laughing from her hiding spot upon hearing me exhaust the limits of my spoken Tibetan. The three of us fell into hysterics at her prank. Amala lovingly, faithfully emptied the altar bowls of water at night, shined them, then refilled them and placed them back on the altar each morning.

One indelible memory I had of that time was of waking in that room in the middle of my first night there. I was startled awake by a loud, strange noise—a kind of humming. I'd never heard anything like it before. At first I was frightened, then thought it was mechanical, perhaps a motor or generator. I waited for the others to wake in fright as I had, but they slept soundly. I waited a long time to see if the motor would cycle off. The sound never got closer, nor did it stop. I fell back to sleep eventually and asked Tashi about it the next day. From then on, in the darkness of the middle of the night, when I heard the deep sonorous droning—which she informed me were the monks in the nearby Jokhang chanting prayers—I'd lie in bed and listen. The Tibetans considered the Jokhang, or Tsuglhakhang, "the holiest of the holy" among what had once been more than 3,200 temples. Sort of like Mecca for Tibetans. The sound, like moans from the earth, reverberated in the darkness beginning hours before dawn. I felt it vibrate the air, vibrate through my whole body, enfolding me. The only light in the room was a red prayer lamp on top of the altar, the shade of which displayed the cut-out Sanskrit word *om*, illuminated by a candle inside. *Ooom shush shush*, it whispered with each revolution, as it spun round and round.

Surrounded by the three-foot-thick earthen walls of the ancient monastery, I felt as though I were in the womb of the earth. The sleeping sisters beside me, the prayers resounding through the valley, punctuated only by wild dogs barking, the glowing, hypnotic *om* spinning round gave me a sense of impenetrable peace and security like I'd never felt before. My body and soul seemed to sigh in relief. I'm home, I thought. Finally. I've landed.

My second morning in town, having made my way around the circular, high-walled cobblestone streets, I watched maybe three dozen Tibetans in grimy *chubas* performing a kind of ritualized, moving yoga in front of the entrance to the Jokhang. They seemed almost in a trance as they repeated the sequence, up and down off the ground over and over for hours—the slate beneath their feet worn slick and shiny. People have been doing that same ritual in that same spot for centuries, I thought. I stood there for a long time, mesmerized by their faith, their concentration, their devotion.

Amala and I also bonded around the heart attack she had that summer, when I fetched the doctor and took her for an EKG test a few days later. I gave her nightly neck and shoulder rubs to relax her and help with circulation. She pushed off one morning a week after the heart attack, a daughter at each arm, to walk the holy walk, the circumambulatory route around the city, even though she was still weak. She had to go out and do it because that day, she said, was the Buddha's birthday.

Years later, I heard veteran travelers to Asia refer to those months as "the golden window" of travel in Tibet because of how freely we could move around. Shortly after I left, the Chinese got organized enough to put certain areas off-limits to foreign travelers, such as around military bases and prisons, both in Lhasa and in outlying areas. A year later, Chinese authorities responded to pro-Tibetan demonstrations with harsh repression and severe restrictions on freedom of movement and association for local Tibetans as well as resident foreigners. But the summer I was there, monasteries were undergoing reconstruction, pilgrims by the truckload visited the few remaining temples, and I never saw or felt a police or military presence on the streets.

Now, as much as I looked forward to seeing Amala and Pala again, I also worried that it would be awkward. I hadn't seen them for many years, and because Tashi had had problems with her flight, she'd be arriving two days after me—she wouldn't be around to help translate or be an intermediary.

Two nights earlier, the night before I left San Francisco, I watched a BBC special on contemporary China. It showed scenes of Lhasa: boulevards with amusement park–like street lamps and busy traffic, sleek-fronted modern shopping complexes, pretentious monuments, masses of people on the streets, and billboards advertising luxury items like perfume and diamond jewelry. Even one of the Chinese officials working there who was interviewed said that after a period of several years' absence, she was shocked upon her return to see the new development in Lhasa. The Chinese urban plan, she said, had never taken into consideration the natural setting or the culture it was supplanting.

I dreaded seeing it.

3
LHASA

AS THE SLEEK train drew near the Lhasa station, all the passengers swung their rucksacks and bags off their berths and stood in the corridors, waiting. The stream from the plumbing leak had coursed beyond the bathroom area and down the hall of the passenger cabins, turning the new red carpet into a wet slog beneath our feet. I hadn't witnessed any potato chip bags popping or shampoo bottles exploding from the altitude, like I'd read about. I felt sleepy and spaced out but had not suffered a headache or any other high-altitude symptoms.

When we pulled into an enormous, spanking-new train station twenty-five minutes early, I walked off the platform, up and down staircases and escalators, and out to the front. That I looked a bit lost I'm sure encouraged the numerous taxi drivers who approached me for a fare. The thousands of passengers cleared out in minutes. I saw Hyvac slip into a cab behind his wife. Then I remembered with slight panic that I had only Amala's and Pala's phone number, not their address. Tashi had never given it to me, despite my asking several times. "My parents will pick you up," she had said. I looked at my watch. It was 8:50. Night was falling.

I stepped off the curb, keeping an eye out for Amala and Pala, and crossed the street, where a vast, empty parking lot stretched out in the darkness before me. The area had been clear of people for fifteen or twenty minutes when, from the far end of the lot, emerging from the darkness, I suddenly saw Pala walking toward me, his hair a shock of white! "Tashi delek!" I called.

"Tashi delek," he replied, with a little smile, shy to meet my eye. Without a word, he took the handle of my wheeled luggage and headed off with me beyond the lot. His hairline had receded and his hair had turned white, but he looked hearty and hale, bundled in a warm Patagonia™ jacket. I was surprised that he moved so normally, didn't seem weak or in pain.

I saw Amala coming toward us in the dark with a little girl. In her hands, I could see a shiny long white *khata*. She raised the offering scarf over my head, placed it around my neck, and tied it loosely in front, talking to me the whole time. "Tashi delek," she said over and over. "Tashi delek," I repeated happily, hugging her, so thrilled to see her again. She spoke a stream of Tibetan unreservedly, as if I understood, while Pala, a man of few words, just wore a little smile. We walked a distance to the outside road, where a jeep was parked. Amala, quite a bit heavier than before, walked slowly; Tashi had mentioned that she had a problem with her ankle.

We drove away from the new station across open, sprawling, undeveloped land; I hadn't a clue where we were and couldn't get oriented in the dark. Then I saw a bridge and realized we were on the other side of the river from Lhasa. I saw in the distance the whole town lit up in the dark and long lines of pale pink lights from street lamps. Lhasa hadn't had lights at night before, let alone street lamps. I remembered this vividly because when Amala had her heart attack in 1986, I had run through the streets at 9:30 at night looking for help and found nothing. No lights, no people, no phones—no sign of life at all. I had been struck with the realization that phone booths, ambulances, emergency rooms, 9-1-1, and the like didn't exist in Tibet.

I saw large, multistory buildings—maybe six floors high—covering the valley floor. After several minutes, I saw the Potala Palace in the distance, dimly lit and peeking out above the rooftops. This gladdened me to no end, even though it was barely visible above all the buildings. The train station was located, I realized, on the other side of the Kyichu River, where there had been nothing before, just raw open land. We crossed another bridge east of the first one, then drove down wide boulevards. I still couldn't get oriented to what street we were on as we passed long stretches of Vegas-style signage—two-story neon signs that continually flashed and undulated, then dissolved and displayed a new image—gaudy, grandiose spectacles like something in Times Square.

Finally we got off the large boulevards and turned down a narrow, bumpy side street. After a few minutes, we stopped and unloaded.

I recognized the compound from pictures Tashi had shown me; her parents had moved to this house several years before. From the monastery, they had moved to another workers' housing unit in the '90s, then her dad had retired, and they'd built this house about a mile from the center of town. One low and one high building flanked a tree-studded patch of lawn. We walked through a kitchen into a traditional sitting room, carpeted seating arranged in a U-shape around a table. A large color TV blared. Pema, Tashi's sister, whom I'd met once before, the mother of the ten-year-old girl, was there as well as a teenage male relative, a young girl wearing an apron who seemed to work for them, and Pema's husband, who looked to be around forty. In the center of the room, in front of the TV, a wood-burning stove with a large kettle on top emitted glowing heat.

We had some tea and later walked around the house. In an adjoining room, three women—friends and relatives—rolled and fashioned dough, preparing pastries for Losar. Trays and trays of the knot-shaped pastries lay in neat rows, positioned on top of lathes and drill presses. This was normally Pala's workshop.

Amala led me to an upstairs bedroom in the other building. She opened the closet to show me that she'd cleared space for my clothes. I hung my jacket on a hanger. I invoked the name of the monastery where they'd lived before, holding up a hanger. "Mindu," I said, meaning "none, didn't exist." I mimed folding clothes and slipping them onto a shelf. Amala laughed and chimed in, telling her granddaughter that at their old home, where I'd stayed with them, they'd kept all their clothes folded in the cabinet; the monastery quarters had no closets. When Tashi had first came to the West, she hadn't known how to use hangers and had hung blouses and jackets inside out with the sleeves folded inward, exactly as they were when she peeled them off her body.

The next morning, it was clear and sunny, though cold. Birds sang in the courtyard trees. Amala moved over and gave me her seat with the backrest, right in front of the stove door. They poured me tea and brought out *pallah*, pan-fried bread. Amala touched the back of my fingers to the round dough to show me it was piping hot. They brought out jelly and a jar of Skippy™ peanut butter—astonishing, because there had been no imported food in Lhasa before, only local or Chinese. Pema fried an egg for me; they thought Americans always ate eggs for breakfast. Amala felt my slippered feet with her hand—I wore knit booties—then left, returning after a few minutes with a short length of board and two small, rectangular Tibetan carpets, which she stacked under my feet to insulate them from the freezing floor. She gave me a lap blanket and tucked it in around my legs. I felt toasty warm.

The son-in-law asked how they knew me, and Amala explained at some length, mentioning Tashi's name. She nodded at the gold band on my right ring finger—bright yellow 24-karat Chinese gold—and I could tell through her gestures that she was explaining that I had worn the same ring twenty years ago. She cuffed her wrist with her hand, mentioning, I guessed, the gold bracelets I'd given her made of the same yellow gold.

Amala used to love to walk the *lingkor*, the holy walk, every day. I asked whether she still did so, and she replied that her ankle bothered her now and, patting her chest and frowning, that her heart beat fast. She rubbed her shoulders and temples and told everyone how I had given her massages when she was recovering from her mild heart attack.

In the light of morning, I saw that the building contained a real kitchen, off the family room—a full-size, sunlit kitchen equipped with built-in dish racks, countertops, a microwave, a double sink with cold running water, and ceiling lights. I remembered the family's tiny, closet-size, sooty-walled, dark kitchen in the monastery with its small, ancient surface for a counter, upon which stood a single, greasy propane burner. There had been no appliances, no sink, no cabinets, no running water, and the barest of lighting. Back then I had been shocked to see how Amala opened a can, of which there were few in town—taking a big Chinese cleaver, she hauled off and whacked the metal top three or four times. Since they had never had canned foods before, they had no can-opening tool or any conception of a can opener. This new kitchen thrust them into the modern age.

Amala led me outside and into the other building, where I'd slept. In the daylight, I saw solid-wood doors and candelabra fixtures hanging from high ceilings. In the old place, a single, dim, bare lightbulb had dangled from a cord in a few of the low-ceilinged rooms; blue-and-white door hangings, featuring a Tibetan design and lined with blankets, had hung in the squat doorframes.

In one room I recognized the cabinet from the old house, from the room where I'd slept, each of the eight panel doors bearing a different hand-painted floral bouquet. I pointed it out, and Amala nodded, Yes, it's the one from the monastery. We told her granddaughter, Tsering, about the place, tucking our heads and lifting our feet high to mime how we had hurdled the high thresholds and ducked through the low doorways to go from room to room.

Amala opened one cabinet door. Inside was the old fifteen-inch, black-and-white portable television we used to watch! We laughed and joked about it to Tsering: Pala used to open the cabinet and hoist the TV onto the top of the cabinet after dinner, then when we were finished watching—mostly Spanish soap operas dubbed in Mandarin, since there was barely any state programming then—he'd put it away again. It wasn't so much a piece of furniture as a toy or novelty. Amala, I thought, remembered a lot of the same things I did about our time together. That was so long ago; Tashi and I had been in our twenties.

"How old is Tashi now?" I asked.

Amala calculated in her head. "Tashi is forty-one . . . her sisters thirty-nine and thirty-seven."

Amala led me through a lavishly decorated large room with wood panels richly carved in traditional designs hung high up near the fifteen-foot ceiling, and more carved panels of female deities on either side of a door opening to a small inner shrine room. On the second floor, she showed me the bathroom, which featured a Western-style, sit-down toilet. The sight tickled me because at the old monastery, the bathroom for all two or three hundred people lay in a pitch-dark catacomb deep in the interior. I had always panicked when I had to go to the bathroom, which started out with groping down creaky, winding, dilapidated stairs in complete darkness. I used to pray just to climb down them safely, without the steps caving in and releasing me into the inky dark. I could sense, though not see around me, spiderwebs, bat guano, rats' nests, and hovering insects. I heard grunting and the flapping of *chubas* as others relieved themselves in the communal room. I would pray not to slip on the floor—which was cakey underfoot in some places, wet and treacherously slippery in others, as the utter blackness made it inevitable that people missed the mark once in a while—because deep below the long, open slot in the floorboards lay a fermenting mound of a thousand years' worth of monks' poop. I used to be mortified at the thought that a decayed board might give way when I was in a compromised position, and I'd drop into the pit of old holy shit.

The whole household was busily preparing for Losar: washing windows, scrubbing floors, sweeping, laundering, dusting, arranging furniture, and making repairs. No one would allow me to lift a finger to help. By afternoon, I was eager to take a walk, stretch my legs, and look around in what had turned out to be a bright, blue-skied, super-sunny day. I asked where the Potala was in relation to the house.

Tsering took me up to the roof, where we could see the Potala to the west at least half a mile away. The family used to live a couple of short blocks from the Jokhang and a ten-minute walk from the Potala; now it looked to be maybe a thirty-minute walk. From the roof, I looked out onto more rooftops; the view was crowded with tall, closely packed buildings in every direction. Some had a set-up with clear solar rods or tubes, not panels, which, I learned later, were for heating water. In the distance in all directions, I glimpsed the beautiful mountains ringing the Lhasa valley. The sight of the bare brown hills flanked from behind by snow-covered, curved peaks lit up my heart with joy.

I donned my jacket, parka, and scarf and told Amala, "Jok e yin. Nga jok e yin." I remembered only a few Tibetan words and, despite my best intentions, had been so busy before I left that I hadn't had time to brush up on the language. "I'm going," I said.

Amala exclaimed, "Aaaaw!" with a worried look and a lean of the head. Then she and some of the others fussed over me: I should hide my gold necklace under my shirt. I should wear my fanny pack in the front, not the back, and hide it under my coat; someone could cut the strap and snatch it if I wore it in the back. I should wear my gloves and hat because of my cough, and put my scarf over my face to keep out dust and wind. I should not take the "moh-dah," the motor taxi.

She and Pala had a long, animated conversation. I think Amala said they should give me the address, the name of the street. And Pala said something like, "That won't help much," probably since I didn't speak Chinese. He took me out the front entrance and down the lane to the main road. He pointed at the communications tower, the tallest thing around for miles.

"Come back to that," he said. "Head for that."

"Okay," I nodded. "Which way is the Potala?"

He turned and pointed into the multistory buildings across the street: "That way."

I ambled along the main road for a few blocks until I hit a gigantic intersection. It extended before me, more than the length of a football field. On my immediate right was some kind of Chinese monument in white stone in front of a Bank of China. On my left, across two crosswalks, was a Chinese Times building. Directly opposite was what looked like a sleek glass and marble hotel. A blue road sign with white writing hung over the car lanes, identifying East Lingkor Road in two directions and three other streets I'd never heard of. Lhasa had not had street signs before, nor wide boulevards, let alone such an intersection. It resembled the Ginza in Tokyo, except much more chaotic. I must have stood there blinking and frozen, taking it all in for ten minutes in stunned disbelief. Was all of Lhasa like this? I didn't recognize anything from before. Not the streets, not the buildings. Tibet had never had these large Chinese commercial buildings before. I could not have imagined anything like it in my life. I understood why Amala had been apprehensive about my going out. I hardly knew I was in Lhasa. I could barely glimpse the mountain peaks around the valley, obstructed by buildings up to eight stories high. Before the Chinese occupation, Tibetans had a strict height limit on buildings, restricting them to two or three stories, so that the Potala Palace loomed above the town in a place of honor.

Walking toward the center of town, I passed hundreds of shops and masses of people. The city was a riot of sound: honking from taxis, buses, rickshaws, motorcycles, double-decker buses, private cars, and trucks competed with Chinese music blasting from shops, beauty parlors, and stalls.

People bustled everywhere. It used to be that a person could see the Potala from any angle in town and thereby find your way anywhere by your proximity and orientation to it. Now I couldn't even see it. Before, in 1986, maybe one or two cars an hour traveled down the main street—old white British ambassadors from the 1950s, with red interiors and white doilies on the backs of the seats, a driver in the front and a Chinese official in the back.

Where before young Chinese had hidden behind their store counters to avoid working their loathed, state-assigned jobs, sometimes even sleeping on the floor behind the counter, they now wore spiky, punk hairstyles and stood outside their shops calling and waving to passersby to solicit business. When I took their picture, they grinned and flashed the peace sign with their fingers.

When I walked into a restaurant for a snack later in the day, I opened the Chinese menu and shook my head; it was only a minute before the chef pulled out an English menu and brought it to my table with a smile. Twenty years ago, the waitstaff in some Chinese restaurants had run to the back and hidden to avoid serving me. If they did talk to me, it took twenty minutes to convince them that I really couldn't read the Chinese menu or speak Chinese.

Swells of people crowded every street in town. Market stalls and vendors on street corners sold New Year's items: candies, firecrackers, fruit, flowers, pig-themed decorations. I was at the Jokhang, the holy temple, before I was even aware of it, buried as it was in a sea of shops. In 1994, Chinese soldiers had blasted hellacious music to keep Tibetans away from it. Now dozens of Tibetans prostrated themselves in front of the temple under brightly colored, new appliqué hangings strung above the entrance. The Barkhor, the circular market around the temple, besides being the religious center, had also been the center of political activity in the late '80s and early '90s. At the first sign of a political protest, security police in riot gear would burst out of the headquarters on foot and in armored tanks. Now the plaza was blanketed with vendors, stores, pushcart peddlers, and amusement park–style shooting galleries with walls of colored balloons and toy rifles on stands. Now they're going to smother Tibet in junk, I thought. Stuff. Junk. Cheap merchandise. Walmart without walls.

I took some photos, then turned around to check the uniformed officer behind me, sitting at a card table in the middle of the pedestrians-only lane. He had a thermos on the table, a bored look on his face. He just turned his head and looked the other way. At one time, the picture-taking would have drawn questioning or a stern reprimand at the least. The Public Security Bureau behind him had only a small, round blue-and-white sign sticking out from the wall to indicate what it was, though its wide entrance was large enough for armored vehicles.

I was aghast at the tremendous visual pollution. Signs were everywhere—shop signs, street signs, advertising—crowding the surface of every wall. Big round blue signs advertising the electric company, Tibet Power, hung from street lamps, which looked like giant metal spiders turned over on their backs. Twisted clumps of electric cables sagged haphazardly across streets and roads. No attention had been paid to any kind of aesthetics. Everybody was in everybody else's way. No matter where one turned, one could not escape the noise and car fumes and crowds.

The beggars in the streets were Tibetan—nuns and monks, old ladies, women with babies. I could tell, seeing the old people, that it was likely they didn't speak Chinese, the language of commerce. They sat on street corners or wandered into restaurants, where they begged at tables, hands outstretched. They didn't fit into the new economy.

Shopkeepers exhorted shoppers through handheld megaphones, making it sound like police were screaming at you to pull over; some shops blared prerecorded sales pitches that filled the air with static-laden Chinese. All the exhortations competed with one another, so businesses just cranked up the volume louder and louder, so that they could be heard above the others.

After walking in the center of town for an hour, I felt like screaming.

When I finally reached home, I reveled in the quiet of the place.

Pema came home from shopping with her daughter. The little girl happily showed me a pink pig wall decoration, two feet high, for the upcoming year of the pig. She asked me to read the label of an aerosol can, written in English. "Shake well," I said, demonstrating. Before I knew it, she was outside in the courtyard, spraying everybody in sight with pink stringy stuff. People started squealing, running out of the way, giving chase to wrest it from her hand.

At dinner, Amala and Pala moved the carpet-covered floorboard to a spot at the table and invited me to sit there. They refilled my rice bowl three times, and after everyone had finished eating, Pema brought a bowl of piping-hot tomato egg-drop soup she had made for me from scratch. After darkness fell, Tsering and the young maid went outside to light sparklers, twirling them in big circles.

The half-Chinese son-in-law spoke to everyone in Chinese—only to Amala, who didn't speak Chinese, did he speak Tibetan. His daughter was the only one who conversed with him in Chinese. She spoke Tibetan in the house, Chinese at school. The teenage relative liked to watch military shows on TV, action programs with men shooting at one another. Pala preferred situation comedies, and the sister and Amala weren't interested in TV at all. They were up and down from their seats after dinner, taking care of chores while others sat glued to the screen.

When I climbed into bed that night, I found a hot-water bottle inside, warming the sheets. Amala had also had someone put an electric heating pad under the covers and preheated them.

Tashi and Lhakyi, Tashi's sister, who also lived in Canada and who, at the last minute, got time off work to come, arrived home the next day in the early evening. I hadn't seen Tashi in more than five years. She had matured, grown fuller in the face and figure, but had the same large pretty brown eyes and impish smile. She looked tired but happy. Because of the roomful of guests that evening—the driver, relatives, and so on—we didn't have a chance to talk privately.

Later, when the guests had left, she unpacked her bags. She'd been shopping for a month, she said, on all her evenings and days off. Her bags weighed sixty pounds each; she had been afraid the airline would flag her for exceeding the weight limit, but they hadn't.

She'd brought fleece jackets for her dad, clothes for the kids, large bottles of omega-3 vitamins and flaxseed, baby bottles, all kinds of pain relief medicine, ear antiseptic—everything in ultra-large bottles: "My mother calls me up and says she wants Advil™, Tylenol™, ibuprofen. She has almost like a clinic," Tashi said. "Her friends call her with aches and pains, and she gives them some. She shares with everyone, so I buy big bottles." She unloaded shoes of various sizes and styles, including winter boots, and then packages from other friends in Canada for their relatives in town.

The next morning, Tashi, Lhakyi, Amala, the little niece, and I headed off to do an errand. Tashi had not been home in three years. "You don't recognize the shops and you don't recognize any of the people," she said, distressed and bewildered as we walked down the street.

I asked Tashi why she thought Chinese liked to come here. When I was here twenty years ago, Chinese practically hung themselves when they got a posting in Tibet; they bitterly resented it and would have nothing to do with the local people. Any moment they weren't at their post office, tele-communications, or other state-assigned job, they were in their quarters, smoking and gambling among themselves. They passed nights and week-ends the same way. To them, Lhasa was a Siberia-like outpost, light years away culturally, politically, and geographically from Beijing. For decades, the Chinese government had presented Tibetans as superstitious and primitive, the shadow side of China—everything the Chinese feared.

Tashi answered that the Chinese could make a lot more money in Lhasa than anywhere else in China. "It's just like the Mexicans who want to come to the United States," she said. "Then they can make better money and send some home to their families." I would learn later that as an incentive to get Chinese, mostly Muslims from neighboring Gansu and Qinghai provinces, to emigrate here, the government had offered triple the normal salaries. I saw a lot more beggars on the streets than before, especially older Tibetans, and monks and nuns.

"And those are the ones who aren't ashamed to beg," Tashi explained. "Others don't have enough to eat, but they're too embarrassed to beg in pub-lic. They can't even afford to buy black tea. They pick up trash in the streets to make a fire. They sublet part of their tiny apartments for income. Those with children who have jobs get help from their children, but if you are old and have no children to help support you, you have nothing to live on."

We saw a man collecting empty bottles in a wheeled cart. Tashi said that the Tibetans were all alcoholics. It was beer mostly, imported from China. I was shocked. I knew there was a problem with alcoholism but not the extent of it. Once they start drinking beer, Tashi continued, they can't stop.

Always the weapon of choice, I thought. If they can get you to kill yourself, it saves them the trouble. It's just like the Native Americans in the United States. Self-annihilation. It's quiet, it's slow—not like a war. And the Chinese government doesn't get bad press. They can say: "Those people did it to themselves." It didn't stain China, reflect badly on its policies.

From my activist days, I knew the Chinese were cognizant of keeping their record clean. The prisons, for instance, would often release an inmate right before the person's imminent death. They might drive the person to his or her death through torture, beating, starvation, and inhumane conditions—China consistently ranked among the world's worst in its human rights record—but would release the prisoner so that the death didn't occur on their watch and their record stayed unblemished.

We headed off to register Tashi and Lhakyi at the Foreign Affairs Office. Natives who lived abroad had to register when they returned to town, show all their paperwork within twenty-four hours of arrival. The sisters answered a battery of questions for thirty minutes or more. Tashi said afterward that you'd think the office would keep records on file with her basic information. She'd lived abroad for more than twenty years and had been back countless times. Lhakyi had just visited a year ago, but the office didn't have any information on her either. They were required to turn in recent passport-sized photos but didn't have any on hand, so they promised to bring photos by later.

We hopped onto a bus outside. Every street seemed to have several large modern hotels. Last summer, Tashi said, her parents had said there were not even enough hotels to accommodate the number of tourists in town. That was the summer the train opened; I would later read that 4,400 people arrived on the train every day that first month, that visitors to Lhasa numbered in the millions. Lhakyi pointed to an old, dilapidated two-story Tibetan building with a dozen white vans parked in front, the drivers milling about: "That's the old monastery," she said.

"No!" I exclaimed. Their former home had been hidden behind buildings before—that couldn't be it.

"Yes, that's it," Tashi confirmed, craning her neck to peer upward through the dirty bus window.

I wanted to get off and see it, but they had to go get passport pictures. I said I'd go myself and meet them at home later.

The steep, almost ladderlike staircase was the same, but the silky smooth ancient wooden banister had been replaced with a new one. The mud and straw exterior walls, full of cracks, leaned and sagged. The balcony railing on the upper floor had been torn out, leaving big gaping holes in the dirt where each post had been roughly pulled out of the floor. New buildings stood in the courtyard, so instead of the feeling of open space and sense of community, the high walls made one feel crowded. Junk and refuse lay everywhere, unlike before, when the tidiness had exuded pride. I was astonished to see the building exposed directly to the street, to the cacophony of traffic. Before, it had been like a hidden oasis, secure and set apart from the outer world of the city.

The woman in Tashi's old apartment spoke some English and let me come in and look around. I went right to the room where I'd stayed before. She said the authorities had ordered the buildings in front torn down so they could widen the road. Then two years ago, they made the front of the building into a car park. I had difficulty hearing her because of the racket from motors revving and drivers blabbing outside the windows. I took a good look at the room: it was chock full of dark furniture but appeared to be barely used. Before, the twelve-by-twelve-foot room with the low ceilings, thick mud walls, and high thresholds had been the heart of the home—a sitting room, bedroom, and altar room.

The quarters had been divided, so what used to be Amala's and Pala's bedroom was part of another apartment. This family used the old woodpile room, a high-ceilinged, windowless space where Tashi had boiled water for tea on top of a wood-burning stove in the mornings, as a kitchen and den.

I thanked the woman and left, shocked and sad to see the place in such an unkempt, deteriorated condition. The building wasn't kept up, wasn't respected; the Chinese, I surmised, were just leaving it to fall apart. It stood in a prime location on the main street, across from the Barkhor. The land would be very valuable.

As I walked home, I thought that the Chinese government could have done right by Tibet, but that was never its objective, to keep the Tibet-ness. It could have planned the growth and prohibited buildings over three stories high out of respect for the Potala Palace and so that you could see the mountains, which were considered sacred, ringing the town. It could have limited the number of immigrants and private vehicles and put in some light rail or streetcars, free public transport that would have eliminated the incredible racket from traffic, the exhaust fumes, and air pollution. It could have offered economic incentives so that Tibetans would prosper, provided business administration training and loans. It could have kept all the old Tibetan architecture and done conservation work on them. If experts could preserve eighth-century buildings in Bhutan, they could preserve ninth-century buildings in Tibet.

But no, the planners had buried the Jokhang. You could barely see the Potala. And the Barkhor was gone—the fifteenth-century circular streets had largely been torn down. That had been the charm of this place, I thought, the ancientness, the architecture.

This was China transplanted. The Chinese had even renamed the main street, from Peoples' Road to Beijing Road. When Amala had said she didn't walk the *lingkor* anymore, she'd cited her ankle, but who would want to venture out on these chaotic, unfriendly, dangerous streets? They were as thickly packed with people as Fifth Avenue during the Thanksgiving Day parade, but without any spirit of goodwill. And this wasn't even tourist season.

I thought about Sonam Choedron, one of my interviewees who had been born and raised in Lhasa and who, when I had known her a dozen or so years ago in Dharamsala, had chafed to return. Sonam had done underground intelligence work—gathering, compiling, printing, and distributing information in support of freeing Tibet from Chinese rule, work for which she'd been jailed for years. I would see her in a few weeks in India. When I'd interviewed her in 1994, only the threat of prison and death had kept her from returning to Lhasa. Were some of these walls the ones where she and her colleagues had hung their posters? Had she come back here? What would she think of this? This was exactly her territory. For some inexplicable reason, she was now living in Australia. The Tibet movement could not possibly be alive here now, I thought. How could people doing that work survive in this environment?

The first time I met Sonam I had expected a grim, toughened activist. Someone with maybe some rigidity in the jaw, or some rigidity of habit, like chain-smoking, or a hardness in the eyes. Instead, I was surprised to see a plump, ordinary-looking woman in her fifties, smiling and holding a baby as she answered the door. She invited my translator and me into the one-room studio where she lived with her family, the walls painted citrus yellow and windows overlooking pine trees. Pear-shaped, large-framed, cheerful, she looked like everyone's favorite aunt or the head of the ladies' church auxiliary.

My friend Lobsang, a nun who had helped me translate for Sonam in 1994, had written me a month and a half ago to say that she'd found Sonam, bumped into her in the Tibetan colony in Delhi, and that Sonam had immigrated to Australia. I could scarcely believe it. Younger Tibetans hankered to go to the West—to the United States, Canada, Europe, Taiwan—but not Sonam; she hadn't expressed the slightest curiosity or interest. Her overriding passion had been winning the country back. I took the news as a bad sign, a disquieting turn. It meant that even the most die-hard dissidents had given up. Nonetheless, I was relieved Lobsang had found her; I wanted to meet with her again.

The next morning, we accompanied Pala on his daily walk, a two-hour circuit. "My father looks good, doesn't he?" Tashi whispered.

"Perfect," I said. "Are you sure the diagnosis is correct?"

"Positive," Tashi answered. "We had someone bring a tissue sample back to Canada and did a biopsy; it's confirmed." But on his last test, she said, results showed his cancer had not grown or spread. I had never asked Tashi about the prognosis, and she'd never mentioned it.

Once again, I was shaken by the new Lhasa, at the deafening noise and nerve-racking traffic. Gone forever was the sleepy, sun-baked, friendly Tibetan town in the gorgeous setting of mountains and river, far removed from the rest of the world.

We were so far removed, that in my first week here years ago, we had heard rumors of a nuclear catastrophe in Europe. The apocalypse had come, we feared, the end of the world, but because we were so far from any sources of news, we couldn't get hard facts on the event—which turned out to be Chernobyl—for several days. We had to track down the one Westerner in town with a shortwave radio.

Above the din of traffic and blaring music, Lhakyi sighed, "I gave up being upset when I was here last year."

In that short time, she said, Lhasa had changed noticeably. There were *many* more people and it was *much* more crowded. She said she had received a long-distance call that morning. I remembered hearing her speak for ten minutes or so in loud crisp Chinese. As we walked along with Pala, Lhakyi said the call had been from a friend in Taiwan, and when the friend had asked about Lhasa, Amala had hushed her in Tibetan: "Don't say anything bad about Lhasa!"

Lhakyi leaned into me: "The phones are bugged," she said in a low voice.

She pointed out that signs, even those over the entrances of the few remaining Tibetan buildings, announced the building's name in Chinese, with the Tibetan name in smaller lettering below. The building is Tibetan, in the Tibetan quarter, built and used by Tibetans, but the prominent Chinese lettering signified otherwise.

When we got to the Potala, I tried not to look at the ugly forty-foot-high white obelisk in the plaza in front of the palace. I turned my back on its two statues of struggling Red Army soldiers and asked everyone to get in the picture I wanted to take of the Potala. Tashi objected to having the Chinese flag in the picture to the right; I objected to having the hideous dead-spider street lamps in the frame on the left. It took a couple minutes to frame the picture precisely, without those intrusions. Tashi told me, translating for her father, that at one point the Potala suffered age-related damage and the Chinese engineers couldn't figure out how to fix it, so they asked the Tibetans. Tibetan craftsmen inspected it and said they would indeed be able to fix it. It had been built by Tibetans, using traditional methods, centuries ago. The Chinese told them to go ahead and perform the work with the understanding that the Chinese engineers would be given the credit. The tradesmen refused. The whole project was stalled for a very long time. Fearing damage to their sacred palace, some elder Tibetan craftsmen eventually performed the work. I remembered the train announcement about the Potala being built by both Chinese and Tibetan craftsmen.

We walked around to the back of the palace to a small lake. On the way there, along the sides of the building, I saw more older Tibetan people than I had seen in two or three days. Aha! This is where they are! I thought. One scarcely saw elderly Tibetans around the Barkhor anymore, there were so many Chinese. They were at the Potala, circumambulating.

Sometimes we'd come to a street corner, and I'd vaguely recognize a place. The streets had been widened and paved, others had been eliminated, and new buildings stood everywhere. Then I'd recognize the hospital we'd taken Amala to twenty-one years ago, or the road to Drepung. Every time I looked out at the unsightly, incongruous line of street lamps or glass office towers, the monolithic complexes with big red Chinese lettering or the multistory hotels cluttered with neon and signage, I felt sick. Angry and sad. All design and policy decisions originated from Beijing, so none took into account the unique aesthetic of the setting or the culture. In fact, there was a deliberate effort to sinicize the appearance of Lhasa, and the Chinese aesthetic now was ultramodern, futuristic.

On the way home, we visited a three-story mall on the main street, a gleaming marble, chrome, and glass creation with an atrium four stories high and a maze of escalators. It was like something you'd see in Hong Kong or the States. Three leathery-faced Khampas in their twenties, wearing grungy sheepskin *chubas* and red-tasseled headdresses atop long braided hair—obviously country boys—rode the up escalator grinning and hooting down to their friends who were watching them from the ground. They rode it like an amusement park ride, like they'd come to the place just to see and experience this new contraption. They craned their necks, gazing up into the soaring atrium as the escalator took them higher, and chattered excitedly when the mezzanine popped into view above. We browsed the shops, and the sisters took a long time choosing a dried flower arrangement for Amala in a store. While I waited for them, I saw one of the Khampas look-

A modern building in Lhasa almost completely obscures views of the surrounding mountains, 2007. Traditionally, buildings were intentionally kept to a height of two or three stories, and the mountains were always visible. Decisions regarding Lhasa are made three thousand miles away in Beijing.

The Potala Palace is barely visible above the roofline of shopping malls and office buildings on the now heavily trafficked and renamed Beijing Road. 2007.

A gaudy Chinese-style hotel in Lhasa, one of more than six hundred, 2007. The year
the railroad opened, 2006, Lhasa had 2.6 million tourists, nearly double the number
of visitors the previous year, and eighty times the number from a decade earlier.

ing panicked at the top of the escalator, shifting his weight as he looked
back and forth between the ground level fifteen feet down and the moving metal steps in front of him. He looked like he was about to jump. He'd
obviously gotten separated from his friends and didn't know how to get on
the down escalator.

When we returned from our morning jaunt, Amala was sitting near the
wood-burning stove, looking small, sad, and worried. Everyone gathered
near her. She rubbed her hands in her lap and talked in a low, fast voice,
sniffling and rocking in place. Lhakyi sat next to her, head bowed, brow
furrowed, listening intently. Within seconds, Lhakyi was near tears. We had
come back energized and in high spirits from the walk—the beautiful bouquet in hand to decorate the parlor for guests tomorrow—but suddenly the
mood changed. The family remained upset and somber through lunch.

Tashi told me later that when we had left with Pala, Amala had gone
back to the Foreign Affairs Office to drop off the passport pictures. A man

In 2007, local Lhasa residents, including a nun in knit cap, peer curiously into a new business offering something unheard of before in Tibet: "Fast Food."

there, not the woman who'd helped them the day before, reprimanded her about Tashi and Lhakyi not registering within twenty-four hours of arrival as the law required and demanded Amala pay ¥500. Amala tried to tell him that her daughters had come the day before and registered, but he was very rude and demanded she pay the fine. From my travels in China, I knew it was common for petty despots like this to use intimidation and threats, to make up false fines if they thought they could put the squeeze on someone. Amala, an acute observer, said she had gotten the impression he didn't really even know how to use a computer, just sat at the keyboard very officiously and pretended to look up their records. No wonder he couldn't access their files from the previous day. I didn't know whether she'd ended up paying him or how the matter had been left.

It made me angry to see how this fool had mistreated Amala. I felt very protective of her, yet powerless; I was a visitor, I didn't speak the language, and I had to keep a low profile.

That day, I thought more about Sonam Choedron, the freedom fighter. Her epic story—she'd lost several family members to the Tibetan cause, witnessed her family home taken and her mother beaten, recalled "the rivers of blood" in the streets after the 1959 Uprising, run an intelligence network, suffered in solitary confinement in an underground cell—astounded me, as did her courage in rising up time and time again against the Chinese, using their own language, and outsmarting them. But nothing impressed me more than her battle with her commitment to the Buddhist tenets of nonviolent action, especially when they directly conflicted with where her passion and outrage led her. The actions of the Chinese, both the government and individuals, had provoked an impassioned response fueling decades of activism, but the biggest battle was always within herself: To retaliate in rage? Or to remain nonviolent, in thought as well as action?

And she had triumphed. The woman I knew, despite all the loss and grief and outrage, was whole and sane. She possessed a huge capacity to enjoy life and give to others. Yet here I was, getting angry just walking down the street, seeing the stupidity and callousness of Chinese policies, just seeing Amala hurt and upset after being browbeaten by a petty official.

The first time we met, in 1994, when Lobsang and I stepped into Sonam's sun-kissed yellow studio, I felt instantly comfortable with her easy, soft-spoken manner. She agreed to be interviewed on the condition we not use her real name or any photographs of her. We agreed on a pseudonym. Then I asked if she was living permanently in Dharamsala or returning to Tibet.

"I want to go back to Tibet, but my daughter in Lhasa has written twice: Don't come back. The Chinese are waiting for you. She says the Chinese come around asking where I am, and when I'm expected back. They want to arrest me again," she said, one hand on the wide-eyed baby on her lap. She explained something to Lobsang.

"The family is considered 'dangerous,'" Lobsang said, translating. She looked uneasy.

"Dangerous?" I asked. The baby eyed us curiously. Lobsang said she wasn't sure of the word in English.

"We have been active," Sonam said. "My husband, my daughters, my son, myself. They call our family . . ."

I nodded my head. I knew what she meant. Subversive. Counterrevo-lutionaries. The name the Chinese use for those who engage in activities protesting their rule. Their term is "seditious and treasonous," which is categorized as an "eighth column" criminal, more dangerous than mur-derers, rapists, or thieves.

I asked about the family's political involvement. Sonam had three daugh-ters and two sons. She told me that her son and husband had participated in hunger strikes and demonstrations, and at one time, she and two daughters were all in prison at the same time. I asked what her husband did, and she said she wasn't sure exactly. They never talked about it. I was astonished. How could they not talk about it?

"People don't talk about it. We were afraid. It's all done in secret," she said.

She knew her husband participated in demonstrations, because he would come home beaten up. She knew the PSB, the Public Security Bureau, the local-level police arm of the state, had interrogated and beaten him. I could hardly believe they didn't talk about it.

Suddenly I remembered something a friend who had lived in China for many years in the 1980s had told me, that her old tai chi teacher had said that people in Chinese society didn't disclose their political positions to anyone, not a spouse, a brother, a best friend. It was a way of protecting the people you loved; the less they knew, the less could be squeezed from them when they were tortured. People had learned this from the Cultural Revolution.

"He was beaten near death a number of times. But he always managed to get home at night," Sonam said. As for her own work, she and a partner ran a clandestine intelligence network in the 1980s. It was extremely dangerous work at the time. The oldest of five children, born in 1944, she'd grown up hearing her parents and grandparents discuss the Chinese threat.

"They had had experience with the Chinese before. If the Chinese come and stay, my relatives said, they will take our country, take *all* our power. My relatives were deeply concerned. It was always discussed in the family, and it influenced me greatly."

Sonam studied Tibetan language from the ages of eight to thirteen, but when she was fourteen, the Chinese recruited her to join their Tibetan Opera Group, and she started learning Chinese. "The Chinese occupied Tibet then but hadn't taken full control," she said. She became a popular singer and dancer in performances the Chinese government put on for foreigners. The Tibetan resistance at that time successfully challenged the Chinese; in Kham, eastern Tibet, for instance, sixty thousand armed Tibetans caused Mao to back off from his plans for the region in 1956.

Sonam remembered the 1959 Uprising. She vividly recalled the blasted bodies strewn everywhere, dead where they had fallen or sprawled on street peddlers' cots. Streams of blood ran down the street, she said. She was fifteen years old. She couldn't sleep at night. She could only think about getting back their country.

"It made you want to do something. Fight back. Do something in response. I always thought about getting our freedom back. Someday we'll have our land back, I thought, and the Dalai Lama will return."

The Chinese took the land and house her family owned an hour outside Lhasa—her father was a successful businessman who traded between Tibet and Kalimpong—as well as their home in town. They took the entire contents of the house. When her mother objected, the soldiers beat her severely. The next twenty years, Sonam said, were nothing but hard labor and political meetings.

"People didn't get educations. People starved. There was not enough food. The Tibetans worked the fields; the Chinese took the harvest. It was a bleak time. A hard life. Sad. Starving."

During this period, under Mao's Great Leap Forward campaign, farms were forcibly collectivized and Tibetans were ordered to grow wheat instead of the traditional crop, barley. Tens of millions, some estimates range as high as forty million, died in the worst famine in world history. Wheat could not grow at high altitude, but the Chinese government did not reverse its policy for years. Sonam and her family worked sixty hours a week and received ¥60 a month for wages. She married at seventeen, and she and her husband lived with her parents. They survived on potatoes, radishes, and other vegetables they grew at home. Tibetans couldn't move about freely, even to other parts of town. They lived in a dark hovel and were interrogated often.

In the early 1980s, Sonam began doing intelligence work. The political climate in Tibet relaxed after the trial of the Gang of Four, whom the government blamed for its repressive policies, and a period of cautious liberalization began under Hu Yaobang, general secretary of the Chinese Communist Party. Buddhist monasteries were rebuilt, Tibetan language began to be taught in schools, some Chinese officials were withdrawn, and Tibet was opened to foreigners. Sonam and her partner gathered and circulated information—posting broadsides, sending fact sheets to the West (her partner met Westerners through his job), and distributing bulletins to outlying areas of Tibet through a courier system that, she said, "crossed the mountains." In 1989, her partner was arrested. Several weeks later, in April, the police raided Sonam's home in the middle of the night.

"We handwrote the originals, so the PSB interrogators held up papers with the two different handwriting styles in front of my partner. They'd taken our writings from the print shop. They said they knew he wasn't working alone. They tortured him and said he'd suffer more if he didn't give up the name of his partner."

The PSB searched every inch of her home, "even the cowshed," tearing out every drawer and cabinet. They took all the family photo albums and all pictures of the Dalai Lama—including, she lamented, her prized picture of His Holiness and the pope. They drove her and her two daughters in army jeeps to Silingpu prison, near the Norbulingka.

"At Silingpu, they separated me from my daughters. They put me in a cell with the windows covered with heavy black plastic. There was no bed or mattress, no chair or table. Nothing. I had brought a mat and a blanket from home; that was all I had." It was so dark in the cell that she couldn't tell day from night or see the color of the food she was eating. The underground cell was also damp.

"My mat became moldy and, in time, began to fall apart. I have arthritis now from all the time I spent in this damp cell. I was only allowed out every few days to dump my toilet bucket. I'd step out the door, take two steps, turn, go through another door, and heave the bucket. My eyes burned unless I shut them, because I was not used to the sun."

Prisoners in Tibet were not even charged for a long time, let alone sentenced; Sonam didn't know how long she'd be in solitary confinement. She was given no water to drink and soupy food to eat. They never let her wash. I asked her what she did in this dark cell alone, day and night.

"I did prayers and prostrations."

Eventually they sentenced her to eight years in prison.

One night, she said, guards came and informed her that her husband was dying and that she'd be taken home to see him. Her husband had pleaded with officials to be allowed to see her before he died. His health had so deteriorated from his prison treatment that the Chinese doctors announced he had contracted a disease "in his winds" and needed an operation. The neighbors all donated blood. I knew that declaring that a person needed an operation was often just a ruse to get blood donations. As he rapidly slid toward death, prison authorities released him to die without the surgery. The guards lectured her for hours on the conditions of her visit: she couldn't touch him or anyone else, she couldn't cry or show emotion, she couldn't talk privately with him, and so on. At midnight, they put her in a vehicle and drove her to her home, escorted by two jeeps full of soldiers to guard her.

Her husband's eyes were open, but he couldn't speak a word. A son and a daughter were there. The soldiers never let her out of their sight. She was taken back to prison late that same night. The next morning, prison guards told her that her husband had passed away. She insisted she be allowed to place a *khata* on him and that her daughter in Gutsa prison also be released to pay respects. She petitioned them in Chinese and just kept hammering at them until they finally consented, giving her just five minutes to lay a ceremonial offering scarf on her husband.

"When we arrived at the house, dozens of neighbors stood waiting outside for us with *khatas* in hand. They yelled: 'Be strong. We're with you. You're in our prayers.'"

The scene in the house was mayhem, she said. Monks did *puja*—chanting prayers, striking drums, and burning incense for the soul of the deceased— while dozens of Chinese guards swarmed through the house, yelling and screaming over a phone line they had set up to the prison. Soldiers hung about everywhere, sitting and lying all over the furniture and floors. They completely trashed the house, even the altar.

In her husband's room, Sonam found a guard sitting on the pillow where her husband's head lay, nonchalantly smoking a cigarette. At the sight, she was overcome with emotion.

"The guard was just sitting there smoking, next to my husband's dead body, like nothing had happened!"

From my travels, I knew the Chinese smoked everywhere without regard for others.

"Can you imagine?" Sonam cried.

I pictured the soldier, blithely waving his cigarette, trailing smoke in the air, fulfilling some ridiculous assignment to guard the dangerous splittist, even though he was dead.

"I don't know what I said or did after that . . . But the next thing I remember, my daughter grabbed me. She said, 'Don't think about it, Amala! Calm down! Keep your wits about you. We've lost father, we can't lose you, too.' The guards jumped up. We'd broken the rules. It was illegal to embrace. They pulled us into separate jeeps and drove us back to prison."

Sonam fell silent for a moment, full of thought. "My daughter was always telling me not to think about it. But when you're in solitary confinement . . . there is nothing to do *but* think."

Five or six weeks later, Sonam got the news that her seven-year-old granddaughter, the child of the daughter in Gutsa prison, had died. The girl returned home from school one evening with severe stomach pains, went to bed, and passed away that night. She had been living with relatives while her mother was in prison. Her lips had turned black, they said. Probing into what had happened, the relatives talked to townspeople along the route from the child's school who said they had seen her and some other children talking with uniformed Chinese that afternoon. The men had given the children cookies and sweet buns to eat. Other children, they later learned, had also died. Sonam petitioned the authorities for a furlough so she could pay respects to her granddaughter.

"I went home for seven days. I said Bardo prayers for my grandchild. The guards chain-smoked and yelled while I prayed. They followed me everywhere, even into the bathroom. During the sky burial ceremony, we saw that her internal organs were black."

I was continually shocked by the PRC regime in Tibet. Some of the things I had heard were familiar, but poisoning children was something new. This was on another level. It reminded me of the story I had heard in the Buddhist community about an American soldier in Vietnam who said that he and his friends had scraped off the white filling of Oreo cookies, replaced it with white plastic explosive, and given the cookies to Vietnamese children for fun. He was still haunted by what he had done thirty years later.

Sonam said she "went a bit crazy" after these deaths in the family, two losses in two months. She lobbied prison officials for better conditions. She knew they got demerits when prisoners died in their care, so she demanded better food and some medicine. She argued that it was their responsibility to treat her better. She had a weak heart and would die without better treatment.

They didn't do anything except take the black plastic off the windows, she said. There was more light, but she felt lonely. She decided it would be better to be in Gutsa prison where her daughter was interned. She steadily lobbied officials for a transfer until they agreed.

She had lived in solitary confinement—underground and in the dark—for six months.

Conditions at Gutsa were worse, Sonam said—the food wasn't fit for human consumption—but it felt much better to have other people in the cell. "With others around," she explained, "if you died, someone would notice."

Her cell was not far from her daughter's, but they were not allowed to talk or even look at each other. The twelve women in her cell were prohibited from speaking among themselves, too, but they had their own inside jokes and, as she said, "good camaraderie."

"Some women could read and others could not, so I urged those who could read to teach the others. We tutored one another in the scriptures. We discussed dharma. We did dharma practice. We encouraged the younger ones, kept up their spirits. At night, we sang songs. I became like the mama."

Sonam laughed, thinking of her friends. "There are twelve people here now from Silingpu and Gutsa, and we still get together!" She reared back laughing.

I was surprised that they had openly defied the authorities.

"It sounds like you all broke the rules all the time. Were you not punished?" I asked.

"Always," she nodded.

Well, I thought, perhaps the punishments were light, so they didn't mind.

"What would they do?"

"They tried to torture us."

"For instance?"

"They'd make you stand outside for a day and a night while it snowed, wearing only *chubas*. No blouse, just a chuba. The snow up to your knees. Other times we had to get on our knees and kneel over a trough of water with our hands tied behind our backs, dunking our chests in the water. We were made to do this for hours. Your legs and back burned with pain," she said, wincing at the memory as she touched a spot on her lower back, "and your clothes were wet for days."

Sonam explained that no one had a change of clothing, so the women had to wear wet clothes for weeks until the garments dried. These people are so tough, I thought. No hypothermia for them.

Sonam grew quiet.

"We were yellow then," she said after a long moment.

"Excuse me?" I asked.

"They drew our blood. It made us weak. People's skin turned yellow. They regularly took our blood."

At one point, Sonam recalled, an official started to give her a lot of trouble.

"He'd say I had to stop what I was doing. If I didn't stop, he'd say, 'We know where your children are.' He kept saying, 'We know where your children live,' trying to scare me. He would taunt: 'Call your Dalai Lama! Yes, he's free, but how is he going to help you now? The Dalai Lama is public enemy number one! He is a wolf with honey on his lips and murder in his heart. He doesn't care about you. Go call him, he can't help you.'" Sonam said the official spoke to her in Chinese, but she saw through him.

"He would always talk like this. One day, I finally said to him, in Tibetan: 'You can say such things now, but one day you'll regret it. Because in your heart, you know the truth. You know who the Dalai Lama really is. He is not a public enemy or a murderer . . . *I know you're Tibetan* . . . I know you're not Chinese. You are a Tibetan, and you know better than to slander His Holiness. Keep talking like this and you'll greatly regret it one day.' He fell silent. Just speechless. He never bothered me again."

Sonam's middle daughter, who was housed in the same prison (her oldest daughter had been released from prison after two months), the mother of the little girl who had been poisoned, was injured one day when guards forced her to run to empty her toilet bucket. After being locked in a cell for weeks at a time, her muscles had grown weak. She slipped and hurt her back. She was unable to walk. The prison offered her no medical care. Sonam lobbied the authorities vigorously for a release so she could get medical attention for her daughter. She carried her daughter on her back to the Chinese hospital in Lhasa. The staff there was of little help, she said; in fact, when her daughter was near death—she had also suffered damage to her liver—they took two quarts of blood from her. Her daughter stayed in the hospital, bedridden, for four months.

Sonam was released in winter 1991, after two years in prison. The Chinese authorities outlined a score of conditions restricting her actions, designed to ensure that she did not return to pro-independence work.

"They gave me a long list of prohibited activities. If I talked to a person one day, I couldn't talk to the same person the next day; I couldn't talk to someone two days in a row. I could not talk to anyone at length. They had a man outside my house at all times who kept track of everyone I talked to—visitors, friends, anyone. Everywhere I went, a security policeman shadowed me. If I wanted to talk to someone for a longer time, sometimes I'd have the children outside wait until the tail wasn't looking, then bolt the door from the outside so it looked like I had left the house. Then I could talk for as long as I wanted inside.

"Twice I was almost put back in prison because I talked to Westerners. One time, an American man, a doctor who spoke Chinese, visited me. The PSB came the same night. They knew what time he had come, how long he had stayed, everything. My son and daughter were also detained. They said, 'We have the *inji* in custody. He has already talked to us.' They accused me of giving him a letter containing political information to take to the West. I said the fellow was going to India, and I had asked him to carry a letter to my children who are in school there.

"Another time, a couple from Holland came; the man spoke Chinese. A friend took Westerners on tours—that's how I came to know *injis*. The Chinese chased this man, shooting their guns. I saw him the next day at the Tsuglhakhang with his wrist bandaged; he'd been shot. He escaped from Tibet by bus, paying off people to get out of the country.

"The police tried to arrest me, tried to get me to talk about our meeting. I said I gave him letters to take to my children in India, in Mussoorie. I already knew that this Dutch man had left town, that the Chinese had no information from him as they claimed. So they had to release me. After this, an order came out in Lhasa forbidding Tibetans to speak to *injis*."

One day, Sonam said, her elder son, a cab driver, picked up a fare to another town. His passenger got very drunk and didn't want to make the return trip to Lhasa that day, as agreed. The man threatened to steal the taxi, saying, "We don't need you, we'll just take your taxi." They argued, and the man pulled a knife and stabbed Sonam's son.

"Witnesses told me that my son begged the man to drive him to the hospital, but the man refused. My son died."

Sonam went to the town and investigated what had happened. She talked to townspeople. She learned that the murderer was an ill-tempered bruiser and Chinese collaborator who often fought bitterly with his wife.

"Even sober," she said, "he was bad."

Homicide draws an automatic death sentence in China; capital punishment is part of party policy. The murderer was found guilty. When the court was about to execute him, Sonam traveled to Shigatse and appeared before the judge.

"I told the judge there was no point taking his life. The judge said: 'You're asking me to stay the execution of this man?!' He asked me why I wanted to spare the man's life. I said, 'It's not going to bring back my son.'"

Sonam was also entitled to financial remuneration for her son's life, something on the order of ¥70,000 or ¥80,000. The magistrate wanted to give her the money.

"Ordinarily a person in my position would use the money to do *puja*, to say prayers for my son, but a Tibetan mother will not use money from the blood of her son to do *puja*. Also, the man was poor, so it would just make his family go broke if they had to come up with this sum. It didn't make sense to make his family go broke and then take the money to do *puja*. I told the judge I didn't want the money."

The judge, taken aback, asked what, if anything, she wanted.

"I said I just didn't want this man ever to come near my house."

Sonam pointed to the wall. Floating on the lemon-colored surface, without frame or flourish, three feet above her head, was a wallet-sized card. "I still keep my son's driver's license."

I squinted to look at the image on the license: a man, about thirty, with uncombed hair and a wild look in his eyes.

"It has his photo," she said.

A moment later, I remembered that the PSB had taken all her photo albums and family pictures on the night of her arrest. This might be the only image of her son that she had.

The restrictions on Sonam's movements and the twenty-four-hour tail continued for three years, making it impossible to get a job or to support herself. She launched a plan to escape. She thought she'd flee to India, where two of her children lived—visit them, get a blessing from the Dalai Lama, then return a few months later when things had cooled down.

In late May 1992, she, her middle daughter, and several other former political prisoner friends obtained permission to travel to Shigatse to do *puja*. They did all their devotional activities, then boarded a truck in secret.

"I didn't tell my mother or eldest daughter I was leaving. If I had told my mother, she wouldn't have let me go." Sonam said her mother was terrified of the Chinese since the time they had beaten her when she tried to prevent their taking the family home. Sonam said her mother used to urge, "Why don't you stop your political work for a few years to make things easier on the family?" Her mother thought that if Sonam continued pro-Tibet work, it would make her children's lives too difficult. But Sonam not only kept up the work; she counseled her children to do whatever they could for their country's freedom, even small gestures. That was their duty as Tibetans, she believed.

Sonam said they drove north for several days. Near Mount Kailash they transferred to horses. They rode all night with three guides, into Ladakh. Ladakh, western Tibet, is culturally Tibetan but politically part of India. They paid someone to help them get around the border posts. In Leh, the capital, they changed into Ladakhi clothing and flew to Delhi. Along the way, they received help from a host of people who knew of her reputation as an underground leader and political prisoner. Everything went smoothly.

In Dharamsala, she had an audience with Gyalwa Rinpoche, His Holiness the Dalai Lama. The ordeal around her son's death had just occurred.

"I told him about the death. He asked what the Chinese government had done about the murder. I explained what had happened, about speaking to the judge. His Holiness responded: 'What you did was very commendable. To intervene to spare the man's life was really selfless. You showed you are a genuine Buddhist.'"

She said she had a second audience with His Holiness just before she was to leave to go back to Lhasa.

"I directed my daughter to say nothing about prison. She'd been in Gutsa two years. I didn't want to talk about anything that had happened in prison."

I got the sense that she had firmly impressed this on her daughter.

"His Holiness knew I had spent some years there, that I'd had a difficult time. He asked what had happened. I didn't answer. He is clairvoyant, I thought; his is the Buddha mind, he can see everything, I don't need to tell him. Besides, newcomers give him reports. I don't need to say anything; it will only depress him.

"I didn't want to get upset either. When I start talking about prison, I get upset and start crying. We talked about other subjects; then he asked again.

I didn't answer. He asked my daughter; she didn't answer. He invited me to respond a number of times."

Sonam told us that an uncomfortable tension grew in the room as the women stayed silent. His Holiness was perplexed that they wouldn't answer. Her daughter finally broke down.

"After a long time, my daughter threw herself at Rinpoche's feet. 'Please come to Tibet!' she pleaded. 'If you do not come, the entire Tibetan people are *finished*!' She sobbed and cried. She cried a long time. She cried so hard His Holiness came near to crying himself."

I was relieved to hear Sonam admit that she could get emotionally upset about her prison experiences; it showed that despite her indomitable spirit, she still had a human side. When I met her, she'd been in Dharamsala two years; she'd been through so much yet was cheerful, gracious, and completely present in mind and body.

I asked her whether she thought there was any difference between men and women who were politically active. Normally, she said, there was no difference. But she noted that women political prisoners were more vocal in prison than men. Men were stronger physically, but "women's mouths are more powerful," she said.

"Women are never afraid. No matter what the Chinese do. Women do what the Chinese don't want them to do, like chant and shout slogans. In prison, the guards could punish us, they could beat us, but we still shouted slogans. We never stayed quiet, we wanted to say *more*. We wanted to do it *again*. Our mouths got bigger! We became *more* determined."

One day, Lobsang and I went to visit Sonam. The baby's head had been shaved. Sonam said it was a custom; Tibetans believe that if you shave off all of a baby's hair, it will come back stronger and more vital. The child's head had a beautiful shape, and her ears looked like perfect seashells. With her shaved head, clad in a dark red sweater, she looked like a tiny nun. It was an interesting concept, I thought: If you let go, you have more.

I realized at some point that this baby was the sister of the seven-year-old who'd been poisoned, and her mother was Sonam's middle daughter, the one who'd been in Gutsa prison and had injured her back. There were some who might be overprotective of this new child, or anxious. But Sonam wasn't afraid to simply love the adorable baby girl nestled in her lap. One time, the baby awoke from a nap and just gazed around silently while we carried on talking. No crying, no fussing for attention, no tantrum. She focused on something on the bare wall opposite us in absolute wonder. In Tibet, it was said that babies seldom ever cried; they were always held and attended to by a family member and so had no reason to cry.

"When I was in prison, I thought, if they kill me, it's all right. I'm not concerned about my life. Freedom is important for the children, the grand-children. Mine is just a single life. You do what you have to and accept what comes. You don't think about your house . . . your family . . . your own life. If you win the country back, you will win freedom for future generations—that's more important than just one life.

"As a human being, I feel remorse for not being able to take care of my family. My mother has sent me messages through others. She is extremely sad that I left Tibet and afraid that she won't see me again before she dies. But whether we are old or young, we have to die. I have no regrets. To my mind, it's not only us Tibetans who are fighting. Democracy is rising up all over the world. People want freedom everywhere. People all over the world fight for their human rights."

As Sonam's story unfolded over many meetings, I was struck by her sheer stamina, not to mention the matter-of-fact manner in which she spoke of events, as if her lot was just what a person could expect in the course of life. She had experienced the shock, outrage, and injustice of the Chinese takeover since her youth and brought to bear every ounce of vitality, will, and intelligence in her efforts to win back Tibet's freedom. Prison had done little to daunt her spirit. In fact, it seemed to have been a test of her commitment.

She wasn't afraid of Chinese officials nor of the punishments they meted out. The prison experience, she said, referring to herself and the other women prisoners, "made us stronger. We became more commit-ted, more determined, more outspoken." She admitted there were times, especially recalling how the guards treated Tibetans, that she had been so angry that she had felt she might lash out. "Some of the guards are *so* bad," she commented. When she thought about all that the Tibetan people had suffered—the thousands slaughtered in 1959, many starved, imprisoned, tortured, and killed since then—sometimes she felt that she could even kill someone, she told us frankly.

She was eight when the Chinese first seeped in, I figured, fifteen when the PLA invaded, and then Buddhism was almost eradicated over the next three decades. Given her personality, her fierce commitment to her country, and all that had happened to her, I could see that she'd had to wrestle with the issue of nonviolence all these years, and this had caused some inner conflict on more than one occasion.

"In Buddhist thinking, fighting is very bad. In Tibet before, we didn't like to fight; we didn't have military camps or fight in wars. We had no weapons, no armies. The Dalai Lama is nonviolent, so it was easy for the Chinese to take control. But since I've lived in Dharamsala and live close to His Holiness, I've taken teachings with him. He always counsels us to be peaceful and nonviolent—no matter what. If they shoot, he says, don't shoot back. We have no guns, but we could pick up stones or steal their guns; he says no. No, that's not the way. Better to follow the nonviolent path."

One day, after the conclusion of our interview, Lobsang and I stayed and chatted longer than usual. In time, we heard knocks at the door. Women appeared, women around Sonam's age, and greeted her with loud delighted hurrahs. Apparently they had a get-together scheduled.

"These are all my friends from prison!" she beamed, by way of introduction.

Within minutes, food appeared and drink flowed. The dozen or so women seemed to all be talking at once, the conversation punctuated by joking and teasing. Sometimes one person would speak and the others would hold back, listening. A pregnant moment, then a collective eruption of laughter at the punch line.

I had thought at one time that Sonam might be putting up a brave front, overstating what a good time the women had had in prison or how close they were. I couldn't imagine how a person could have a good time in a Chinese prison, but after seeing her with her friends, I didn't doubt it for a minute. No wonder she could still be affectionate and joyful after everything she'd been through. Not bitter, not despairing, not paralyzed by rage or grief. Resilient, openhearted, content. So ordinary. Yet perfectly extraordinary.

That night in the family room, Pala and Lhakyi looked over the papers from the foreign registration office Amala had brought home that morning. Upon closer scrutiny, they found Lhakyi's gender listed as *male*! Everyone howled. They saw her birthplace printed as *Nepal*. Peals of laughter broke out. This rude man had turned Lhakyi from a Tibetan woman into a Nepali man—at the touch of a button! People rocked in laughter, torsos heaving. "I told you!" Amala cried, imitating him hunting and pecking cluelessly at the keyboard with an officious chin in the air. Yes, truly, people joked, he really did *not* know how to use the computer!

We watched a TV interview of a young man, a modern-looking guy in his thirties wearing all black—some kind of modern dance or aerobic exercise entrepreneur. Lhakyi shook her head.

"He is Tibetan and not even speaking Tibetan."

He'd been speaking Chinese the whole time, so I hadn't known he was Tibetan. And this was Lhasa's local programming. When his name flashed on the screen, sure enough, I saw it was a Tibetan name.

We watched a DVD Tashi had brought of a Kalachakra celebration in Bodh Gaya, India, which had taken place a few years before. Every person watched, unlike on other nights, when Amala and Pema had shown scant interest in TV fare. The DVD began with ritual dances for over an hour, the performers in colorful native costumes from a dozen Himalayan regions, part of the cultural programming that preceded the teachings. Then the Dalai Lama appeared on a throne, in a close-up frame, and began the discourse. Everyone sat transfixed—the household help, everyone.

After fifteen minutes, someone got up and adjusted the controls at the bottom of the TV set. The color—his skin tone, the background—was too red and made it hard to see him clearly. I fiddled with the controls for a long while, but they were complicated, labeled in Chinese, and I made little improvement.

"Can I turn the volume up?" I asked.

"No, don't do that!" Tashi blurted out.

"Why not?"

"Because we are not supposed to be watching."

I looked at her.

"It is illegal."

My stomach tightened. Of course, I thought, if Dalai Lama pictures are against the law, then tapes of him would be, too. Three months in jail, minimum, I heard later, for just possessing a photo.

I cast a glance at them, attention glued to the screen, looking like a frieze, watching the Dalai Lama's image. I turned around and checked the large window behind the couch. It faced a public lane, and passersby had a clear view in. Since it was dark outside, people could be looking in, but we wouldn't be able to see them. The curtains were drawn, but the right corner flapped up, exposing a triangle of glass the size of two hands. I crawled back over the couch and flipped the corner down, then tucked it in.

A few minutes later, Amala picked up a bolster and placed it at the center of the windowsill, where the curtains tended to part.

I was missing so much, both positive and negative, because I didn't speak the language, I thought. How blithely I go along, insulated from the daily tensions that are part of their lives.

The next morning, I asked Tashi if she'd place a call for me to Mrs. Paljorkhyimsar. I wanted to meet her sometime and interview her. I leafed through my notebook, looking for the number. "First, ask if we could just meet. Then at another time, we'll do the interview," I said. I wasn't sure how well Mrs. Paljorkhyimsar would remember me, or what her physical condition was. From her granddaughter's e-mails, I wasn't sure if Mrs. Paljorkhyimsar would be able to speak or comprehend. She was living in Lhasa now, having moved back from Switzerland.

"We'll do it after Tuesday," Tashi said. That was four days away. "We are very busy until then. Guests are coming over." I found the number, and she dialed. As we waited for the call to go through, she added, as an afterthought: "But we shouldn't use the word 'interview'; we'll say we want to meet her."

I looked at her, puzzled.

"The phones are bugged," she said.

Someone answered. Tashi spoke into the receiver. The number was for Mrs. Paljorkhyimsar's nephew, Karma, who as a boy had stayed with Mrs. Paljorkhyimsar and her sister, his mother, in Tibet in 1959. They talked briefly.

"What did he say?" I asked when Tashi put down the phone.

"He said to come over tomorrow."

"Tomorrow?!"

She nodded. "Around noon."

Pala and Amala breezed into the family room in midmorning with color in their cheeks from walking in the nippy morning air. Light of step, in good spirits, Pala peeled off his leather hat and coat; Amala wore a smile. They had been able to straighten out the paperwork at the registration office and dispose of any talk of a fine. All was well. I felt relieved.

The household continued to prepare for Losar. Everyone helped Amala and Pala drape *khatas* around the *thangkas* in the shrine room. They built elaborate altars with the fried pastries, lining up offering bowls of candies, nuts, and dried fruit at the base and adding a ram's head fashioned from dried *tsampa*. Pala made chalk drawings on the cobblestones leading to the house entrance, graceful billowing curves depicting traditional images of sacred Buddhist vessels. Then he did the same for the neighbor's entrance across the lane. The women colored their hair; the men got haircuts. From the second-story balcony they hung fluttering white and navy blue awnings.

"I'll give you one job," Tashi said in the family room, a heavy black camera in her hand. She had brought a video camcorder and a borrowed SLR camera from Canada. She asked me to take pictures. She said she always brought a camera with her but never remembered to take pictures. Being as how I, their esteemed guest, was not allowed to do a lick of work, I was happy to be of use.

The next day, Tashi and I took a bike rickshaw to a busy spot near the Barkhor and then placed a call to Karma. When I had met Mrs. Paljorkhyimsar in Switzerland, she had often spoken about how much she missed Karma and her relatives in Tibet and wanted to see them again. She had stayed in Europe only because her son, grandchildren, and husband lived there and she'd been separated from them for so long. When her husband fled Tibet in 1959, Karma had been eight years old and, being a member of a politically disfavored family, was denied an education. She was very proud of him because despite this, when the government policies relaxed, he taught himself to read and write, then passed an exam and became a teacher.

Within minutes, a congenial-looking middle-aged man wearing a knit cap and dark jacket approached us, followed by two young women. We offered greetings and made introductions all around—the two were his daughters—and then walked along the circular lanes, passing an unusual mustard-colored building, which, Karma told us, had been the fifth Dalai Lama's residence before the Potala Palace was built. After a few minutes, we stepped inside a traditional building complex, the courtyard full of people and activity. Karma led us up two flights of stairs. In the small, cramped living room of one of the apartments, an old person bundled in a sheepskin *chuba* sat on a couch, inches from a fan-shaped electric heater, its orange rays splashing eerily against the plaster walls.

Karma approached her and gestured us to come over. I knew this must be Mrs. Paljorkhyimsar, but I didn't recognize her. She was bone thin, her face dark, weathered, and sunken. I was shocked but tried not to show it as I greeted her.

"Tashi delek," I said, bowing slightly and looking directly into her gray, watery eyes.

She didn't seem to comprehend. Her nephew explained who I was. She murmured something in a breathy, almost unintelligible voice. He said she did not remember meeting me in Switzerland; she had met many people there. I took out a photograph of her wearing a bright pink polo shirt, which I'd taken in Zurich in 1991, sixteen years ago. If I hadn't known it was her, I never would have recognized her; not only was her face thinner and darker, but her hair was hidden beneath a knit cap and she had only two teeth.

She was ninety now, her nephew told us, and since she was not able to follow the conversation and spoke little, he would answer questions for her.

He and his family had lived in Penpo until two months ago. His wife had died in August after a long illness, and he had stopped teaching because he had so many people to take care of: three old people, including this aunt. He had moved to Lhasa so it would be easier to care for them.

Mrs. Paljorkhyimsar's husband had passed in 1991, just four months after I'd met her. She moved in with her son Tenpa and his wife in Zurich. When everyone left for work in the morning, Mrs. Paljorkhyimsar felt trapped and frightened there alone. After Tenpa's unexpected death from a stroke three years later—he was only in his late fifties—Mrs. Paljorkhyimsar continued to live with her daughter-in-law. But she didn't speak the language and couldn't relate to the culture. She wanted to return home to Tibet. A year after Tenpa's death, in spring 1996, she returned to Tibet with her daughter-in-law and oldest granddaughter.

I asked after her health. Her knees were bad and she had some arthritis, Karma said, but the advantage of living in Lhasa was that he could take her around the Barkhor and the Potala in a wheelchair.

Mrs. Paljorkhyimsar fingered her prayer beads in her lap while we talked. I told them that her story was a centerpiece in my book, a moving account that inevitably touched people who heard it. Mrs. Paljorkhyimsar's strength was prodigious, having survived what she did and then having outlived her husband and son, even though they'd had a better standard of living in Europe while she was trapped in the gulag. Karma commented that a doctor friend of theirs believed the old Tibetans were hardy because the food they ate was pure; the younger people these days had a poorer diet of processed foods.

I felt a little odd talking to Karma and not to Mrs. Paljorkhyimsar herself. However, I trusted he knew her as well as any person alive, better, even, than her own husband, since he and she had survived the ordeal of the camps together for twenty years.

I asked about her impressions of Tibet when she first returned after a fifteen-year absence.

"There was more freedom of movement," Karma answered. "You could come and go as you pleased—something not allowed in 1981." After her grief over the deaths of her husband and son, she had been overjoyed to see him. Because they had been through so much together, she trusted him to take care of her. In their old hometown, all her old friends came to see her. Their visits were very happy occasions when they could meet again to share tea and talk about old times.

I asked what she thought of the changes in Lhasa.

"There are lots of nice buildings," Tashi answered, translating. I didn't understand. She and Karma spoke. There were lots of new buildings, Tashi amended. In other words, the outsides were pretty, but the buildings hid a lot of poor people who did not have enough to eat. Behind the impressive-looking fronts was a lot of suffering. Tibetans sometimes couched criticism in roundabout language, for both cultural and political reasons.

The whole time we were there, I felt sad and shocked to see this phenomenally strong woman in such a frail state. In Switzerland years ago, she had been hale and hearty, slow in movement but completely lucid. This was a woman who had endured when half the women in her slave labor camp had died from the brutal conditions—the torture, the workload, the lack of food, for three years a tablespoon of roasted barley flour a day—who had outlived her husband and son even though they had been free and enjoyed far better lives.

I remembered her tattoo, a hand-drawn blue swastika, the Bon symbol of good luck. Did she still have this tattoo? I asked. I think I needed irrefutable physical confirmation that the person in front of me was the same woman I'd met before. Karma spoke to his aunt, and she mumbled something. We both leaned close to look at her hand.

Yes, it was there on her left hand, quite faded, especially now that her skin was darker. But it was there. I told Karma that during my visit in Switzerland, she had often sniffed snuff off the back of this hand, and that was when I'd come to notice the tattoo. Karma said she had kept up the habit until just three years ago. Tashi commented that her own grandmother had had this tattoo on her hand as well. Perhaps it was a custom or fashion of that time, for that generation.

Karma said his daughters were nearly finished cooking lunch. Even though we had thought this was just going to be a short first visit, Tashi and I knew it would be impolite to leave; customary hospitality includes offering a meal. The daughters laid out a lovely five-course lunch on the table. A granddaughter brought out a steaming bowl of food for Mrs. Paljorkhyimsar and set it on the folded apron in her lap. With shaky, exceedingly slow movements, she dipped the spoon into the broth, captured some rice and vegetables, and lifted it to her mouth.

Several times throughout our visit, she would utter, "Choe . . . choe," meaning "Please have tea, please eat," in a raspy, breathy, barely audible whisper, turning her palm up in the traditional gesture of invitation. Every time Tashi or I paused, she noticed and indicated the food with her chin, urging, "Choe." I was astonished by the Tibetan sense of hospitality, this generosity and sense of caring for others no matter their own condition.

Mrs. Paljorkhyimsar ate with purpose and gusto. I remembered her words about having nothing to eat in Tibet but so much work to do. And then plenty to eat in Switzerland but nothing to do. Now, I thought, she had enough to eat and she was back in Tibet, where her heart had so longed to return.

I had jotted down a few questions to ask her. The first had to do with the many changes she'd experienced in her life. She came from a poor background, but her fortunes changed after she married a wealthy landowner. She had a very good life for a time, but after the Communist invasion, her fortunes turned again. After surviving years in labor camps, she went to live in Switzerland and then, after fifteen years abroad, returned to Tibet. She had undergone many turns of fortune. How did she now see the totality of her life?

Karma answered that she had had a comfortable life in Switzerland and was reunited with part of her family. But deep down, she was unhappy. In Switzerland, she was always thinking about her nephew because they had endured so much together. So she felt extremely glad to be back in Tibet.

Historical memory, I thought. She wanted to be back with the person who had shared that central and traumatic period of her life, who knew intimately what it was she had been through, and who had helped her survive. That was important. Even more important than food.

Karma told us that at one time they had thought they would move back to Penpo, because it was too cold in Lhasa. All the high buildings blocked the sun. Buildings in Lhasa used to be low, with lots of space between them, so that every structure was warmed by the sunlight. But this wasn't true anymore, and their home was very cold. But his daughters preferred to stay in Lhasa because it was livelier, more exciting for young people. They got a heater and that helped, so they decided they'd stay.

"What did people do in your hometown?" I asked. From the description I'd gathered years ago, it seemed to have been mostly agricultural.

"In spring and fall, people work on farms," he said. "In the winter and summer, the young people look for construction work, and older people stay at home."

He told us that the Chinese government planned to make Penpo into the second-largest city, after Lhasa; it was planning to build a tunnel through the mountain, so that travel between the two would take only forty-five minutes by car. The same route, I thought, that had required an all-day horseback ride when Mr. Paljorkhyimsar rushed home from the capital in 1959 after seeing the Chinese army troops.

"They did the same thing on the route to the airport," Tashi commented.

I remembered that the airport trip used to take two hours because you had to climb up a high mountain pass and then descend into the Lhasa val-

Mrs. Paljorkhyimsar enjoying steamed dumplings at New Year, Lhasa, 2007.

ley. A few years ago, the Chinese blasted a tunnel through the mountain; now it took forty-five minutes to drive the fifty-five-mile-long route.

Tashi and I had to get back to the house as there was a full schedule of New Year's activities and we'd already been away longer than anticipated. I decided I'd return when I wasn't pressed for time, probably to pay respects during New Year's. We thanked Karma and his daughters.

"Kali shu, Mola," I said to Mrs. Paljorkhyimsar, squeezing her hand. She breathed something in reply. I felt she knew what was going on some of the time, but all the responses were delayed. I could see and feel the diminished life force in her. As I left the apartment, I felt shaken up.

Later, I reflected on Mola. She had married in her early twenties and was in her early forties when the Chinese invaded. In her early sixties, she arrived in Switzerland. I met her ten years later in July 1991. Around age eighty, I figured, she returned to Tibet. Now she was ninety.

After darkness fell that night, loud fireworks began—not localized, but all over the city, surrounding us. Tashi's brother-in-law, who was half Chinese and who had been collecting a large stash of fireworks all week to celebrate Chinese New Year, the night before Tibetan New Year, headed up to the roof and asked me to follow. From there, we saw fireworks filling the skies—streaking colors, bursting rockets of light, explosions of sound. He delighted in setting off his arsenal for more than an hour. After a time, I noticed that only he, the young children, and I were up there, and I came down.

The noise was too deafening to carry on conversation. The unremitting booming became tiring and stressful after the first hour, like we were under siege, being bombed. Sometime deep into the second hour of fireworks, Tashi looked at me warily. She sighed. Without moving an arm, she unpeeled an index finger at the sky: "You see how many Chinese there are here now?"

I was roused from sleep early the next morning before dawn by a lot of noise—doors slamming, voices echoing, footsteps pattering. It went on for so long that I gave up on sleep and got up to investigate, even though it was still dark. In the adjoining room I saw Tashi's and Lhakyi's empty beds, their blankets folded and stacked. I wondered groggily where they were. I remembered Tashi saying something about the activities starting very early in the morning, but it was still the middle of the night.

At that moment, the three sisters burst through the door, grinning broadly, each carrying an object: Tashi, a portable trough-shaped altar adorned with dried colored reeds; Lhakyi, a silver pitcher; and Pema, an ornate wood and silver bowl.

"Tashi delek!" they yelled, stopping in front of me with their offerings, like the three wise men at the birth of Jesus.

I looked at my watch. "Tashi," I whined, "it's 5 a.m.!"

"Yes!" she agreed happily. "Happy New Year!"

They instructed me in performing all the rituals, pinching *tsampa* into the air three times, tasting a bit of the dough, sipping a palmful of water, and downing a spot of barley beer. They'd already visited their parents' bedroom, Tashi said, and brought them tea in bed.

We ate a special breakfast, consumed only on New Year's day, a *tsampa* porridge cooked with sweet potato and yak cheese and flavored with *chang*, molasses, and yak butter.

The family spent the whole morning dressing, particularly the women. The *chuba* required two people to put on correctly—the pleats hanging long in the back, the collar lying flat, the men's sash cinched above the waist to allow movement. The women wore theirs ankle-length over a colorful silk blouse; the men wore theirs knee-length and more like a light coat. Then came makeup and jewelry, shoes and hair. I took formal family pictures in the shrine room, everyone dressed in shimmering silks and satins, with Pala's beautiful carvings as a backdrop.

We ate a lavish seven-course lunch. The family served a host of meat dishes: a succulent, flavorful pig Pala had slow-simmered in a large pot over the outdoor wood-burning stove. The pig, raised in the hills in Kongpo, a day's drive to the east, had been fed only peaches and plums; it tasted mildly sweet. Different meats had been drying outside under the roof eaves, and we dined on them: homemade yak sausage, mutton sausage, ox tongue, beef. Following the main meal came a stream of snacks and treats: passion fruit, pistachio nuts, plump fresh cherries, mandarin oranges.

For the evening meal, we had a special noodle soup, which came with one oversize dumpling per bowl. Each dumpling contained an object that represented your character—a bit of wool or broken pottery, seeds, or pebbles. A chili pepper meant you had a smart mouth, Lhakyi explained, and glass meant you were pure.

Tashi got wood, meaning beautiful.

"Every year I get the same one," she said.

One sister got charcoal, meaning her mind was dark. I got a piece of paper. Tashi explained: "It means you're always going places; you never stay in one place." Not inaccurate, I thought.

We left a few bites of noodles unfinished and tossed them into a large washbasin on the floor, which was then taken outside to the courtyard. Amala lit a cross-shaped bundle of straw on top of the basin, to drive away evil spirits. Pala lit the tip of a long, torchlike bundle of straw and ran around the courtyard with it. To chase away ghosts, Tashi said.

Later, inside, the sisters brought out a metal washbasin holding balls of *tsampa* dough. In turn, we each took one cookie-size ball in hand and pressed it into a part of our bodies to remove bad karma, like washing away sins. We watched and roared with laughter, as each person held the dough against his or her forehead, stomach, toes, crown of the head, wherever the person thought bad karma had accumulated.

Fireworks cracked in the night sky. They lasted only about an hour, unlike the nerve-racking marathon the night before for Chinese New Year.

We watched special television programming, mostly large-scale dance performances filmed in a television studio, a lot of spectacle that was supposed to look like entertainment and appear apolitical. We saw traditional Tibetan dance from different regions of the country, the dancers wearing the local dress of their region, and then modern acts with dancers wearing skimpy, glitzy sleeveless *chubas*, in which they'd freeze to death if they actually wore them outdoors in Tibet. Various bands of lithe, tousle-haired youths played Tibetan rap music. We watched a very stylized contemporary opera, the performers in tight-fitting, green PLA uniforms and heavy makeup. Tashi said the lyrics were all about the "peaceful liberation of

Tibet." She knew all the words because the opera had been popular when she was growing up in the 1960s.

We saw one dance act in which the performers waddled around in over-size extreme-weather parkas and climbed a pyramid-shaped set, a symbolic Mount Everest. One of the public monuments in town displayed this same image. The government evidently liked to keep the image in the public's mind; China's claim to the highest mountain in the world boosted nation-alist pride and enforced the notion that Tibetan land was part of China.

The emcees were always a pair, one Chinese speaker and one Tibetan speaker. About four or five times that night, the station broadcast a ten- or fifteen-minute segment featuring the governor of the Tibetan Autonomous Region (TAR) touring Tibet. He appeared at development projects, factories, hospitals, dams, always cheered by crowds of smiling, clapping Tibetans. Never a better time to get in propaganda than when you have a captive audi-ence. Like the ads during the Super Bowl.

I woke up the next morning thinking: Living well is the best revenge. Tibetans were still taking pleasure in life, still celebrating their traditions. I felt heartened and relieved. Enjoying this most important holiday was an act of resistance, a triumph over those who would see you destroyed. It was so comfortable at the family house that it was easy to forget the atrocious conditions in town.

I asked Tashi about the schedule of activity for the day. I was looking for an opening when I could have some time to myself.

"We get everything ready for guests," she said.

"Then what?" I asked.

"Then they come over."

"And then?"

"Then we clean up."

"Okay," I said, confirming that the activities would then be over. I thought I'd plan when I might go for a walk, get to an Internet cafe, or have time to write. But I didn't want to be absent for anything or appear rude.

"Then," she continued, "we do it all over again."

I looked at her as if to say, "And then?"

"The same the next day," she said.

I nodded.

"And the next," she said.

I looked at her expectantly.

"And the next."

"For how many days?" I pressed.

"Many," she said. "The first day is family. The next day is friends. The next day we go to other people's houses . . . " Her voice trailed off as if there were many more customs.

"What time are they coming today?" It was about eleven. I thought maybe I could have a leisurely morning. Perhaps it was the altitude, but I couldn't move very fast.

"Anytime now," she answered.

"Until when?" Maybe I could squeeze in a walk later this afternoon, once everyone left.

"All day."

"All day?!"

"Yes . . . and night."

That day, about thirty or forty people came over. Kids attached themselves to Tsering and ninety-year-olds who'd lost their vision were planted on the couch, where relatives leaned in toward their ears to speak. Tashi described everyone's relationship to the family. Her mother's family was huge. There were Amala's brothers' widows and her brothers' first wives, with whom they kept up relations and liked better than the current wives; there were granduncles and second cousins Tashi and her sisters had run around with as children; and adult children of relatives. I couldn't keep the relationships straight. The family cooked a nine-course feast and served it buffet style. A handful of people played mah-jong. Company stayed until eleven o'clock that night.

The next day, after breakfast, we all climbed up to the roof to install new prayer flags—brilliantly colored flags in turquoise, scarlet, goldenrod, emerald, and white on a stand like a tall sapling. The cousin slipped it into a hole in a corner of the roof. The middle sister, donning the traditional fur hat in the cold brisk air, performed ablutions at the small trough altar decorated with spikes of dyed magenta, yellow, and green reeds stuck in *tsampa* dough.

All the family members lined up, pulled their arms back, grasping a pinch of *tsampa* between their fingers, and then called out together in one spirited shout: "Tashi delek, phun sum tshogs a ma bag gro sku khams bzang gtan du bde bat hob par shog!" and tossed the *tsampa* high in the air. It meant, "Good luck and good fortune in all aspects of life! May all sentient beings be well! Peace and happiness!"

We had tea and gazed at the tops of the mountains, their base obscured by all the tall buildings. In the distance, we saw plumes of smoke wafting from high up on a foothill. Pema said she had climbed up there before to make incense offerings, but the altitude—she patted her heart and pretended to gasp for air—made her short of breath.

Maybe it was the ceremony, or the fresh winter morning air, or the view of the mountaintops, but the mood felt light and happy.

Tashi told me that the Paljorkhyimsars' nephew had called me that morning and invited me over for New Year's. I had wanted to go anyway, to pay my respects and give Mrs. Paljorkhyimsar an offering for Losar.

"When should I go?" I asked.

Tashi said a lot of people were coming over today, and that they'd stay all day. I didn't doubt her, judging by the day before.

"Now," she declared.

I left shortly before noon and walked through empty streets. It was the first time I'd seen them without mobs or walls of traffic. For the first time, I could really appreciate the mountain air and broad vistas I associated with Lhasa. For the first time, I enjoyed just being in the streets of town again.

I found the building easily enough. When I climbed up the side staircase to the second floor, an unfriendly woman answered the door of what I thought was the right apartment. She shooed me away when I asked for the Paljorkhyimsar house. I went up to the third floor and saw an unfamiliar gate. I was in the wrong building. I left and walked around the narrow, winding old lanes.

In one lane, I saw pony rides for little kids. The twisting lanes hemmed in by traditional-style buildings almost made me think I was in old Lhasa. Everything was on a different scale. The narrow, circular design and uneven stone paths made people slow down, made all transport move at a slower pace. China created exactly the opposite conditions when it wanted to develop a town: it widened the roads and built boulevards and huge plazas, to facilitate mass movement—military processions, tank convoys, splashy Party ceremonies. I remembered that from 1986.

After walking a bit more, I was sure that I had been at the right building complex before, so I went back. I climbed to the third floor but found the right door this time, spying the orange glow of the heater dish through the curtained window.

Inside, Karma and his daughters were working at the small living room table rolling dough and cutting meat on a big thick chopping block. Mrs. Paljorkhyimsar sat at the end of the couch in her spot. When I entered, they cleared the table and moved to another room.

I sat down next to Mola on the couch. This time, she talked directly to me in a kind of hoarse whisper. Her words were not intelligible because so many of her teeth were missing, but I wouldn't have understood what she was saying anyway, since it was in Tibetan. I took her hands in mine. Very warm and quite fleshy. How wonderful to have that direct connection, without intermediaries. In our last meeting, I had felt some awkwardness because we'd all never met before and Tashi and I had needed to get home to help greet guests. This felt a lot more relaxed and leisurely. I gave Mola a red envelope with some money, the traditional offering at New Year's. She slipped it inside the front of her *chuba*.

The large color television displayed a Chinese rap band—all quick camera cuts, hard-hitting bass lines, and young, muscled guys jumping and jerking on their guitars behind Mrs. Paljorkhyimsar's head. What a contrast: the old century and the new. What China had wrought then and what it has wrought now. One dark, weathered, nearly mute and losing life force, and the other spasming and roaring into the future, loud, noisy, and self-conscious.

We sat together alone for quite a long time while the rest of the family kept busy in the kitchen. Periodically, I studied my Tibetan phrasebook; otherwise we sat there quite contentedly without speaking. The family's New Year's altar—with the pastry totem, ram's head, and candy bowls—stood along the top of a cabinet on the wall opposite. One of the girls came and turned down the TV. At another point, when it got cold, she came in and turned on the heater. I found it very peaceful. I realized that there was always activity at Tashi's. With the house and all the family members and household help and goings-on, I could never hunker down for a period of time and be silent with my thoughts. How great it would be, I thought, to just tuck myself away for a day in a library, somewhere quiet and cozy.

I felt heartened to be able to see Mrs. Paljorkhyimsar and make an offering to her. In the States, I had become so miserably despondent about this project at times, what with the scores of rejections over the years from agents and publishers. Clearly the material was important; one graduate school professor of mine said, "You're sitting on a gold mine." But the endless frustration of hiring editors, scraping together funding, and rewriting the book countless times in different genres—oral history, historical narrative, dharma book—not to mention the lack of support for artists doing political work, had beaten me down.

But when I had enough distance, like now, from the comfortable American life and its daily concerns, I saw things differently. Nearly eight thousand monasteries demolished, and thousands of years of culture destroyed in twenty years. To give twenty years of my life to unearthing this women's history and getting it out was just a thimble in an ocean, the blink of an eye. Look what these people had suffered, what they had sacrificed: their whole lives.

At lunch, Mrs. Paljorkhyimsar constantly urged me to "Choe, choe," when I paused in eating or drinking. Her family gave her a serving of *momos*, handmade steamed dumplings, and a bowl of hot savory milk to go with it. I was pleased to see that she enjoyed eating so much.

When I finally got up to go, I faced her and took her hands. I suddenly felt deeply sad. The others bustled around, looking for a *khata* for me. It was the last time I'd see her, I thought; she was ninety, and I didn't come to Lhasa often. My throat felt dry and tight. Tears sprang to my eyes. Her story was so important and her survival so miraculous. It was such a privilege to have met her and to have her share her life story with me. Her chapter was the one I workshopped and reworked so much; it was the one that moved people, the tale that set the tone for the scope and depth of the women's life experiences and revealed how different these were from what had been known as Tibetan history.

Karma and one of his daughters walked me out to the street, to an intersection a stone's throw from the Jokhang. He kept saying something to me and gesturing, pointing back at the house and then down at the ground. I think he was telling me to come back and visit. Come anytime. Nobody has hospitality down like the Tibetans, I thought. He was just so kind; I could see it in his face, even though I never understood a word he said.

At the Barkhor, more market stalls were open today than the day before. People were wearing their finest *chubas* and walking the *kora*. Some did prostrations in front of the Jokhang. I could feel a sense of peace from the temple, from the people doing prayers. It didn't move me like the first time I had been here years ago, but I could still feel some tranquil, tender feeling in the air around the temple when the pilgrims were there. It required an effort to see the mountains, but I thought, What a wonderful thing to have the Jokhang and the Tibetan faithful and the mountains still here.

It was a change for me: to just appreciate what was there and not be focused on what was not there anymore, on what had been taken away. That always put me in an angry state, agitated and embittered.

As I walked home, I passed the family's old monastery house and hardly gave it a glance. I noticed that I was more able to be in the present the longer I was here. Day by day, I was letting go of the past. Moving on. Once, I met a rock climber in an airport. I told him I had liked the sport well enough when I dabbled in it years ago; the problem came when I looked down after climbing up. I had no trouble going up because the concentration it required forced me to be totally in the present moment, but when I looked down three thousand feet and saw the distance I could fall, I freaked out. The remedy for that, he told me, was to camp out on a high shelf for a few days, at two or three thousand feet up. Then the perspective that used to bring terror would become normal, and the fear would vanish.

When I arrived home, several dozen people sat on the carpeted couches of the large living room. A small hill of canned drinks, mostly beer, stood near the door. Pema, Amala, and Lhakyi poured from large thermoses, refilling people's cups with either Tibetan tea or milk tea; they filled shot glasses with beer, always right up to the brim, as per custom. Something about the altitude or the dryness of the air made people thirsty, even if they were sitting around doing nothing. "Choe, choe," they urged with a little hike of the chin. Drink, drink.

At one point, Tashi introduced me to a distinguished and kind-looking couple of Amala's and Pala's age. He was tall and broad shouldered, and she wore a modern shorter hairstyle, not the long upswept braids Tibetan women traditionally wear. They sat on one of the couches by the window, and I could tell Pala liked them, because he went over, sat next to them, and engaged in conversation. Lhakyi once said that her father didn't talk very much, even with Tibetans. It was their mother who kept up the social ties. Tashi said the gentleman was a journalist and the woman, a high-level administrator.

A woman in a dressy red coat entered, maybe in her forties, with long hair and curled bangs, and wearing makeup. She cried out at the sight of Tashi and enclosed her in a bear hug. After long minutes, she loosened her embrace, rubbing her red, wet eyes with the back of her hand. She linked her arm in Tashi's as they sat down. Tashi said they had been best friends in high school and explained her friend's emotional state: "She is close to my parents, and she knows about my father's condition. Plus her own father died last year."

The woman took a good long look at me, then turned to Tashi and said something. Tashi responded, before calling out in English to me, yelling through the noisy room to where I sat on another couch several feet away: "Is it twenty years, Canyon? About twenty?"

"Twenty-one!" I called back. "Tashi, let's meet again in twenty years in Tibet!" I added.

"Okay," she hollered back.

Around evening time, three men arrived—one, tall, large-framed, and gimlet-eyed, the second, chubby with a boyish face, and the third, a skinny man with a small camera. The chubby guy made a beeline to the altar on the hutch and performed ablutions: three pinches of *tsampa*, a taste, then a quick bow, carrying himself with confidence, almost a swagger. Either he was Tibetan or he was a very well-trained Chinese, I thought. After a few

minutes of watching them, I decided there was something about them—
the way they quickly, almost instinctively scoped out the room when they
came in and held themselves a bit apart from other people—that gave me
the sense they weren't Tibetan. The skinny one went around taking pictures
of everything in the room with his point-and-shoot camera.

When the journalist and his wife got up to leave after a long visit, they
talked to me on their way out. He spoke English. I suppose Pala or Tashi
had told them who I was. I was a little surprised because we hadn't interacted at all aside from being briefly introduced, and I had no idea he spoke
English. He shook my hand and looked me in the eye.

"Always remember Lhasa," he said. "There is no place like Lhasa."

I nodded—I agreed of course, wholeheartedly—although it was the Lhasa
of many years ago that I held fondly in memory.

"Your whole life . . . " he said, holding me in a steady gaze, "don't forget
Lhasa." He continued to clasp my hand in his own. "There is no place like
Lhasa . . . "

By now I had begun to sense a deeper urgency beneath his words, as if
he were trying to transmit something more than the words.

". . . because of the *clean air*."

Tashi told me later that the woman had been dismissed from her high-
level job because she had helped monks at the local monastery. The Chinese
government had been coercing monastery members to denounce the Dalai
Lama and sign official documents to that effect; certain monasteries were
strongholds of noncompliance. Security forces had injured monks in clashes
there. When it became known that she had lent them humanitarian assistance, the government sacked her. As for the husband, Tashi told me that
he couldn't ever leave China, because he was a journalist. "They won't even
let him go to Macao," she said. The couple was on holiday in Hong Kong
recently and applied to go to nearby Macao; he was refused. The government gave her permission, but not him.

"Why not?" I asked.

"Because he is a journalist and Tibetan."

If he were a Chinese journalist, she explained, he could obtain a visa to
leave China, or if he were not a journalist even though he was Tibetan, he

would also be permitted to leave. But as a Tibetan journalist, he was not allowed to travel into the outside world.

Later, in the smaller, more intimate family room in the other part of the house, I came upon the chubby-faced man standing with Lhakyi and a few others by the TV. He was pontificating very loudly and elaborately toasting someone. People laughed. He turned and did the same thing to another person. They all raised their glasses, smiling. He did the same to another man to my right. He was making his way clockwise around the room. I was in a corner by the window; he came and spoke to me in the same self-important tone.

"Wo buzhidao," I shrugged, meaning I didn't know what he was saying, hoping to convey that I didn't speak Mandarin. Someone explained to him who I was, and his face lit up. He turned to me and raised his glass, continuing his loquaciousness.

"Buzhidao, buzhidao," I protested. "Guangdonghua," I added, telling him I spoke Cantonese.

Someone told me in English that he was "the boss of the railroad." That he wanted me to drink with him, to toast. I humored him and took the small shot glass he offered. I'll take a sip, I thought. He tipped the Budweiser™ can to my glass. Along with Skippy's peanut butter, Budweiser had made its way to the Roof of the World.

"Bu, bu, bu," I cried after two ounces, signaling him to stop, but he ignored me and filled the glass. He talked incessantly in a loud, patronizing tone of voice. Someone translated, saying that he wanted to take me out when he visited the United States. He wanted to give me his phone number, so I could call him.

He tossed back his beer and displayed the inside bottom of the empty glass. "Now you," he indicated. I shook my head. I didn't mind taking a sip, but I wasn't going to imbibe the entire full glass. He scolded me like an old-fashioned schoolmaster.

He filled his glass again and threw back another drink in one gulp. "Like *that*," he said, showing me the empty glass. He's drunk, I thought. A voice in English said, "He says it's a shame that you are Chinese and don't speak the language."

He filled his glass a third time, sloshing beer on the sofa because his hands shook so much. He leaned back and downed the brew, then tilted close to me.

The head of the railroad coming on to me? That's too ironic, I thought. It's a good thing I didn't speak Chinese, I realized, because if I did, we'd have real fireworks.

By now, half a dozen people stood shoulder to shoulder with him, facing me. I was boxed into the corner—the crowd, the coffee table, and the couch blocked my escape route. I couldn't get out unless I broke through. For a split second, I considered how I might make a polite exit but then thought it wouldn't matter—he was too drunk. Hastily, I plucked my vest and camera off the couch. "Zaijian. Zaijian," I called out, as I started to bolt. He reached out to shake my hand, still talking a blue streak. I felt his fingertip scrape across my palm. I bristled. A come-on.

The next morning when I came downstairs, Lhakyi said that the railroad boss had called and asked to take me out. They had covered for me, she said, told him I was still sleeping and couldn't come to the phone. I think my being American excited him. They filled me in on what he had said the night before, that he'd boasted about how much money the Chinese government had spent to build the rail line and how much progress it would bring to Tibet.

"A lot of political rhetoric," Lhakyi said.

Hey, I thought, just like the commentary they played on the train.

To Lhakyi he had quoted the Chinese proverb "Ru xiang sui zu, ru jing wen jin" (When you're in my country, you should follow my customs). He must have the script from the train memorized, I thought. Maybe they were required to memorize it! She was incensed: "Here he was in *Tibet*, saying that when you're in *my* country, you should follow my ways!" she shrieked.

She said she replied simply, making a great effort to contain herself: "I, myself, was born here." And let it go at that. He was a guest, so she had to be courteous to him, she said, but she hadn't liked those three men from the beginning. They were not invited by the family. The Chinese wife of a relative invited them. Tashi said he assumed that all Tibetans drank alcohol; that's why he insisted that everyone toast with him.

His obnoxious behavior, his posturing, his party line talk, and the sexual come-on disgusted me. They think they own the place. It scared and angered me that the railroad head could be in the house, in the cozy family room, and could just take over like that.

The next morning, I awoke early and sneaked out of the house to take a walk. I needed to clear my head, especially after last night, and after the many full days we'd had. I walked maybe half a mile to the edge of the city toward the river. I passed some new block housing, eight stories high, made of concrete and very institutional-looking, with no character or charm. It looked like something that belonged in a crowded urban center in China. It didn't look right here. Tibet was unique in its wide open horizons, its boundless sense of space. At one time, it held the lowest population density in Asia, less than two people per square mile.

I reached the river but found it dry and all dredged up. After a few minutes, a dog barking loudly on the river path frightened me and discouraged me from going much farther. Then a Tibetan man came along, walking in a sprightly manner with great purpose. I followed him in the direction of a bridge, far in the distance, and as we got closer, I was relieved to see that the dog was chained. The sun was in my eyes, and there was a lot of mist or haze in the air. I could hear whoops and cheers and a lot of noise from the direction of the bridge, which continued unabated for several minutes.

Figures were streaming across the bridge. Because of the smoke and haze, I could see only silhouettes and the vigor of their movements. The figures floated in and out of view, obscured by great plumes of smoke; it was not morning haze, I realized, but smoke, something burning on the far side of the bridge and on the hill across the river. The people were Tibetan, I realized from their *chuba* cloaks, their braids, and the stalwart way in which they moved. These were not the fashionable modern types you saw in town and in shops; these were the common folk. Many carried sacks in their hands or on their backs; some toted stands of colored prayer flags over their shoulders.

I figured I couldn't make it over there, cross the bridge, and still get back to the house at a reasonable hour so that the family wouldn't worry. So I turned home and made a mental note to return another day.

When I arrived home from my walk, the family was getting dressed to head out—Pala in his handsome gray wool *chuba* and leather hat, the others in the final stages of pulling on dressy *chubas*. They planned to visit other families today, Tashi said. I tried to beg off. I was exhausted from all the entertaining. I'll just stay here, I told her. She translated my remark to her parents, and they conversed for a couple of minutes.

"They are afraid you will be bored," she said.

"I won't be bored!" I cried. I longed for a quiet day. After the third or fourth hour, it was exhausting to be around people when I couldn't understand conversations. Amusing myself with picture-taking and people-watching only went so far. Plus I normally had a lot more time to myself.

"I have plenty to do," I said. "I'm going to write . . . take walks . . . read."

A flurry of debate ensured. Tashi emerged after several minutes: "My father says to come. It will be interesting for you. He says you'll see that not everybody lives the way we do."

Tibetans cross a bridge over the Lhasa River carrying stands of new prayer flags and sacks of incense on their way to a pilgrimage mountain at New Year, 2007.

We hopped on a public bus to the town center, then headed on foot toward the Barkhor. As we walked the crowded stone lanes, Tashi said that when she was growing up here, there used to be a lot of open space where she and other kids played hackysack and just ran around. The buildings had all been two stories high.

"They've torn them down, and made all the buildings three or four stories," she said.

We entered an old traditional building with a long narrow courtyard. A woman with a fresh-scrubbed friendly face stood wringing laundry at a water tap. When she saw us, she brightened and spoke briefly with Amala and Pala. We climbed to the top floor and followed the balcony around three sides of the building until we came to a residence at the end. A woman I recognized from Tashi's house the other day—fortyish, plainly dressed, with thin, almost gaunt features—greeted us warmly and invited us in. Eight of us filed into a small, plaster-walled sitting room, where we occupied all the space on the two couches. Our hostess left the room.

Elaborate shrines lined the walls, glass cases holding scarf-draped statues of different Buddhist deities. The woman from the courtyard appeared and left. The woman who had invited us in brought tea settings and a thermos and poured tea. Later, an elfin woman, maybe in her seventies, entered to a hue and cry; apparently, she was the person we had come to see. She greeted the family warmly and fluttered around and refilled teacups. She talked freely in a raspy, soft voice with Amala and Pala, who seemed delighted to see her. Lhakyi told me that the woman had been a priestess, an important figure in the religious tradition.

When she finally sat down, she took the only seat available, a place at the end of the couch, near me. I looked more closely at her—she had bulbous cheeks and expressive, light gray eyes. She was so utterly distinctive looking that I couldn't take my eyes off her. I asked Lhakyi who she was. She is the widow of Amala's older brother, Lhakyi said, who died thirty years ago.

"How come she wasn't at the house?" I whispered, referring to two days before, when all the relatives had visited.

Lhakyi replied, keeping one ear on Auntie talking, that her aunt said she had intended to come. Lhakyi listened further. "But she says she was drunk."

The word made me laugh. Lhakyi was still mastering English, so there might be a better word—like "hungover" or "tipsy." It was hard to imagine this lovely, gracious elder drunk. But I found it amusing and very refreshing that she admitted it so openly.

Auntie spoke at some length. The room got quiet, the mood serious. Amala and Pala, Lhakyi and Tashi all nodded sympathetically: "Tsk tsk," they intoned, or "La . . . la . . . la," which was the equivalent of our "uh huh" when we're listening. Amala at one point inhaled softly, "Aiiiiee."

The entire family paid rapt attention. Even the ten-year-old stopped fussing and fighting with her cousin. After a long time, Lhakyi translated: "She has like a depression. She is sad all the time; she cries a lot. She is sad for no reason."

I wouldn't have known that just looking at her, I thought.

"That is why she drinks," Lhakyi continued. "She misses the old Lhasa; she doesn't like the new Lhasa. She doesn't see anyone she knows on the streets anymore. Every time she goes out, she comes home crying . . . "

Now I was really concerned.

". . . because the city has changed so much. There are so many people moving here. She said the Muslims are worse than the Chinese."

I turned and stared hard at Lhakyi. That was a shocking statement. Poor woman, I thought. Living right here in the Barkhor where the throngs of new émigrés were most dense, she was especially hard hit. She could never get away from the impact of these disastrous Chinese policies. Our family lived farther from town, so we got a respite, but she lived in the thick of it.

Eventually, people started to straggle off to other parts of the house. Lhakyi and I wandered outside to get some fresh air. Another of Auntie's daughters sat outside on the tiny, fenced-in porch. She and Lhakyi talked. She is my age, Lhakyi said. Apparently, all the children had grown up together. Lhakyi told me afterward that her cousin was talking about the difficulty of finding housing now. The train brought tremendous numbers of people, and the huge influx had sparked a housing crisis.

We had *momo* soup for lunch. Auntie said she was really happy to have visitors.

She explained that they didn't get many visitors because, in Lhakyi's translation, "their status is low." She said she worried a lot these days about her children's future. Since they didn't receive good educations, they didn't have good jobs. She was a single mother of five, "without any connections" after her husband died, so she had struggled to bring them up. Her children all have health problems, Tashi told me. They struggle to make ends meet.

Lhakyi said that Auntie felt she had done a good job raising them, in terms of their character—they are all good people—but as far as their economic situations, she was anxious.

"If you don't have a good education, it's hard to get a good job in Lhasa," Lhakyi explained. "She says there also is talk that the government plans to demolish their building . . . she worries that they'll be homeless." Lhakyi whispered that Auntie said she prayed every night and every morning to Kundun to protect them.

Later that afternoon, Tashi's best friend from high school, the woman who had worn the red coat to the party, came over. Tashi told me that her friend lived in Kongpo, east of Lhasa. She stayed for hours, through dinner and into the night. She and Pema started drinking at about five in the evening—Budweiser Lite™ in shot glasses. I remembered that she had drunk a lot the other day and started collaring old friends—a whole group of them, eight or nine, had grown up together—to sing out loud with her in the middle of the room. She and Pema sat in the family room after dinner and pulled down shot after shot of beer.

Around eight o'clock, the friend started delivering long soliloquies. Tashi sat beside her, a smile frozen on her face. No one could engage in conversation because the friend carried on so loudly and nonstop.

At about nine, the friend toned down, looking balefully at her shot glass on the table. She spoke in short rhapsodic phrases as if reciting traditional poetry. Tashi translated: She had many sorrows. Enough to fill a stream. The stream could swell into a river. And the river swell into a veritable ocean. She wished she could utter them aloud, lift the heavy stones from her heart. She didn't want to upset the parents though, she said, so she would not name them. She stared at her shot glass. She fills every glass, she said, with all her tears. Then swallows them again. She looked at us, eyes bloodshot, torso swaying.

Around ten o'clock, Tashi told me that her friend was starting to repeat herself. I suggested to Tashi that she could beg out, say something about being tired herself, but Tashi said she couldn't. That would be considered very rude. I turned in for bed around eleven thirty, leaving the friend droning and Tashi mute beside her.

The next morning, Tashi told me that her friend had left around half past midnight; she had walked her to the main street and helped her get a cab. Tashi said that all her friends and former classmates were very upset about all the changes they were seeing. She and I sat on the sofa bed in the family room alone. Everybody had already cleared out for the morning. Her friends, classmates, and cousins had all been talking about it these last few days, Tashi said. Everyone was uneasy and upset.

I asked her what people had said.

"Chinese workers were paid ¥50 a day for building the railroad. The Tibetans only ¥25," she said. "When officials first told local people about building the railroad, they said that food would be cheaper, and people would be able to buy more goods, and the project would give a lot of good jobs to everyone. But once it was finished, the good jobs only went to relatives of railroad officials."

Her friends told her that no one is allowed to get near the railroad; if they do, the authorities said they would be shot. Armed guards patrolled sections of the tracks. The government warned them that if children or animals got too close, the adults would be held responsible; if children trespassed during school hours, their teachers would be held responsible.

The government, in grabbing Tibetan farmers' land for the railroad, routinely undervalued the properties. Tashi said that when China took land from the farmers, it gave each family ¥20,000 to build a house closer to the city. But then the family still owed another ¥10,000 mortgage on the house. These country people had been farmers for many generations and had no other job skills. They couldn't grow food anymore. So they had no job, no land, no food, no training for any other job.

"Near Shigatse, the government found a big copper deposit," Tashi said. "Officials said the train would make travel easier and help develop Tibet, but actually they'll use it to take this copper to China. The Chinese government has a partnership with a Canadian company to mine the copper."

She said that the Chinese government had found oil in Tibet, and something she described like a "white gold." A couple of years ago in Chamdo the Chinese had found a big lode of another valuable mineral—she didn't know the English word. The government knew the Khampas—known as proud, stubborn, and rebellious—would never agree to leave their ancestral land, so it struck a deal: the Khampas could move to Kongpo, Lhasa, and elsewhere with license to do as they pleased, as long as they stayed away from Kham for three years. Khampas could now rob, smuggle, even murder, with impunity. The government didn't want any trouble with the Khampas; it just wanted them to stay away so it could extract this mineral, supposedly one of the purest lodes ever found.

"People are angry . . . but they can't say anything," Tashi said, shaking her head resignedly. "They have a joke," she added, perking up a bit. "When the train comes to Lhasa, it makes the sound *dingdingding*. And when it leaves Lhasa, it makes the sound *duuung . . . duuung . . . duuung . . .*"

I laughed. The first sound was spritely and quick, an empty train running light and fast on the tracks. The second sound was lumbering and slow, the train heavy with cargo. It was funny, but painful at the same time.

"The government also built a line to bring water from Tibet to China," Tashi continued. "The Chinese are trying to take Tibet's water to China, but the line doesn't work right. In winter it freezes, and in the summer, there's some other problem." She couldn't remember exactly what the other complication was. I knew China had polluted its rivers and water sources so badly that the water was unsafe to drink. During my 1994 visit, I'd seen a television commercial trying to sell Tibet's "clean, pure, Himalayan water" to eastern China.

"The government has cut down all the forests in Kongpo," Tashi said, referring to something her friend had talked about last night. "There's a special tree there . . . "—she didn't know the English word for the species—

"They took all the wood to China. With the trees gone, the birds and animals left. The hills are bare now; there's no more life. No more birds singing. Nothing. The Tibetans in Kongpo are very sad about it.

"A lot of people from Canton are moving to Kongpo," Tashi said. She described Kongpo as a fertile land with a temperate climate, not as high in elevation as Lhasa, and with lots of room still to own land and put up a house, which you couldn't say about most parts of China. Her friend had explained that the Chinese in Kongpo were allowed to buy land easily, to build a house and purchase lumber and materials without difficulty. But Tibetans who wanted to do the same thing were required to obtain twenty different permits and authorizations. The impossible obstacles forced Tibetans to move to the higher elevations to live.

"China is just robbing Tibet." Tashi shook her head and fell silent for a long moment. "There'll be nothing left. They say they'll bring development to Tibet, but they're just robbing it. Lots of Tibetans are angry—all my friends," she said.

She told me that her friends didn't want to send their kids to college in China because when the children returned to Tibet, there wouldn't be jobs for them. And it was very expensive now to send a child to college.

A college education is required for a government job with a good pension, so competition among Chinese youth is intense. She explained that there were quotas for Tibetans to go to college in China but Chinese people took the spots. Chinese students claimed they were going to major in Tibetan so that they could take advantage of the special spots set aside for such students, but once they were in, they changed their major and never studied Tibetan. Chinese students also came to Tibet to take the college entrance exam, because lower scores are required for applicants from Tibet, Tashi said.

Young Tibetans who want a good job and a decent future, she added, have to pass tests given in the Chinese language, so they are essentially forced to master Chinese. "Few Tibetans study Tibetan language these days. So Tibetan is becoming a useless language. Tibetans who care about their country try to find a way to move to the West . . . to India . . . the U.S. or Canada."

She indicated that corruption was rife. "For instance, Beijing gives Tibet big subsidies, but many people along the way take a chunk of it. By the time it reaches Tibet, the money is tiny."

She mentioned that most stores in Lhasa are now owned by Chinese and Muslims, not Tibetans anymore.

Before I knew it, we'd talked for nearly an hour. All this time, I had thought Tashi and her friends were socializing, having a good time. That hadn't been the case at all. Now I knew what Tashi and her classmates, friends, and relatives had all been talking so intensely about. Her high school pal, the one who had drunk too much and talked late into the night, lived in Kongpo and was very upset by these changes. She had needed to confide in Tashi, to share her grief, fear, and anger with her old friend during all her late night visits.

A couple of days later, Lhakyi and I headed back to visit Auntie. I had asked if we might meet again. Lhakyi and I walked a different route to the Barkor, down a road I hadn't been on before. Nightclubs and bars sported larger-than-life-size ads for Chivas™ scotch and Budweiser™ beer. Images of raging bulging-muscled men from Western films were plastered across the fronts of video stores. When I'd lived here before, there were no ads for anything—let alone for products so incongruous with Buddhist values. Closer to the town center, screechy, scratchy, screaming recorded sales pitches and bouncy Chinese pop music blared from shops. I saw a gigantic black SUV with tinted windows nearly mow down a tiny Tibetan granny when it sped onto a narrow lane; slow in step, the woman stood blinking in shocked disbelief at the near miss. Drivers were extremely aggressive and honked incessantly, making the streets resemble a scene from downtown Bangkok.

"I know no one here. It feels like I'm in another country," Lhakyi said as we navigated our way down the sidewalk. Junky signs hung on every available surface, and swollen tangles of electrical wires stretched every which way. "These past years in Canada, I always said, I'm going home to Lhasa. But last year, for the first time, I thought, Hmm . . . I might stay in the West . . . It's cleaner, there's more freedom. Then this visit . . . after what they did to my mother . . . ," referring to the registration office official who had tried to shake down Amala, "I said, I'm only going to come back to see my family. Because under this government," she frowned and shook her head, "you are not free."

We walked to Auntie's home. I wanted to talk more with her about the changes in Lhasa, especially since she lived at ground zero, in the Barkhor. When Lhakyi had said the other day that Auntie suffered from depression, it was the first time I'd heard anyone mention emotional disorders here. Her admission that she cried a lot, felt sad "for no reason," and had begun drinking and taking snuff brought to my mind the phenomenon called hysterical blindness, which had plagued women in Vietnam during the U.S. war there. I'd read about one woman who lost seven of her eight children in the war. Women, I thought, bore the emotional toll of what was going on in the social environment. Especially, I thought, someone extremely intuitive, like Auntie seemed to be.

Inside the building complex, with its cracked walls and faded, peeling, paint, boxes of trash were strewn about, along with abandoned metal buckets, piles of pots, bags of stuff in piles, and drying mops; clothing hung on clotheslines. Upstairs, as we walked the balcony along three sides of the old Tibetan building, I saw shaven-headed men wearing white skullcaps loitering outside many of the other residences, tracking us as we made our way to her unit at the end. I tried to smile at them, but their stares were hard, even predatory. I felt very uneasy.

We were invited to sit in a tiny front room, on a bench seat beside a large window that offered sunlight and heat. Auntie, with long ears and deep trenches of wrinkles across her forehead, sat at a right angle to us. Her oldest daughter, the one who had visited our house the other day, sat on our left. Tea was poured, pleasantries exchanged. Lhakyi recalled that when she and Tashi were kids, they used to play hooky from a particular loathsome math teacher's class and found refuge with this aunt and her brood. Pala would come knocking on the door looking for them, and Auntie would cover for them. When the coast was clear, she'd cook a delicious lunch for everybody.

Lhakyi told me that Auntie's hearing was bad. The mistreatment she had suffered during the '60s had damaged her eyes and ears. Her daughter would help answer questions.

I asked about Auntie's background as a priestess. Auntie, who was seventy-three, said she came from a line of such priestesses. Her mother and grandmother had held a special place in society. They could remove sickness and help people overcome obstacles. When she was thirteen, her mother passed away and she inherited the position. After the Chinese invaded, the authorities made her stop doing the work. They called it poison and confiscated all the special garments and objects she had used. She was twenty-five at the time. She suffered very much, Lhakyi translated.

"Do you mean she was tortured?" I said, asking for clarification.

"Yes," Lhakyi replied.

From their reluctance to offer details, I got the impression that the experience had been traumatic, so I didn't pursue the subject. Lhakyi told me that the family was shunned because of their political status. Throughout this time, the 1960s and 1970s, there was no food and no money. They couldn't even afford shoes. They barely scraped by. They lacked what in China was called *guanxi*, the connections needed to get anything done.

Auntie's father, an official in the administration of both the previous and the current Dalai Lama, had been branded a Big Hat. In the Chinese system of categorizing political enemies, a Big Hat was the highest degree of an enemy of the government. He died, she said, in 1961. Her husband was also in government, a surveyor of some sort. I noticed that they avoided talking about the circumstances of his death.

"*Lots* of Muslims and Chinese are moving in," Auntie said in her croaking voice. "The Tibetans are having a hard time surviving in society now. Prices keep going up, and it's hard to get good jobs. For example, vegetables imported from China are very expensive. If you have a salary, it's okay when prices climb . . . but our family doesn't have high salaries or regular paychecks. We can't afford the price increases. The vegetable selection in years past was more limited, but more affordable.

"Tibetans who speak up are put in jail," she said, "or driven out of the city. This is what troubles me the most. Especially at certain monasteries, the government is very repressive: they demand that the monks denounce the Dalai Lama, but the monks refuse. Then the government cracks down hard on them."

She went on to say that in the countryside, the Chinese government promised to pay a farmer for his land but then gave him a paltry sum, not fair compensation. After that, the family must make mortgage payments to the government for a new house or a little studio apartment where the government wants them to live. They live in a brand-new building but have nothing to eat.

"Here in Lhasa, the government builds new apartment complexes with scores of tiny rooms and rents them to immigrants who've just moved here. The government razes Lhasa people's homes so they can build these complexes for the new immigrants.

"There are so many people in Lhasa now, it's frightening," she said. "Lots of Muslims have moved here, lots of Bonpo people. Last year, when the train started, the majority of those who moved to Lhasa were Bonpos." She went on to say that the Muslims are even worse than the Chinese. I was shocked by this comment and asked what she meant. "At least," she explained, "the Chinese have similar values. Before this government came, they were Buddhists. They have that background. The Khaches have a completely different religion and treat Tibetans despicably. They go to the Jokhang temple and steal sacred objects; they brutally beat monks who try to stop them. If there's a dispute between a Muslim and a Tibetan, the Muslim will come after the Tibetan with a big gang. They operate in gangs. Big bosses hire young guys to do the work. They beat up Tibetans. There is no law enforcement over them. Even if people are arrested, they bribe their way free."

The Khaches arrive dirt-poor, Auntie told us, take over businesses Tibetans used to operate, and go back to their own province very wealthy. They sell cheap imitations of products for the price of the genuine articles. They also sell drugs, cocaine and marijuana.

She explained that the Khampas came to Lhasa to trade *yartsa gunbu*, an extremely expensive medicinal herb from Kham. It's a grass in summer and a caterpillar-like worm in the winter, and very laborious to collect. The Khampas painstakingly gathered these caterpillar fungi and brought them to trade in Lhasa. When the Khampas did business with the Khaches, the Khaches drugged the Khampas' tea. The Khampas lost consciousness, and the Khaches stole the herbs.

"Common Tibetans can't afford to live here in Lhasa anymore. This building, for instance, used to be very clean and orderly. Now it's got rubbish and debris strewn all over. Life was much simpler before; food was not expensive and was fresh and flavorful. Now we have all these services, but we also have all these bills—for water, trash, electricity."

I asked whether she saw anything positive in the changes to Lhasa—cell phones or plumbing, for example?

"We have no running water, just the cold water spigot in the courtyard," she answered. "The older generation doesn't use these things. None of these have improved life. Along the public roads where tourists travel—to the airport or on the main roads to tourist attractions—there are new buildings. But these are just for show," she added.

Her only hope, she said, was to see the Dalai Lama before she died. Conditions were bad, but could be even worse—held in check, she believed, by his influence.

"The older generation only wishes to have the opportunity to see him before we die. We are just waiting for the day when he comes back. When that happens, order will be restored and life will be good again.

"The older generation . . . we don't go out now," she said. "We just stay home, because it's too crowded in the streets. The older generation knows the truth, but we can't say anything because the government will crack down."

I noticed when we left that theirs was the only residence whose tiny front porch was covered in chicken wire. Not enough to keep out a determined thief, but enough to deter someone from just reaching in and helping himself. Are they sitting ducks here? I wondered. A household of Tibetan women living among these steely-eyed, skullcapped strangers in this dilapidated Tibetan building? (I would read later that these men were largely unskilled laborers and small traders lured by wages three times higher in Tibet than in China. Tens of thousands had come on the train.)

Lhakyi told me as we walked home that Auntie, according to Amala, had been stunningly beautiful as a young woman and that Auntie's husband, Amala's brother, had died in a tragic accident more than thirty years before. Lhakyi remembered her father rushing to the site of the accident and not coming home until very late at night. Auntie's husband had been

The Jokhang Temple, center of the Tibetan religious world, in the heart of Lhasa, 1986. Note the small number of people, only Tibetan faithful.

The Jokhang Temple, 2007. Note the crowds and the Chinese Muslim peddlers, wearing white caps, who have taken over traditional Tibetan businesses.

trapped in a building that collapsed under construction, and Pala had spent hours trying to dig him out. Lhakyi said she had a vivid childhood memory of the sight of her father's shredded, bloodied hands.

Since the day I had ventured out on an early morning walk, I'd wanted to hike up the mountain on the other side of the river. From a distance, I had seen several hundred Tibetans crossing the bridge on foot, carrying stands of prayer flags through thick clouds of burning incense. I had seen more Tibetans there than I'd seen during my entire stay in Lhasa. This mountain was the same one we'd seen from our rooftop, shrouded in plumes of incense smoke, which Pema had said she'd climbed before. My days in Lhasa were limited now; I had to push on to Dharamsala. I pestered my friends every day about taking the hike.

A week after New Year's, a group of us finally set out for the bridge, about a mile or so from the house. One helper carried a bag that looked like a Santa Claus sack on her shoulder, and the other bore a load the size of a big day pack containing several rolls of prayer flags and a jug of *chang*.

Once we hit the main street, four of our group jumped into a cab, ending my fantasy of a healthy hike together. Tashi and I continued on foot. As we ambled down the wide main street, she told me that there were many houses of prostitution on the avenue.

"You're kidding!" I exclaimed. I'd been up and down the street numerous times and had never noticed anything.

"They look like teahouses," she said and explained that the brothels displayed a sign for a certain Tibetan beer on the front window, indicating that they were brothels. "There are Tibetan girls and there are Chinese girls," she continued, "but the Chinese cost more. You can get a Tibetan girl for, like, a bowl of noodles. But a Chinese girl . . . " she squeezed against my arm for a millisecond, "*that's* ¥100."

Tashi said that the prostitutes, often as young as fourteen or fifteen, were called "cats" by the townspeople. They hailed from rural areas of Tibet that were poor and had few job opportunities. She said the girls were marketed to visiting Chinese businessmen and government officials attending conferences and Party meetings. The men were promised the "Complete

Dragon—from the top of the head all the way to the tip of the tail." That meant the whole package of first-class accommodations, dining, liquor, and women. A top selling point was the promise that the girls would perform sexual favors that the men couldn't secure from their wives.

We passed one storefront where four plump adolescents—with teased spiky hairstyles and cheeks round with baby fat—idled on a ratty old sofa that had been pulled out onto the curb.

"Those are 'cats,'" Tashi pointed out. My eyes popped in disbelief.

(When I brought up the subject with Lhakyi later that evening, she told me that the small teahouse on the corner, where we turned off the main street to reach the house, was a front for a brothel. I was absolutely shocked. We passed the place every day. The neon sign said it was a teahouse, but it looked more like a bar. I had never seen any patrons inside. Lhakyi said that last year when she was in town, she overheard a girl bitterly arguing with a john one night when the windows were open: "Pay me ¥8! Give me my money!" Eight yuan was about a dollar. Lhakyi said she had once chatted with a young Tibetan girl and asked her why she did this kind of work. The girl replied frankly, "Because I didn't want to become a thief." Stealing was greatly frowned upon in Tibetan Buddhism, and she had no other means by which to support herself. She'd made the decision to keep ethical conduct according to her Buddhist upbringing.)

Tashi and I passed a huge complex near the river, an apartment block eight stories high, sterile and dreary. Tashi told me there was talk that the government planned to appropriate the neighborhood where her family's home stood, tear down all the single-family houses, and erect big apartment complexes like this one to address Lhasa's acute housing shortage. My heart sank. The house had taken Pala years to design and build. He had earned the option to buy the land as part of his pension from his state job, where he'd worked for thirty years. Tashi and Lhakyi had sent money from Canada to help pay for the expenses. It would be absolutely devastating if the house were demolished.

Citizens here had no power against the state. The government could just come in and take someone's land or home. In the early 1950s, Chinese built roads right through people's property, without permission or compensation. Eighty percent of Tibetans lived in the countryside as nomads or farmers. Their land was their only asset. It was what they passed down to their children.

At the bridge, I saw that the mountain looming ahead of us was criss-crossed with long lines of prayer flags. I stopped on the span and gazed a long time at the river. I remembered the river so fondly from our picnics on its banks that summer twenty-one years ago—wide and clean and mighty, with a steady full flow. Now I saw nothing but opaque, stagnant, dark green water. Two ducks floated along on the murky surface. It had dried up so much that I could see the rocky bottom. Tashi didn't know anything about what had happened to it. Dirty and dead, it bore no resemblance to the river I remembered. I felt terrible sadness, sheer despair, and anger.

Cement-block housing in Lhasa. To address the housing crisis caused by the sudden influx of Chinese immigrants, numbering in the tens of thousands, the government plans to tear down residential neighborhoods and build more such housing. 2007.

The polluted Kyichu River, a northern tributary of the Yarlong Tsangpo, Lhasa, 2007. A prime picnicking site in pre-1950 Tibet, its Tibetan name means "river of happiness." According to a 1996 Tibet Autonomous Region report, 4.9 million tons of liquid waste had been discharged into the river, presumably in 1996 or around that year.

We started up the mountain's rocky dirt trail. The others who had taken the taxi were already halfway up. My heart pounded loudly in my chest, and my throat quickly got dry from panting. We ascended about nine hundred feet. About two hundred feet from the top, Tashi begged off; she staggered and leaned against a boulder, winded. She felt she might throw up, she said. She didn't want to continue. Don't wait, go ahead, she urged. I lugged one heavy foot in front of the other.

From the high vistas, I could see the breadth of Lhasa for the first time—block after block of gray, industrial-looking sprawl. It spread eastward about three miles along the river, then jutted north. I couldn't tell how far it went beyond that. Pollution in the form of a thick brown layer of haze hung over the entire city. Lhasa's air used to be so sparkling, so invigorating—crisp and clean. I'd never before breathed such fresh, life-giving air.

At the peak, the lines of colorful prayer flags strung across the mountain face looked magical. Each of the colors—red, green, blue, white, and yellow—stood for a different element: fire, metal, water, wind, and wood. The flags, which bore printed prayers, were commonly strung from high places, like the tops of mountain passes, where the wind could take the prayers directly to the gods. We went around tossing *sang*, and offering *tsampa* and *chang* at several small fire rings along a ledge. My friends murmured prayers as they watched the smoke billow, then stood wordlessly watching the *sang* burn, as if in a trance. A young man with the coarse, sunburned face of country people appeared and squatted on the ground, talking to Pema. She had hired him to climb up and rig the prayer flags we'd brought.

Pema was the most traditional of the sisters in maintaining religious rituals, I thought, as I watched her stare into the fire ring, clouds of smoke framing her figure. One night in the courtyard, at about ten o'clock, when everyone was inside glued to the TV, I'd seen her burning *sang* on a metal stand, a purification ritual Amala performed in the early mornings. Pema had no interest in going to the West, like her siblings. She was precious— talented, sensitive, hardworking, strong, and poised. I wondered what her fate would be.

Here a Tibetan had a quickly shrinking, tiny acre of space to occupy. Tibetans were not allowed to do this and were prohibited from doing that. They might go about in what looked like relative freedom but in fact had little. The government controlled everything. They lived in a country under duress, people under house arrest. Slowly being smothered to death.

What kind of future would Pema's kids have? They'd have to become more Chinese than the Chinese if they hoped to get decent jobs. They'd have to neglect their Tibetan language and heritage so that they could attain a decent standard of living in this Sinocentric world, returning home every night from their "good" jobs to be entertained by television propaganda.

I remembered something Mrs. Taring, one of my interview subjects, had said, referring to 1959: "Before, we only lost Tibet from the outside, but if we lose the culture, we will also lose it from the inside. And then the Chinese will have won." Hearing it had sent chills up my spine.

I had read Mrs. Taring's book, *Daughter of Tibet*, on a two-week trek into the magical Rongbuk Valley. It was the second book about Tibet I'd ever read, and it completely transported me to the world of Lhasa in the 1940s and 1950s. I was thrilled to have found a book by a Tibetan woman. A member of one of Tibet's oldest families, Mrs. Taring learned English in Darjeeling in the 1920s. Her book, an intimate account of Tibetan society, ended when she escaped Lhasa in March 1959. She was renowned for founding the Tibetan Homes Foundation in India, one of the most highly regarded Tibetan institutions in exile, which housed and educated thousands of children orphaned by the 1959 takeover. And she was closely associated with the Central Tibetan Schools in Mussoorie, which her husband had founded and directed for fifteen years. These two institutions had trained many of Tibet's present-day leaders—government officials, scholars, and business figures.

I wanted the sequel to her book: the second half of her life, in exile. How had she been able to create these institutions, and what personal mark had she left on them? Whenever I mentioned her name among Tibetans, whether in India, Switzerland, or Nepal, the response was inevitably an outpouring of respect and appreciation. Many of her former students remarked that she had cared for them like they were her own children. What made her tick? What choices had she made? What challenges did she face? What role did spiritual faith play? I wanted to hear it in her own words, get a sense of what she was like as a person. She also had a unique partnership with her husband, a multitalented, brilliant, dedicated man who was as admired, respected, and loved in the Tibetan community as she was.

A friend in Dharamsala, a relative of Mrs. Taring's, used the word "dynamo" to describe her eighty-four-year-old great-aunt. It made her tired, my friend said, just thinking about what her great-aunt accomplished in a day. She rose early, said prayers, studied scripture, answered letters, and bathed—all before breakfast.

I met Rinchen Dolma Taring on a scalding-hot day in May 1994. I was perspiring on the back porch of her house, dusty and disheveled, relieved to be in the shade. Mrs. Taring, called out from the house by her maid, who wore burgundy nun's robes, stood in a moss-green lightweight *chuba* with a perplexed look on her face.

"How do you spell that?" she asked after hearing my unusual name. I spelled it.

I told her I had written her letters from the States.

"When did you write me this letter?" she asked. She spoke English with a Tibetan accent and a tinge of British inflection.

As I answered her questions, she scrutinized me, one eye closed against the sun. She was taller than I had expected, with a square face and eyes that sloped down at the outside corners, like Bobby Kennedy's. The local Indian lad who had so graciously offered me a ride when I was stuck in the middle of nowhere had driven through a lovely area with verdant poplar trees and old temple ruins to the outskirts of a peaceful village near Dehra Dun. On a residential side road, he stopped, opened a black iron double gate, and then drove onto a property with a large two-story home. I got off the bike and straightened my rumpled clothes. It had taken hours to get here—a ninety-minute shared taxi ride down the mountain, a long time getting my bearings and waiting, then the dusty, fourteen-mile ride on the back of the scooter in 104-degree heat. I was meeting a dignified personage, a living legend. Under the dust and sweat, I was desperately afraid that I wasn't making a good impression.

To my shock and distress, the emissary who had preceded me two weeks earlier, charged with informing Mrs. Taring of my visit, had somehow fouled up: Mrs. Taring didn't have a clue as to who I was. She had no phone, so I hadn't been able to ring in advance. She leaned forward and peered into my face.

I had a headache from heat exhaustion. I mentioned the Nuns Project, I mentioned my visit to Tibet years ago and living with the Lhasa family, I mentioned my performing, the oral histories—summing up years of involvement in a few short sentences. I was struck by her pearly white, soft-waved hair; I had only seen images of her in her book, with jet black hair. A birthmark the size of a quarter colored the bridge of her nose. She looked skeptical. I feared she might refuse to talk with me.

After ten minutes of cordial but rigorous screening, she said, with only the slightest apprehension in her voice: "All right then. Come Monday at 10 a.m. We will talk."

When I returned on Monday, the *anila* maid who had first greeted me on the back porch invited me in. I waited in a spacious, comfortable living room, painted muted mustard and off-white and adorned with three large colorful Tibetan *thangkas*. Large windows opened onto views of the hills. The room's atmosphere exuded warmth, refinement, and, at the same time, simplicity and solidity.

The bookshelf in the hallway looked like the rare book collection in the central library in Dharamsala: *The Cultural History of Tibet*, the 1939 edition by David Snellgrove and Hugh Richardson; *Some Forgotten Kingdom*, by Peter Galard, 1930; *Lost Tibet, The Historical Status of Tibet, and Return to Tibet*, by Heinrich Harrer; *Tibet and Its History*, by Hugh Richardson. Books by Dervla Murphy and Lowell Thomas and Kripalani. All first-edition hardcovers, it seemed. There were also newer titles, including *In Exile from the Land of Snows*. On the lower shelves, I saw books on Mahatma Gandhi and a volume titled *Nutrition for Developing Countries*.

"Excuse me," Mrs. Taring said, entering briskly after a few minutes in a powder blue *chuba* over an eggshell-colored blouse. "I was writing a letter." I handed her a bouquet of yellow daffodils from town. She looked quite touched and excused herself, taking the bouquet. She returned with the flowers, arranged in a vase and basket, and placed them on a small table beneath a *thangka* of the Buddha, which had a small framed picture of His Holiness on one side and an image of her husband on the other. She stood in prayer, hands clasped for a few silent seconds. I sensed a lovely poise and great dignity about her.

We sat down, and she lifted something to the side of her head: "Sometimes I lose my hearing," she said, fitting a hearing aid into her ear.

Aha, I thought. This is why she studied my face so intently the other day. She couldn't hear everything and had to rely on what she saw. I asked if we could switch sides so I could reach the electrical outlet to plug in my tape recorder. She rose energetically from her seat. She had a directness about her and great vigor.

The *anila* came in with tea on a tray, complete with fine china cups and saucers. It reminded me of high tea in Britain.

"Would you care for some tea?" Mrs. Taring asked.

I thought about it, then shrugged my shoulders: "Sure." I was suddenly overcome by a wave of embarrassment, mortified that I had transgressed some law of propriety. I should have inclined my head, clasped my hands, and said, Oh no, thank you. I had forgotten that Tibetan tea was an elaborate extended dialogue of formal offerings and polite declines. I felt like some kind of bohemian, a woolly California beach bum. I was used to drinking tea from a plastic commuter mug, brandishing the name of the local camping store while flopping around in gym shorts at home.

I recovered my composure, commenting on the small sugar spoon—engraved silver, quite old and very beautiful. It was from Lhasa, Mrs. Taring said, a gift from a nephew.

I asked about her escape, the event that ends her book. Her husband, Jigme, the prince of Sikkim, whom she married at age nineteen, had followed His Holiness's entourage to Mussoorie, a former British hill station at eight thousand feet in the Indian Himalayas, close to here. Jigme Taring, being a fluent speaker of Hindi and English—he had translated for the Dalai Lama on his trips to India in the 1950s—had been critical in helping the government get settled in exile. Meanwhile, Mrs. Taring found her way to Kalimpong, via Bhutan. She stayed with a niece and was asked to teach English to some local girls. Her fifteen-student class mushroomed quickly in size. After a year, Jigme was put in charge of creating the Central Tibetan Schools. In late 1961, she received a letter from the Kashag, the Tibetan Cabinet, directing her to move to Mussoorie to help her husband. By then, she had a small thriving school for girls with one hundred devoted students. She told the Kashag, "I'm in the middle of building up this school, I can't leave. The children depend on me."

A year later, the Kashag wrote another letter, this one more forcefully worded, requesting that she appear in Dharamsala, where the government-in-exile had permanently settled, and promising to find a replacement for her at her girls' school.

"Well then, what could I say? I couldn't say no. I went to Dharamsala to discuss the matter with His Holiness," she explained.

In the 1950s, Mrs. Taring had traveled with the Dalai Lama and his family on three separate trips to China, each several months to a year in length. She'd been in daily contact with the family then, tutoring the Dalai Lama's younger sister in Tibetan and visiting often with his mother. The Dalai Lama knew and trusted her.

She excused herself and left the room. Reappearing several minutes later, she handed me a yellowed letter from a sheaf of papers. Typed on a manual typewriter on a plain sheet of paper, it bore the seal of the Dalai Lama of Tibet stamped in red in the upper right corner. The date was 1962. She had a copy in Tibetan as well, she said; this English version was to help with fund-raising.

It stated that the Dalai Lama sought to organize four model schools for Tibetan orphans and had appointed Mrs. Taring to serve as general secretary. The mission was to "give protection and help to needy and destitute Tibetans in India, particularly Tibetan children, on all levels of human life: physical, social, cultural, religious, and spiritual." The last line read "You will act under my direct authority." At the bottom of the page, in a florid black Tibetan script, was the signature of the Dalai Lama.

She said she and the Dalai Lama talked at length.

"His Holiness believed that we lost our country from not being able to cope with modern change. So he felt modern education was essential for the young people. He also wanted to find a way to care for children who'd been orphaned, who had no parents or family here in India. There were hundreds of children like this. So he and Pandit Nehru developed the idea of the Tibetan education system to care for these children and to produce what they called "seeds of a free Tibet." She said the Dalai Lama took a keen personal interest in the project.

I knew that he had been talking to India leaders throughout the 1950s, and when he fled Tibet in 1959, he had expected that India would lend Tibetans military support to help them take back their country. Nehru counseled instead that the best way to keep the country was to preserve the culture and educate the children.

Mrs. Taring recalled that she had felt terribly reluctant to take the job. The scope and nature of what the Dalai Lama wanted her to handle was enormous—fund-raising, construction of the physical plant, design of the educational curriculum, creation of all legal, financial, and administrative structures, the hiring and training of staff. She had no experience in these things, she claimed. She had done little in Tibet before, she said, except keep up good social relationships.

"How did you finally agree to it?" I asked.

She said His Holiness had looked her square in the eye and said, "Just do your best. Do your *very* best. Do it *every* day." She paused a long moment, visibly moved at recalling the conversation. "This really struck my heart. I still remember it. I kept this in mind through the years. He said I'd always have his full support. I should report directly to him."

Her first assignment was to teach Hindi and English to the fifty bodyguards who had escorted His Holiness across the Himalayas. She rented one of the many vacant houses in Mussoorie, left over from when it had been a popular mountain resort for the British. After a year, the bodyguards turned out and found jobs, and the first group of seventy-five children arrived. They'd come from transit camps where Tibetan refugees worked road construction, hard manual labor involving long hours, leaving the children without supervision.

The children arrived, she said, their stomachs distended from malnutrition, their bodies covered with scabies and lice. They clutched small bundles of clothing and personal items—all their worldly goods. They had worms. They were withdrawn and miserable. They'd had no medical care, and several died every week. She, her daughter Betty, her niece, other friends, and some of the older children started to give the new arrivals baths.

"Their eyes were full of pus from conjunctivitis, their bodies covered in bleeding sores. We arranged for medical care first. Then I worked with the ones who needed health and hygiene. The others my husband took into the Schools."

Eventually, they found systems for doing things: "We had one room for children with scabies, one room for TB, like that. We'd boil water and organize hot baths and change dressings. There's nothing better to heal scabies than washing in hot water."

The children would gather leaves, twigs, and newspapers for the fire, where the adults heated water in six or seven big boilers they'd made from galvanized iron sheets. In those days, they couldn't afford water heaters, so they fashioned their own.

Over time she found more help: "We had doctors from the American Community Hospital in Mussoorie, volunteer medical people from the Swiss Red Cross and Catholic Relief. Western volunteers helped us a lot—dentists, nurses, teachers, general helpers. Ladies from the airline hostesses association. One couple was from Hawaii, the Matsuuras. Husband and wife, both doctors; they came in 1960 or 1961. We had four or five hundred children by then.

"We bought food from the local grocers. Food was much cheaper then. The main staples were rice and flour. The first years were the most difficult time because we didn't have enough money. If we gave them food for breakfast, we couldn't afford lunch and dinner; we could only afford to give them one meal a day. There weren't enough clothes to clothe them.

"We built a kitchen with wood-burning stoves; we didn't even have propane in those days. My husband designed the kitchen. He invented a nice stove built into the wall; the smoke vented outside. Later, we could give the children two meals—tea for breakfast and then food for lunch and dinner.

"We had a huge steamer for making *ting momos*. We gave them nice *ting momos*, nice dal, good vegetables. Fruit once a week. An egg once a week. Week by week, you could see them get better.

"We went everywhere on foot. We had no cars, no jeeps. We had no phones. Even Dehra Dun, the big city twenty miles away, had only a few taxis then."

Often Mrs. Taring, or Amala, as she asked me to call her, would respond to my questions with a frown or grimace and a short silence while she thought hard. "Oh, I'm so forgetful," she'd say, or "It was so long ago, I have so many other things on my mind now." Or "I haven't thought about this in so long." She graciously tried to answer my questions, but I realized after a while that these events had taken place more than thirty years ago. The story of the early days, when new refugees built what had become a renowned institution from humble beginnings, held an urgency for me that she did not feel anymore.

Because of our slow progress, I thought I would need to talk to her more. I asked if it might be possible for us to talk a couple of hours every day this week.

She asked where I was staying, and I told her I had rented a room in a guesthouse up in Mussoorie. It was twenty degrees cooler at the higher elevation, and I didn't tolerate heat well. She asked how I got down to Rajpur, and I said that I waited at the taxi stand for someone to share the ninety-minute ride down the mountain.

"Come down and live here. Stay a few days. We have plenty of room," she responded.

I was delighted and honored. Not only would it save me the three-hour commute, but I'd have the opportunity to get to know her more informally. Luckily, she said, a group of guests had just left on Thursday, and another group would arrive on the weekend, leaving a few days open in between.

The next day, I moved from Mussoorie to Amala's house. I was in awe of being in her presence the first couple days. Each time we met or had a meal, it felt like I was being called to a formal audience. She impressed me instantly with her erudition and warmth, her intelligence and manners and social grace. Yet, as with most Tibetans, she possessed a down-to-earth manner.

She had three children, eight grandchildren, and fourteen great-grand-children. Her two youngest daughters had suffered intensely in occupied Tibet. The offspring of one of those daughters, a granddaughter about my age, and her two children lived with Amala, but the children were away at school and the granddaughter was in Delhi for a few days. A grandson's wife and two children, about seven and eight years old, were staying in the house for the summer before they moved to the States as part of the Tibetan Resettlement Project.

Around the third day, I asked Amala if she had any pictures from the early days. She led me to a suite on the first floor, which would be her daughter's room in August when her daughter retired, and showed me a trove of photo albums. Amala had painstakingly organized the hundreds of loose photographs her husband had taken through the years—black-and-white photos, mostly from the 1960s—into dozens of albums. The photos had been neatly mounted but lacked captions; I would have to ask her about the images. She kept all her important files and documents in three-ring binders and left the binders for me to peruse as well.

In the afternoons, after we talked, I went through the photo albums and binders.

I found a proclamation from the Sixteenth Legislature of the State Senate of Hawaii, dated April 1994, honoring her, a "true daughter of Tibet," for, among other things, her "undaunted faith in mankind." It bore the signatures of about fifteen senators. The attached letter, dated October 1992, read, "Dear Mrs. Taring. It's been over twenty-three years since I last saw you. . . . I remember your dedication and devotion to serve the children of Tibet. . . . Whenever I think of great people that I've met in my lifetime, you're at the very top of that list." It was signed by a senator named Richard M. Matsuura.

A tribute to her and her husband from a Tibetan organization in Canada read, "In honor of twenty-nine years of service to the Tibetan people."

I found a quote from a former student—now a school principal, who'd been orphaned as a baby—while thumbing through an annual report of 1960. He had been one of the original seventy-five children who arrived in November 1962: "We were treated to delicious noodles and then a warm, dignified lady gave a speech. I did not understand much of what she said, but I could feel the concern and saw the love in her eyes. A sense of security pervaded my bewildered little being. We were cared for in a way I had never experienced in my young life."

He recalled a happy, busy childhood. Besides classes and homework, they had chores such as sweeping, collecting firewood, chopping logs, laundering clothes, and digging dirt for construction: "I see now how essential these were to making us well-equipped for life." He remembered his housemother as a pivotal figure in the home: "From morning until we went to bed she was there checking how we made our beds, how we dressed, if our nails were cut, how we cooked, and most importantly how we talked. Words cannot express the importance and magnitude of this institution's work."

Instead of asking her questions in an interview format in the more formal living room, in our morning sessions I took to leafing through the photo albums in the studio with her. I'd ask her about the images. Girls in uniforms sitting outdoors eating a meal on the grass, in a square formation facing each other: "We didn't have dining rooms then, we just ate outside under the trees." Eight-year-old boys engaged in horseplay at the water pump: "That's where we bathed them." A construction site of two- and three-story buildings: "First we learned under the trees, we didn't have any classrooms. These are the new classrooms coming up in the late '60s."

In time, they set up a kindergarten with a Montessori program and a medical dispensary, staffed with the senior girls and boys, who received nursing training. With medical care and good nutrition, the children's general health improved, and the death rate went down.

"We organized them into groups of twenty-five. We built homes with the financial help of Western agencies, and the children and houseparents lived like a family, twenty-five children with two houseparents. Everything was organized on the number twenty-five: the baths, the classrooms, the size of the houses. Older children helped younger children, just like in a family. I took great care in choosing the houseparents. The children would imitate them, so I chose very cultured, kind, loving people."

Tibet had not had the tradition of public schools. The new educational curriculum in India included five subjects and three languages—Tibetan, English, and Hindi. Amala said she and her husband felt it was essential to teach the children both the old and the new, the traditional and the modern—to root them in their own culture, religion, and language but also prepare them for modern life. This would arm them with the knowledge and skills they needed to hold responsible jobs and serve the Tibetan community.

I asked about a photograph of eight tousle-haired boys, perhaps eleven to fourteen, in sports uniforms boisterously hoisting a trophy: "This is Tashi Wangdu, he is now minister of information and international relations. This is so-and-so; he is now director of education. This is Dorje so-and-so, a good boy; he is a businessman in Canada. This is so-and-so, he went to Mount Hermon; he is now a big trader, he's become very rich. This one is one of the best—he became homes secretary after Khandro-la. This is Tashi Tobgye; his education was very high, he's in Canada. This one's a wonderful boy; he is teaching at the International School in South India. This one's a male nurse in Denmark."

She could look at a photograph and recall the child's name, even if it showed the child from the back. She could look at a picture with a dozen bright ruddy faces and tell me their names, their educational histories, what they now did for a living, the names of their spouses, how many children they had, and their skill in English and in Tibetan. She had an astonishing, encyclopedic memory for people. She uttered the names of a dozen countries all over the east and west where former students now lived. The prophecy of the thirteenth Dalai Lama flashed to mind, something he had said in 1932: "Tibetans will be scattered all over the world like ants."

I asked her about a photo of dozens of twelve- to fifteen-year-olds with shovels and sacks on a rock-strewn hillside, a dilapidated Victorian mansion on a hilltop in the background. The building, she said, was the original schoolhouse: "My husband had the children break down a small hill to level the ground for a new building. Every Saturday, they had to work a few hours. He did the work himself, so the children couldn't complain."

The children helped with the manual work, she said—fetching flour rations from the mill, mending their own clothes, gardening, cleaning, cooking. The program went up to grade eight, then the children went elsewhere for secondary school. She and her staff secured scholarships to top-ranked schools throughout India for the most promising students. She rattled off names: Mount Hermon, Woodstock, St. Andrews, St. Peters.

One photo showed the Dalai Lama's private secretary, looking to be in his mid-twenties: "Yes, this is Tenzin Geyche when he was a monk. His father taught in the Schools."

A photo of a fortyish Indira Gandhi and Amala, looking pleased, walking among uniformed students standing in formation in a school yard on a sunny day inspired a vivid memory. She had wanted to invite the minister of education, Mrs. Gandhi, to be on the board, she recalled, but "never had the guts to ask." Her friend Maurice Frydman, an old British hand in Bombay, through whom she'd first met Indira Gandhi, encouraged her.

"I said, 'I can't ask her! She is the prime minister's daughter!' He said, 'She is a noble lady of India, and you are a noble lady of Tibet. There's nothing to be afraid of. Go talk to her, I know she will receive you well.' He gave me all the courage. He used to tell me, 'Don't worry, I know you will be one of the great general secretaries.'"

Mrs. Gandhi indeed agreed and served on Amala's board for many years.

She recalled a crisis in the mid-1970s, when the Civil Service Academy of Mussoorie wanted to clear the Homes Foundation off the land and take the site for itself. Mrs. Gandhi intervened on their behalf to halt the action.

"I had wonderful people on my governing board. Good backing," she said.

I was intrigued by a photo of a small Tibetan temple with prayer flags fluttering, with a dozen children and Amala climbing a steeply inclined road in the foreground. The temple stands on a high promontory with a range of low hills in the background.

"One of the first buildings we built was the temple," she explained. "This was very important. My husband designed it. We had to raise money, of course. One of our volunteers, Dervla Murphy from Ireland, had gone back to the West and written a book. She donated the royalties to build the temple. Without her help, it would have taken a much longer time to get built.

"We celebrated all the Tibetan holidays there," she recalled. "We held prayer sessions and ceremonies. The biggest holiday, of course, was Losar. Then Monlam and March 10th. For Uprising Day, we had a procession through town and dramatic skits. These are all the traditional holidays. In July, we celebrated His Holiness's birthday with picnicking and dancing. Autumn Festival we held under tents in the meadow."

I asked Amala about a photo of herself sitting with a plump, white-haired European woman amid mountains of neatly bound packages: "It was Losar. Mrs. Miriam Dean was helping me put together Losar gifts. At New Year's we made two thousand bundles for the children. We used donated toys and clothes, and sometimes bought them little gifts. Children at the Homes, at the Schools, and in all the settlements got a gift."

A photo of several hundred people sitting in a circle under a tent pavilion in a huge open meadow watching children perform Tibetan dance: "We taught the children traditional dances. We wanted them to keep the culture, not forget it. At that time, we thought we'd be returning to our country soon . . . that living in India was only temporary. We taught them music and dance as part of the education. We had good lamas teaching. One lama was very good at dance, so he taught dance." She paused a moment. "It's all stopped now. My successors say, 'All this is going on in the monasteries. It's not our job.'"

I sensed uneasiness in her voice.

We all had lunch every afternoon on the veranda, where it was cooler. The veranda overlooked a lovely, large garden with hibiscus bushes, roses, and camellias. In the center stood a tree in a circle of grass, and off to the side, a single *chorten*, then trellises and more trees. The house stood on maybe an acre and a half of land, including the adjacent vegetable garden. Amala said her husband had kept the garden—it had been his hobby. He died three years ago. She had built the *chorten* as a memorial to him.

One daughter was in Delhi but would move here later in the summer; one was in Calgary; the youngest was in Seattle. In 1959, her younger daughters, in the chaos of the moment, had been left in Tibet. They had suffered intensely under the Communists, beings members of the loathed aristocratic class. They were reunited with their parents in India, in 1980.

I asked how her husband's institution, the Central Tibetan Schools, and hers, the Tibetan Homes Foundation, worked together.

"Ours was a registered charity, and I was general secretary. His was entirely separate. He was the principal of Central Tibetan Schools, set up by the Indian government. Of course we would advise each other and helped each other. Like I would tell my husband, 'Take some children from the Homes to attend classes at the Schools.' Or I'd say, because he had new children arriving from the transit camps, 'If you come across any orphans, hand them over to me.'

"In later years, I could give the Schools financial help for things they needed. The Schools were funded by the government of India, so funds were very limited; the government didn't have extra money. The Homes received aid from all directions, all over the world. I could send extra money to the Schools to build the new football field, or the basketball playground, or make an improvement in the diet. It was all for Tibetan children, so my sponsors agreed to it."

I asked her what had been the most difficult, or biggest obstacle she had faced.

"In those days, the government in India was very restrictive about our expanding. They wanted to stop me from creating more homes."

She said that because the Homes Foundation was a registered charity—although the foundation had purchased the land, the land was technically Indian government property—it was subject to the laws and regulations of the Indian government. Officials called her down to Delhi once.

"They said: 'Stop buying homes, stop organizing homes. You've already got eight hundred children; that's enough. Why do you want more? They're spread all over Mussoorie, all over India.' When we wanted to add a house, we had to get permission from the External Ministry, the Central Relief Committee for Tibetans, the Rehabilitation Office in Delhi, and so on. Everything required a lot of permissions—permits and licenses; there was

Mrs. Taring and Indira Gandhi, a member of the governing board of the Tibetan Homes Foundation and Indian minister of education, tour the Homes grounds amidst its resident children. Mid-1960s. Photo courtesy of R. D. Taring.

Rinchen Dolma Taring and her husband, Jigme, founder and principal of the first Tibetan school, Central Tibetan Schools, Mussoorie, India, 1960s. The two had a close working partnership. Photo courtesy of R. D. Taring.

so much bureaucracy. And every time we wanted to send children to foreign countries for college, we needed all these permissions. First from the government, then from various offices. It was a *lot* of administrative paperwork."

It wasn't the case anymore, she said; the policy had changed. Now the Homes Foundation was twice as big, and there were no problems. Eventually those government offices became very friendly with the Homes Foundation.

Another problem in the early days was that the Indian government objected to foreigners working at the Homes and demanded that she employ more Indians. But the foreigners are *volunteers*, she had protested, they are unpaid. The government pressured her to send them home. She had had to negotiate hard to keep them for three or six months before sending them off.

I asked what she was most proud of. She had also been instrumental in founding the Tibetan Women's Center in 1963, a carpet-weaving industry

Mrs. Taring and her husband lead the Dalai Lama through the art studio of the new *thangka* painting course at Central Tibetan Schools, around 1970. This four-year course and other vocational programs were developed after the academic curriculum had been established. The Tarings strived to teach the youth traditional art, religion, language, and history in order to keep Tibetan culture alive. Photo courtesy of R. D. Taring.

that created economic self-sufficiency for local women, and, in 1975, the Tibetan Old People's Home, a residence for seniors.

"The Homes Foundation," she said immediately, "because through it we fed everybody. Having so many connections with volunteer agencies around the world meant I could just help anybody. I worked especially hard to get medical care. It gave me the authority to send anybody who needed care to the community hospital—poor people, old people, sick Tibetans from the road crews. If someone needed a major operation, I could send the person to Delhi. I just had to get the proper bill and submit it, and everything was covered."

In large part, I commented, her effectiveness was due to her skill in making connections with Westerners.

"Yes, I had Western friends in Lhasa; I was used to talking to foreigners. The key was knowing a little bit of English. I was able to make a bridge.

"Everything went smoothly. The constant help was wonderful. The world sent us help through its voluntary agencies. Swiss Aid to Tibetans, German Aid to Tibetans, Ockenden Venture, Save the Children. We received wonderful support."

I learned later from perusing its annual reports that funds for the Homes Foundation came from Holland, Norway, Canada, the United States, Australia, Japan, New Zealand, and Britain.

"It is a great pleasure to work when you are given all that you need to do the job and you are keen to do it. It's like being a rich man. It's still going on—the Homes and the Schools. The government of India is spending tremendous amounts of money on Tibetan education, so it must be used well and not wasted."

One day, we planned to visit the Tibetan Women's Center. About four hundred people worked there, including one hundred women weavers. We were late getting to the bus stand, so since it was morning and still cool out, Amala suggested we walk the two miles. Her left leg gave her trouble when she went downhill, but the route was level, so she put on some white leather tennis shoes and we headed out.

As we ambled through the small village of Rajpur, a mixture of broken-down old houses and newly constructed concrete homes, we passed Tibetan people lazing on their porches or thumping melons at the vegetable peddler's cart. They stood and inclined their heads and clasped their hands at the sight of Amala. Tibetans swiveled around in doorways, townspeople emerged from their homes. Even handicapped people resting on porches dropped what they were doing, struggled off their cushions, and bowed. Indian and Tibetan townspeople alike, their palms clasped together, stood in place until we had passed.

One old Indian man with a half-shut eye hobbled over with the help of a walking stick and spoke to her, tilting his head back to display his eye. They conversed briefly. We walked on, and she mentioned that she had arranged an eye operation for him. Another Indian villager waved to her. She explained in passing that his roof leaked and he got sick every winter from the dampness, so she engaged a donor in Canada to pay for a new roof.

As we passed a Tibetan family, the woman, about sixty, carrying some groceries, offered a friendly greeting; Amala said that the woman had almost died from tuberculosis, but she'd arranged an operation, and the woman was fine. The whole way through town, a distance of maybe a quarter of a mile, people stood bowing while she passed. I could feel the genuine affection and respect they held for her. I'd never seen anything like it, except for a religious leader. It felt like walking beside a beloved queen.

An old sahib dressed in white called out in Hindi, waved, and lifted himself from his cross-legged position behind a hanging metal scale. I didn't think she'd heard him, so I stopped and called her attention to him. He pointed back down the street, in the direction we'd come, and said something in Hindi. They exchanged brief words. Once we were under way again, she explained that he was her Hindi tutor and this was the day that he came to her house for her lesson. She had had to cancel.

"I thought you already spoke," I said.

"Oh! I really need to improve my Hindi. It still needs work. It's okay for everyday things, but I want to speak it a lot better."

I was flabbergasted. She was eighty-four. She had built and run these institutions in India for thirty-five years with her current level of Hindi but still wanted to improve her language skills!

On another day I asked her if she had any unfulfilled wishes.

"Everything is fulfilled," she said. "There is nothing left. I am very, very satisfied. I have no regrets. Whatever I've been able to do and the tragedy we've encountered—a tragedy not just of the Taring family, but of all the Tibetan people—all these have been turned into very valuable teachings. I'm still very grateful for having the family reunited. We never thought it would ever happen. First of all, I'm very grateful for my health. Then I'm very grateful for the livelihood we've received. For our good friends. What can be better than these things?"

I asked about her morning routine. My friend, her grandniece, in Dharamsala had told me that what Amala accomplished in the morning was prodigious.

"I am reading the 108 verses of *Chon Joog*. It is all about voidness and impermanence. A wonderful scripture. I've read it a dozen times. This is

my thirteenth reading. It's called "The Eight Thousand Verses." I am studying about impermanence. I want to study more dharma, get the house fixed
up nice, and go like that. I am more and more interested in my religious
studies, to get everything prepared."

She said she also penned several letters every morning. This didn't surprise me because the mail she received, which the postman handed to her
after lunch on the veranda every day, read like a *Who's Who* of modern
Tibetan history. She'd sort through the letters, bearing ornate penmanship
and all types of foreign stamps and postmarks, commenting, "Oh, Hugh
Richardson has written. Oh, wonderful, a card from Professor Tanaka. Mm,
this is from Melbourne . . . oh yes, it must be Geshe so-and-so. This is from
Frau so-and-so in Geneva." I recognized the names on the return addresses
as distinguished figures in Tibetan history, government, and religion.

I asked her how she had come to write her book, *Daughter of Tibet*. She
said a well-known British publisher, John Murray, approached her in late
1966 through her Irish friend, author Dervla Murphy, and asked her to write
her life story. She sought advice from His Holiness and then agreed to do
it. She took a leave from work and stayed in Lismore, Ireland, with Dervla,
who was pregnant at the time, in late 1968.

The publisher asked for a synopsis, so she outlined a chapter on school,
a chapter on life before marriage, one about after marriage, and so on. The
editors agreed to it, and she wrote the chapters accordingly. It was very difficult, she said, because she had to bring back all these memories of living
in Tibet, and it was very sad for her. She wrote it in a hurry because she was
anxious about the Homes. She couldn't be gone more than four months
and had left the place in the care of a niece.

She'd write and pass the pages to Dervla, who would look over the English
and then send it out for typing. Someone else checked it, and then the editors came from London and reviewed it. They cut a lot, because they wanted
it to be a standard length, eighty thousand words maximum. With the support of Murray and Dervla and a wonderful editor named Jane Moore, her
book came out in 1970. She had had no idea at the time that it would be so
popular, that people would appreciate it as they had, but she was pleased
about it. She felt proud of the book, she said. It was translated into German,

Italian, and Japanese. Someone was supposed to translate it into Tibetan, because she didn't have time to do it.

One day, we ran about twenty errands in Dehra Dun. It gave me an opportunity to see how Amala interacted with the outside world. She jumped right out of taxis and marched into places and asked for what she wanted. On our first errand, by the time I had climbed out of the car in the broiling heat and trudged into the phone center, the clerk was writing down the phone number in Delhi that Amala was dictating to him. The same thing happened at the optician's. She just had a commanding presence, but it wasn't aggressive or pushy.

She had a tremendous sense of organization. If I said I wanted to speak to a person or be somewhere on a certain day, she'd work out mentally how to get it done. Given that few homes or businesses had telephones, the plans were very involved, centering on making calls from places with telephones—settlement offices or the carpet center or the school—to ask a certain contact of hers to look for the person whom I wanted to find. And since she didn't have a vehicle, she had to engage a car and driver to get to the places with the phones.

She impressed me very much because she demanded a lot of herself in what she accomplished every day. She was always supervising something or writing letters or tutoring her granddaughter or entertaining a visitor, yet she was kindly in all instances. Unfailingly appreciative, she wasn't demanding and didn't impose.

Once, when a storm blasted the house and we lost power, we all ran around with flashlights battening down the storm windows. She sat at the table in the candlelight, unconcerned about the furniture getting wet or objects blowing over, and urged me to come back and finish dinner because the food was getting cold.

After I'd been there a few days, she told me she'd been invited to an important conference put on by the Tibet Foundation in London on the subject of education. All the heavyweights in the field were going to be there, including His Holiness the Dalai Lama, Samdong Rinpoche, Sakya Rinpoche, and Rinchen Khandro-la. But she had declined, citing the difficulty of traveling at her age. She and her husband had always traveled to such events together, she said, a trace of sadness in her voice.

"I still feel I can help people. That is the real religion, isn't it? To make yourself useful until you throw away your body. So I told Phuntsog Rinpoche, who invited me, that I wouldn't be coming, but I will send my views in writing. I'm going to write it in Tibetan. But I also want a good translation in English."

I knew that not all Tibetan officials read Tibetan.

"I want a good translation in English, so more people can read it. I want everybody to read it—the government of India, everybody. It won't be long, but I want it to really express my feelings well."

She asked for my help with the English version. I'd brought my laptop and a portable printer with me, so I said I'd be happy to help.

From then on, our informal talks often turned to the subject of education, about which she felt passionately. It was the key to the preservation of Tibetan society, she felt, and it was in crisis.

"The main thing is, there is something wrong with the education of our children—the Tibetan education. Without proper education, we will always be making mistakes. Whatever we do will be a mistake, because we don't have a good basis for understanding. We lost our country through mistakes.

"We need to take a closer look at Tibetan education, at the children coming out of the present system. The language is going from bad to worse. It's frightening. It scares me. The language is all mixed up: Khampa, Western, Southwestern. When the children speak now, it's very improper. At the conclusion of class twelve, the young people cannot speak well, they cannot write well. Their main goal is just to get the graduation certificate and get a job. They don't think of the importance of keeping the culture, through language and religion. I know, I can see it. Young people come to my home, and they speak very odd Tibetan.

"And along with the language, you have to instill the religion, because character forms on the basis of that—the practice of kindness, of right speech, right effort, right views, and so on. If we don't teach children culture and religion, they will lose their moral character."

I remembered her saying that preservation of Tibetan language, culture, and religion had been a major focus in the vision they had for the Homes Foundation and the Tibetan Schools when they were developing their educational goals. I quickly saw that this was where her passion lay, not in the thirty-year-old memories I was asking her about.

"We have only one million people. Those abroad are getting quality educations, but in India, there are still many who are not getting schooling. You don't see them, but there are many poor families with five or six children. The parents can't feed them, let alone give them an education. Lots of children are being wasted, and this is not going to be good for the future of Tibet."

She was concerned that the children of the poor were hidden in pockets in Tibetan settlements all over India.

"A lot of children are being wasted, left illiterate. It's our responsibility to find these children. We can't wait for them to come to us. It's our responsibility to our community, and to our donors and sponsors.

"I have seen little babies grow up and become parents. If children are not educated now, they will grow up to become uneducated parents and their children will be uneducated. And it will go on and on, generation after generation. I see this clearly because I've been doing this for many years."

In her opinion, only a few of the current Tibetan-language teachers were suitably trained. With most of them, their knowledge of written Tibetan, spelling and grammar, was poor, and their religious education was inadequate. Part of the problem was that key policy makers were not really educators; the exile government would take a staff person who'd been the manager of a carpet center, for instance, assign him to teach music in Dharamsala and then, after a couple of years, assign him to the Education Council.

"No one wants to talk about this," Amala explained. "But if we keep quiet to avoid hurting people's feelings, we will be hurting our own country.

"People will say that we've got schools in every settlement, the Indian government gives scores of rupees, so what more can we do? The Indian government looks after the Hindi curriculum, it takes care of the English curriculum, but *we Tibetans* need to take care of the Tibetan curriculum.

We need to set standards for Tibetan education. High standards. *Much* higher than they are now.

"In the beginning of our time in India, we had to learn foreign languages to survive, but now is the time to keep up our culture. Our own language must be the top priority. We might have very good textbooks, but we need qualified teachers to teach them," she insisted passionately.

"We now have a thousand children in the Homes Foundation, about five or six hundred in the Schools. In the Schools, the Tibetan language is taught by Tibetans, and the other subjects are taught by Indian teachers. In the Homes, Tibetan teachers teach math, history, English, and so on, in line with Indian standards. But the Tibetan-language teachers are not adequate." She paused a moment, her eyes full of thought. "One of the best schools now is TCV. The teaching staff is good because TCV pays better. If we don't pay well, we can't attract good teachers.

"I feel you are like a Tibetan," she said, her voice trailing into a slower rhythm, "because you take such an interest. Otherwise I would not be talking about these things . . . showing what's wrong with our society. How can you say we don't have one proper grammar teacher? It's embarrassing."

Every day I spent with Amala, I grew to appreciate more who she was and what she'd done with her life. Her role, if put in modern-day terms, stretched from chief executive officer, visionary educator, superintendent of schools, development director, chief operations officer, overseas ambassador, public relations officer, and more.

She claimed with characteristic modesty that she hadn't done much in Tibet except socialize and maintain good relationships with people. Yet I felt that this very quality seemed to form the basis of her successful, often delicate navigations among people from many cultures and stations in life with whom she had to work—from local Indian grocers, to government bureaucrats in Delhi, to European heads of charitable organizations, to refugee roadworkers. Everyone from children, teachers, and volunteers, to the Dalai Lama and the queen of England, with whom she'd had several audiences.

She said that when His Holiness convinced her to undertake the task— she'd felt inadequate to its daunting scope—he'd finally prevailed by just requesting that she do her best. Her very best—and to do it every day. That had been the guiding principle for both her and her husband, all these years. She said she would ask herself all the time, What is the best way to do this to benefit people? She wasn't concerned about a title or winning accolades, just how she could help people.

"You see, my husband and I never realized what we were doing. We felt anxious about what we were doing. We were never proud about our work. We just kept going. We were never satisfied; we always wanted to improve the programs. Other people saw it, but not us. When we retired, we both thought, Well now . . . we did our best.

"And after things started to deteriorate, people came to us and said, 'Now we realize what you did. Now that it's slid downhill, we see all you did.'"

I asked if she had had many guests here at the house.

"Constantly," she answered emphatically. "Family. Friends. Up until last Thursday."

For instance, a grandniece had held her wedding at the house a couple of weeks ago. Relatives from Lhasa and from abroad had come. People stayed at the house. A guest had fallen ill, and been taken to the hospital. The person had to have an operation and recovered at her house. Next week, guests from the States were arriving.

"You came just at the right time. If you had come earlier, I would have been fully occupied with many things. The place was *full* of people. It was nonstop. Just now I am having some peace. A good rest."

She outlined her schedule through the rest of the summer; it was a constant stream of visitors, family gatherings, and other events, beginning with people arriving that weekend. I thought how lucky I was to have landed there when I did, in that small window of opportunity in her schedule. She paused a long moment.

"Our house in Lhasa was the same way."

"A lot of activity?"

"Yes, we had all the parties there. Some relatives didn't have a nice house or a nice garden, and they'd say, Please let us hold our wedding here, please let us use the house. From the roof terrace, we had a good view of Sera—it made a nice place for gatherings. Or somebody had no home for a while, and they'd stay with us."

She said her husband used to grumble, "What is this? A hotel? What are you doing?" And her response was along the lines of "We have it, we may as well use it." He had designed the house, and she had coordinated the construction and done all the purchasing. She had written about it in some detail in her book, and the account gave a vivid picture of Tibetan society. The house had been located on the outskirts of the city, east of the Potala. Built in the traditional style, two stories high, it had seventeen rooms. Now the city had expanded so much that the house was no longer east of the city but in the middle of it. They had built the residence in 1939 and lived there until their escape twenty years later.

I asked if she ever missed Tibet a lot, or wanted to visit.

"Oh yes. I do. I do miss my country a lot. My country and my people. But you always try not to, don't you? I got very much hurt the day my grand-daughter told me last year that they had torn down the house. I heard the Chinese had been using it for offices. I felt so sad. So much trouble we went to building a solid house . . . it hurt me very much. So now I think, I'm glad we used it so well, now that it's gone. Whatever you have, you share, and then you have no regrets."

I had gotten the sense these last few days that the big project on her mind was preparing for the transition of death. She said her main occupation now was religious study, especially on the subject of impermanence. She had just built an addition to her house for her older daughter in Delhi, who was retiring in three months. She was establishing tributes to her husband at the Central Tibetan Schools, a statue of Milarepa and the Taring House sports shield. She was getting the financial books in order for the various organizations she was involved in and arranging for the education of some of her grandchildren.

Knowing that she was preparing for death, I felt even more acutely the privilege of being able to spend time with her. She was one of the last surviving links with the old ways, the old Tibet. I felt sad that she knew her generation was fading out, and that she was extremely concerned about the loss of the language, culture, and religion, especially because they laid the basis for becoming what she called "a good, valuable human being."

One day, while we were discussing the topic of Tibetan education, she talked more about the critical need to cultivate good teachers. When they first arrived in exile, she explained, all the learned lamas had been newly flushed out of monasteries in Tibet. Early students at the schools and the homes received the best-quality Tibetan educations, because these highly educated lamas taught them—she recalled the names of several *geshes* and *rinpoches*. In the intervening years, however, these men left India and emigrated abroad. Now there were no highly qualified teachers, and learned monks no longer left their monasteries to teach children. She and Jigme had both felt strongly about the subject.

"My husband and I wrote to His Holiness about this a few years ago. There must be proper teacher training. We have to cultivate good teachers in the language. The first batch did so well because the *geshes* and lamas taught them. Then there must be a body that has the authority and knowledge to check on the quality of the teaching. *Every* year. Not every few years, or two years. *Every year* . . . or it will slide downhill."

She said that now the children were just made to memorize prayers, not given instruction on the meaning or practice of the teachings. "They are not really teaching them the religion. The language, the culture—these are *very important* for them to know. If we don't teach the children our culture and our Buddhist principles, they will lose the moral character. Now we are in a dangerous time. If we don't guide it well, the Tibetan culture will be lost.

"It's just what the Chinese government wants. We lose Tibet from the outside, and we lose Tibet from the inside. Then . . . China will have won."

She said she could understand why Tibetans went abroad—developed countries had a higher standard of living and it was hard to find a good job in India. The disciples of these lamas had also left. In the '60s and '70s, she had arranged for higher education for scores of her students. They were supposed to come back and serve the community. After a long pause, she said in a low voice that only three or four had come back. Eventually, they returned to the West as well. Only poor Tibetan refugees were left in India. And the learned *geshes* were teaching religion to *injis*, foreigners. "One day," she said, "I fear we will have to learn our own language and religion from foreigners."

I felt chills up my spine hearing this.

On Friday afternoon, I gave Amala the first draft of her letter. Then about an hour later, at afternoon tea, I gave her another version. We had a visitor for tea, a cousin who lived nearby and spoke good English, a lovely middle-aged woman who had lived in Switzerland for many years and had retired nearby. Amala was very pleased with the letter. The cousin read it, too. They were both quite impressed.

That night when she went to bed, I gave her the most recent version. Then the next morning at breakfast, she returned it with copious edits—she had read it either early in the morning or very late the night before! Her notes were about tone, not content. I'd been taught to get rid of qualifiers, not to say "I'm a bit concerned," but to say "I am concerned"—to sound authoritative and definitive. She asked me to replace the declarative sentences with phrases like "these are my humble and sincere opinions," "let us consider," and "I would appreciate." I suppose in the Tibetan world—where the language is honorific and changes according to your relative status to the speaker—my Western-style phrasing was too bold. Indian authorities would also be reading it, I thought, as well as high lamas—parties to whom she deferred. I incorporated her changes.

What did she mean, I wondered, about Tibet outside and Tibet inside? I thought about it a long time. Their "Tibet-ness" was internal, I thought. Though Chinese forces had obliterated almost all the monasteries, seized the land, killed a part of the population, banned Buddhism, and run tens of thousands out of the country, including their leader, the Chinese were never able to destroy the spiritual faith and values Tibetans held inside. Not in forty years of "reeducation." That was the key to the culture. But if this unique moral character were lost, the Tibetan nation would in fact be destroyed.

I thought about what she had said about all the finest lamas now teaching foreigners. In the West, we'd experienced a surge of interest in Tibetan Buddhism beginning in about the mid-1990s. Adherents of Tibetan Buddhism had grown exponentially. The Chinese takeover had been a catastrophe for Tibet and for world civilization but indirectly benefited the West: The ancient wisdom system of Tibetan Buddhism, previously locked inside a remote, inaccessible corner of the world, had spread to the West. High lamas and *geshes* taught abroad. But I had never realized that this benefit came at the expense of the Tibetans. That our having such access to these precious teachers meant the Tibetans themselves had lost them. Westerners, instead of Tibetans, reaped the benefit of the Tibetan Buddhist teachings.

One day Amala showed me a booklet she and her husband had published ten years earlier on the occasion of the Dalai Lama's forty-ninth birthday, "The Six Perfections." They had printed a thousand copies. She flipped through the pages of Tibetan writing.

"This is on giving alms . . . why you give alms, how to give alms. The second one is discipline . . . the third one is how to endure, about restraint. The fourth is effort, you must make an effort. Then meditation, how to meditate, why you need to meditate. The most important of the Six Perfections is wisdom. These are the essentials. They should be taught to children *right* from the beginning. Because they are beautiful. Whether you become enlightened or not, at least you'll know how to be a good person. Now they have them memorize prayers, but they don't *teach* them. It's like these trees. . . " She gestured out the window at a pine tree. "Now I can't straighten the line of the trunk. I could have done it from the beginning though, when it was young and still growing. It's better to teach the essentials from the very beginning.

"Tibet is a Buddhist country. We are helping other people understand the teachings, but we have to make sure our own children understand them as well."

She turned the pages, reading.

"It says that if you have the highest intelligence but you're lazy, that intelligence is useless. If you are not very clever, but you put a lot of effort into study, you will inspire yourself to learn more. If you want something, you can't say, 'I'll do it some day, I'll do it another time.'" She mused on this: "In a way, life is very long; in a way, life is very short." After a few moments, she turned back to the book.

"You must not waste a minute, the scripture says. If you have no effort, it doesn't matter how much education or intelligence you have." She glanced up. "It's like a car without the engine. Everything is nice only on the outside. You have to always be alert, *always* put forth your best effort. If you do, there is nothing you cannot achieve."

Amala Taring, the author, and two of Mrs. Taring's great-grandchildren on the veranda of the family home in central India, summer 1994.

4
CROSSING THE
HIMALAYAS

ALL THROUGH LOSAR, I'd been periodically checking the road conditions for the overland trip to Nepal. Snow blocked the road at the higher elevations, near Nyelam, at between sixteen thousand and seventeen thousand feet, and there was no telling when it would be cleared. I really wanted—since I'd come this far—to try and see the land, the pristine high desert between Lhasa and the Nepal border where I'd spent a lot of time twenty-one years ago. But I had to make it brief because, in my scramble to make this trip happen, I'd overlooked getting an Indian visa. Now I'd have to halt in Kathmandu to get the visa, and I knew from experience that the process wouldn't be quick. I admonished myself about it for days, as it would cost precious time. I hadn't heard from my friend in Dharamsala about whether she'd been able to locate Mrs. Namseling and Sonam Choedron; it could take days to find them. The women didn't have phones, and Sonam was just visiting, so there was no telling where she'd be staying. Mobs of people would be in town for the Dalai Lama's teachings.

I met a Japanese woman and her young German companion, and we agreed to share a ride, but the weather, or fear of the weather, and other circumstances kept delaying our departure. One evening, the woman called while I was packing my bags for our departure the next morning. She wanted to change the plan. It was the third time she'd changed the plan in as many days. She wanted to leave earlier, at five instead of nine, and go straight through. No stopping as we'd agreed. She was worried about the weather. She didn't want to get stuck at that twenty-mile stretch of snow near Nyelam.

I was livid; every time we agreed on a plan, at the last minute, she changed her mind. "It's only a short stretch that's bad," I protested. I'd heard that only six or seven miles were really impassable, and local people could guide us across on foot. I said I'd found out that there were two guesthouses in Nyelam; the proprietor of one spoke a little English. Worst case scenario, I told her, was that we'd walk six miles. I had to repeat everything three times because of the horrid phone connection, and she had to repeat everything five times because of the bad connection and my inability to understand her heavily accented English over the bad connection. It's doable, I argued. Six miles is not far. Even with bags. We'll find some locals to guide us. I'd trekked in adverse weather in Tibet before. I had the image of us bent against the snow, led by a couple of hardy locals.

She wouldn't budge. She wanted to leave at 5 a.m. and go straight through. We'd negotiated and renegotiated the trip for days, and now she was pulling this at the eleventh hour. I was beside myself. Wimp, I thought, risk-averse wimp. I was so furious, I could have strangled her. I'd had it with her last-second, unilateral decisions. I felt ready to cry.

I didn't have any backup plans, I worried. If I waited any longer, I wouldn't get to Kathmandu until Friday, and I'd have to wait over the weekend to apply for my Indian visa. Then I wouldn't get to Dharamsala until midweek and would have only three days to get my work done before I had to leave on Saturday. The Dalai Lama was teaching every day, so I'd have only evenings to work.

Amala wanted me to take the weekly plane that left Saturday, fearing the roads were not safe. Pala will pay your airfare, she pleaded. February was the worst month for weather here; delays of several days on the overland route were common. But if I flew on Saturday, I'd experience the same delay with my visa and arrive late in Dharamsala. I'd be in a sheer panic trying to get everything done in just three or four days.

I'd need to find the women, find a translator, find a place to stay. When I had tried to reserve a room from the States, I'd found that hotels and guesthouses were booked solid for months because so many people were coming for the teachings. My reservation was at a place forty minutes away, but I had hoped to find something closer in.

Lhakyi and I went to a neighbor's house to use the Internet. I tried to e-mail my friend Lobsang in Dharamsala to let her know I might be late and ask if she could line up the two women for interviews. We checked the exact dates of the Dalai Lama's teaching. My understanding was that it was March 4 through 14, but I wanted to verify. Surprisingly, the Google search went through, and the list of sites appeared—Tibet.com, DalaiLama.com, and so on. When I tried to open them, though, every screen came up "Page Not Available." Thank you, Google.

That night, I took two Valium™ to sleep, but I still twisted in bed with frustration and worry. Amala was worried, too. Stay here, she said. Stay here a few months. Don't go to India, don't go to the States. Learn how to make delicious Tibetan dishes and how to keep the fire. You'll learn the language well. The roads are not safe.

With each day, I grew more anxious about getting out of the country so late. I'd barely have enough time to get my work done in Dharamsala before my flight back to the States, where I'd been accepted into an artist's residency back East.

I finally left Lhasa one evening at the end of the month, having wrestled my passport from the Nepalese embassy, where I'd dropped it off earlier that day to get a Nepalese visa. In truth, I also found it hard to leave the warmth and security of the family. When I'd first announced I'd be leaving, Tashi told me that everyone expressed sadness over my departure. The family all said they'd miss me and wished I could stay. One night, they made me a special *momo* dinner. They wanted to give me a Tibetan carpet as a gift to bring home, but I begged off, claiming I wouldn't be able to carry it. One morning, Pala exclaimed: "When you leave, we're going to give you a *khata* two yards long!"

For days, the middle sister had been making me special teas and home-made hot soups. I gave Amala and Pala framed enlargements of the photos I had taken on the first morning of Losar, of the family dressed in their silk and satin finery, standing in front of the beautiful panels Pala had carved.

In the end, six of us stuffed ourselves into a Land Cruiser for the trip. I saw a billboard in English on the outskirts of town. It towered over the road from the airport into Lhasa: "A Fresh Chapter of Lhasa History. A New Image of Lhasa City."

That's why Auntie had said she didn't like the new Lhasa. The government had been touting a "new Lhasa" as if it held any appeal for Tibetans or was anything they had wanted.

The sight of Shigatse, the second-largest town, shocked me. Before, sleepy dusty Shigatse had been notable for Tashilhungpo Monastery, seat of the Panchen Lama, the second-most important personage after the Dalai Lama. It had comprised maybe ten blocks at the most. Now I didn't recognize it—a sprawling, neon-lit city of broad boulevards and gaudy restaurants springing out of the desert night like Las Vegas.

The drive was so smooth I could have been on any highway in the West. Twenty-one years ago, these roads had been corrugated rough dirt tracks, still unpaved. I'd endured many a bumpy, twelve-hour ride on the public bus over these roads to get to the countryside. In 1986, the majority of vehicles on this road were army trucks and the occasional public bus, used 1950s or 1960s Soviet-era vehicles: the windows didn't close, we had to stop every hour to fill the radiator, the shock absorbers were shot, the upholstery on the bench seats had worn thin, and the engine was so weak that every time we approached a mountain pass, we had to get out and climb on foot. Going uphill, at the high altitude, the bus barely moved with the weight of passengers.

I thought about the first time I'd visited Dharamsala in August 1986. I had been simply astonished. After being in Tibet for months, where there was barely electricity, few cars, and no real stores except the government department store, to be among Tibetans who spoke English and dressed in Western clothes made it seem like Tibetan civilization had instantly jumped ahead a century. In Tibet, no one spoke English. Tashi and a young tour guide were the exceptions, but their English was very basic.

Tibetan culture thrived in Dharamsala. In Tibet in 1986, I had seen no magazines, no newspapers, no libraries. The most popular item people read were comic books. Certainly there were no books confirming Tibet as a different culture or a one-time independent country. That was something the Chinese government had worked hard to erase; it sought to have everyone think Tibet had always been part of China. I had interviewed a young Tibetan woman who lived in Amdo, in northeastern Tibet, close to the border with China, who had gone through the entire school system, graduated at the top of her class, and didn't realize until she was in college that she was Tibetan. Finding books, bookstores, films, magazines, and indeed an entire English-language reading room in the Dharamsala library dedicated to Tibet and related subjects felt to me like discovering gold.

Dharamsala, perched in the foothills of the Indian Himalayas at the site of a former British hill station, had served as the seat of the Tibetan government-in-exile since 1960, after a year in transition in Mussoorie. The refugee community had established a medical center, a school system, centers for the study of traditional arts, and temples and monasteries. In 1986, when I'd lived there for four months, the town had been a very friendly, relaxed place with mostly local Tibetans, a small sprinkling of Indian merchants, and some Westerners interested in Buddhism or some aspect of Tibetan culture. For Westerners who did not have an interest in Buddhism or Tibetan culture, the town held little charm. For me, however, it was a treasure trove; I spent hours every day reading in the library and just nosing around town. After I stumbled onto Buddhism, I took daily classes at the library and moved to a Buddhist retreat center up the mountain, enjoying the environment in the pine-forested foothills, which provided a peaceful refuge in which to explore my new interest.

My next visit, three years later, was totally different. Instead of the blissful experience I'd enjoyed earlier, I lived and worked in the government compound and saw the inequities. I saw the indifference, the power abuse, the obstructionism. Previously, one very rarely saw a motor vehicle—most certainly a government car—but in 1990, cars first appeared in the form of a whole fleet of Indian-made Maruti vans. Incessant noise—because the drivers honked loudly and often—and pollution followed, and the narrow mountain paths became dangerous obstacle courses for pedestrians.

By the time I returned to interview the women in 1994, nearly four years later, the place was overrun. Before, for instance, one just showed up and sat down at the Dalai Lama's teachings—there was plenty of room—but four years later, his teachings were mobbed with people. Aggressive paparazzi crawled all over the temple building as he spoke, even sticking their long lenses in from rooftop parapets above him. Well-heeled Indian merchants owned high-end stores selling Tibetan artifacts. I will never forget seeing one old monk parked on a stool beside a display case, staring longingly through the glass for hours at a prayer wheel. I didn't know if it had belonged to him at one time, or whether he recognized it or just wanted it, but it was heartbreaking. Westerners threw wads of money around to buy high-priced dharma souvenirs and sat in the cafés loudly comparing the Tibetan Buddhist initiations they'd taken across the globe. Along the steep road to the Central Temple, construction had begun on high-rise luxury hotels, a rather dangerous proposition, since the whole area lay in earthquake country and had been completely flattened in a big shaker a year after the 1906 quake in San Francisco. Dharamsala had been a spiritual refuge that my friend Doc and I had always dreamed of coming back to, where we had considered buying land with other Buddhist-practitioner friends, but after the 1994 visit I thought, I never want to come back here again.

"I know what you are," white-haired Daniel said, in a soft, confident American voice, eyeing me across the white tablecloth in a coffee shop in downtown Kathmandu. He held me in his cool gray eyes. "I misjudged you before." He was a friend of Lhakyi's, a kind of Renaissance man, I would discover—poet, philosopher, statesman. We'd talked over the phone briefly a couple of times and now met in person. He had asked what brought me to Kathmandu, and I told him about the book, its many incarnations, and my long quest to get it published. "You're a soldier-artist."

I'd never heard the term. Someone had once described me as a soldier, but I hadn't heard the term "soldier-artist."

"You're driven," he said without judgment.

I'd never thought of myself that way before. Persistent? Yes. Committed? By necessity. Determined? Sure. But driven? Somewhere inside though, the minute I heard the words, I knew he was right. What other kind of person would try to convince traveling companions she didn't even know that trekking over the Himalayas in winter, at night, was just a small, inconvenient hardship?

But what was driving me?

"It's such important work you're doing," he said. "And quite lonely."

That was so true it stung.

"Because your only palette is yourself. So the story mirrors your own inner struggles."

Riding home through the rainy streets that night, I pondered, What *was* driving me? Karmic debt? I had distanced myself from the northern Han people of the People's Republic since visiting China in 1986. One earlier version of my book had included the story of my learning in the mid-'90s that my family's original name in Cantonese, Lok, meant "camel," indicating that we'd descended from a tribe of camel tenders and riders. (Sometime at the turn of the twentieth century, in the United States, the surname Sam was mistakenly recorded.) I was Cantonese, southern, I'd insisted. But after the horse's legs and mane, the camel's hump, and the woman rider were pointed out to me in the Chinese pictogram of the word *lok*, I'd realized it was irrefutable. My family, at least on my father's side, was from the north, where there were deserts and dunes. Around Mongolia perhaps. The rice fields and river deltas of Canton were no environment for camels. Tibet and Mongolia were like cousins—ethnically, culturally, spiritually related. My connection to Tibet made sense then.

A Jewish woman commented years ago that my going to China for a year and coming back a Tibetan advocate was like her going to Israel for a year and coming back a Palestinian supporter. I didn't see it that way. I had felt little affinity for China before I'd first visited.

But I did feel a sense of responsibility toward the Tibetans when I came back from my year away—after all I'd seen and all I'd learned. I'd traveled in Amdo and Kham after the two months in central Tibet. I knew I'd had more access to the Tibetan world than a white traveler would have had. I'd been invited into people's homes, into their tents and caves, called over to join picnics, all over Tibet. Children had befriended me as I'd walked down the street in remote towns, taken my hand, led me home to meet their extended families. I was assumed to be a Tibetan from Dharamsala when I was in Tibet, and a Tibetan from Canada when I was in Dharamsala. Compared to the average Western traveler, I'd been given a bit more of a glimpse into the Tibetan people's lives, their humanity and character.

But there was more driving me.

I wanted to know how these hardy, cheerful, kind people had survived the brutality they'd suffered. Was it their faith? Was it their inherent disposition? What gave them the physical and psychological resilience, the forbearance, not just to endure, but to emerge with clean hearts?

I arrived in Dharamsala on a sunny Sunday morning, March 4. I found the streets strangely deserted. I learned that thousands of people had assembled at the Central Temple, where, in an hour and a half, His Holiness the Dalai Lama would start the first of ten days of public teachings. With the streets clear, I hit the ground running. In ten minutes, I'd found a room—centrally located, private bathroom, friendly Tibetan proprietor, budget price. I felt lucky. The town had been booked solid for months. A good sign, I thought. An auspicious beginning.

Besides reinterviewing Mrs. Namseling and Sonam Choedron, I had another task here.

"Can you take a gift to His Holiness?" Tashi had asked me, translating for her mother a few days before I left Lhasa.

"Of course," I had said. "Is it small?"

"Yes."

"Is it light?"

"Yes."

"Okay then. I can't give it to him personally, but . . ."

"Oh, no, but you must," she cut in.

"But . . ." I sputtered. I thought I could just drop it at the Private Office.

"*Please.*"

That would require an audience, I thought. "Tashi, he is teaching all day," I declared.

"Yes," she agreed. She held me with her warm brown eyes. "Please try."

I turned to Amala. She was looking at me the same way. I looked at Pala. He sat as usual, half smiling, fingering his prayer beads on the couch, absorbed in prayers.

"Just try."

They knew I'd had a private audience with the Dalai Lama in Dharamsala, a few months after I'd left Tibet years ago. That didn't give me any pull, I thought. *Everybody* wanted to see him, everyone made demands of him.

"The man is *teaching*; the man is *busy*," I cried. I didn't want to add to his burden.

Tashi and Amala just looked at me.

"What's inside?" I asked finally.

"Some clothes."

Shouldn't be too difficult, I thought.

"Small package, right?" I confirmed in a wary tone.

"Right," Tashi assured me.

I'd had Tibetans ask me "to take a few things" to relatives on previous trips, and after they'd stuffed my backpack, which I painstakingly kept lightweight, with all their packages, two of them had to sit on top of it to zip it closed. In 1994, I'd even lugged a VCR to a friend's family.

When I started packing my bags, I asked for the package. Tashi gave me instructions as she handed me the gift, the size of a folded shirt but heavier, encased in two plastic bags: "Remind him who my parents are," she said. "They met him in Toronto in 2003."

I nodded.

"Get a receipt."

"A receipt?" I yelped. I'd never heard of that. I didn't want to have to ask him for anything.

"And a prayer bead," she added.

"A prayer bead? What do you mean?" I squeaked.

"A bead from his *mala*."

Still another request, I grumbled to myself. I wasn't even confident I could complete my work, let alone try to get an audience with the Dalai Lama. Now I was supposed to ask him to take apart his *mala*. The Tibetans counted prayers with a string of beads called a *mala*; His Holiness said several hours of prayers every day.

The thought flashed through my mind that they might want the prayer bead because of Pala's health. The bead would have His Holiness's blessings, the imprint of his prayers for *bodhicitta*, or loving kindness. It would help Pala get well.

"Okay, no problem," I said.

She explained that the robe had been left at the Norbulingka in 1959. An aunt—one of the people I'd met at the house on one of the first days of Losar—had been employed at the palace and had saved it. They thought that the garment might have belonged to thirteenth Dalai Lama because it appeared to be antique silk. Then there was a shirt that Amala, an expert tailor, had sewn for him from some other cloth the aunt had saved. That meant, I calculated quickly, she'd saved the robes for nearly fifty years.

"Even if he doesn't keep it . . . just gives it away to someone else," Tashi said, " . . . it's okay. But they want to give it to him."

"Tashi," I asked, "shouldn't we get a bead for your aunt? She's the one who saved the fabric all these years."

"Yes," Tashi shook her head, agreeing. "Okay, get two beads."

Receipt and two beads. I made a mental note to myself.

"Look, I'll *try* to give it to him," I said in a doubtful tone. "But I can't promise."

"I know, Canyon," she broke in. "Just try."

5

DHARAMSALA

NARROW BHAGSU ROAD looked much the same, with the rusty, ramshackle tea stalls, except that instead of mostly Tibetan-run stores, now there were also Indian-run laundry shops and a Western-style bakery attached to the Hotel Tibet, businesses catering to tourists. Some storefronts had fitted windows and straight plumbed lines, superior in construction to the tinny stalls of years ago.

A line of two dozen Westerners snaked out into the street from the Security Department branch office. Apparently, foreigners had to register to attend the teachings and obtain a security badge. I dropped off my luggage and grabbed a bite to eat. By the time I got back to the office, it was closed. I stopped at a shop to buy a transistor radio—necessary for tuning in to the English translation of the teachings—and headed down to the temple; I'd heard there was an area where people could sit outside without a security pass.

On the main street, rinky-dink grocery stalls had been replaced by Internet cafés, travel agencies, and high-end gift shops selling cashmere shawls and fine jewelry. Farther down the road near the temple stood glass-walled, four-story Indian hotels with marble lobbies, which I'd seen under construction the last time I was here, more than a dozen years ago.

I spotted a companion from the bus, sitting with a monk and two others by the rear railing in the outdoor sitting area, a big open space behind the temple where about two hundred people had gathered. An attractive, longhaired Tibetan woman named Kunsang, who to my surprise hailed from Northern California, immediately moved over and gave me part of her carpet to sit on. The scores of people, both Tibetan and foreigners, sat facing a three-story pale yellow building, one of the monastery's housing blocks, all listening intently, the foreigners through earphones to a translation and the Tibetans to His Holiness's baritone voice booming through the sound system.

Tuning to the English translation on my radio, I heard the translator's voice introduce the topic of the teaching: Shantideva's *Guide to the Bodhisattva's Way of Life*. I knew the text was His Holiness' favorite; he'd given me a copy of it years ago at the end of the private audience I'd had with him.

"The education of the heart was critical," His Holiness said. He sat on the other side of the building, in the temple courtyard, in front of the thousands of people who had security clearances. Translations went out in Korean, French, Japanese, Chinese, and Mongolian. "Modern education emphasized the development of the material world, but this alone was hollow," he said. He went on to explain how learning and promoting sound human values such as consideration of others, compassion, and ethical behavior could reduce greed, corruption, and other afflictive emotions plaguing society today.

I didn't want to turn around because you're not supposed to turn your back on the Dalai Lama, even if he was on the other side of a three-story building, but I couldn't resist looking over my shoulder to catch a glimpse of the snow-blanketed, craggy mountains of the Dhauladhar range. The western Himalayas. I breathed a sigh of relief. I was so thrilled, so humbled to see them again, shining in the sparkling morning light. Imperturbable, solid, majestic. I felt anchored. Right with the world again. It was one of the reasons I'd loved Dharamsala and why I imagined His Holiness and the Tibetans had felt comfortable here all these years.

Twenty-one years ago, I had sat in the library down the road, the Library of Tibetan Works and Archives, reading a *National Geographic* look-alike magazine on Tibetan culture with a bright yellow-bordered cover. This had led to my curiosity about Buddhism, and then my exploration of it, and then a dream, and then a fluke opportunity for an audience with His Holiness, and eventually a change in the entire course of my life as I came back to the United States and worked for Tibet. A chain of events I never could have imagined.

Our human rebirth was so precious, so rare, said the translator, it was important to use it wisely, to develop our minds. Never be complacent with your study. And have a sense of joy in your dharma practice. His Holiness discussed the need to practice what he called the "Ten Virtuous Actions" in order to reduce suffering, and he said that in order to clear the ground for that practice, one needed to be free of the "Eight Worldly Concerns."

At the end of the afternoon session, I chatted with some of the others. Kunsang was from Nepal, though she lived in Northern California now with an American husband and their eight-year-old son. She was warm, engaging, and self-confident, and the two of us hit it off right away. Thousands of people poured from the temple and out onto the road along two intersecting thoroughfares—the crowd so thick it seemed that one could take one's feet off the ground and still move forward, carried by the crowd. Kunsang pointed out her cousin's house, a stone's throw from the temple, and invited me over. She was headed there, but I told her I had to stay around for a while. I stood at the juncture where the road went up to town or down the mountain to the government area, trying to see if I could spot Lobsang, my old friend who'd been my contact here, or Mrs. Namseling or Sonam Choedron.

I had chased Mrs. Namseling all over the map. She didn't have a phone or mailing address. Lobsang had written in an e-mail a couple of months back that Mrs. Namseling, astonishingly, was in the United States, so I finally got a number for her on the East Coast and called her daughter's house. The voice-mailbox was always full. I tried all different times of day for three weeks. Finally a woman answered—she'd been out of town and was a cousin, not a daughter—and told me that Mrs. Namseling was not in America but in Switzerland, visiting her daughters. She would be returning to Dharamsala for the Dalai Lama's teachings.

The other person I was looking for was Sonam Choedron, whom I also hadn't seen since 1994. When I'd heard she would be in Dharamsala as well, and would return to Australia right after the teachings, I decided to save myself a trip to Australia by adding a stop in Dharamsala to my trip to Tibet. I had no idea where Sonam would be staying, but I did know that I had to be on the ground to find either of them. One thing was certain:

they'd be around His Holiness. Most certainly they'd be in attendance this first day of his public teaching, an annual tradition for forty years.

I scoured the crowd for their faces. I hadn't seen the women in more than a dozen years and didn't know if they'd changed much in appearance. There looked to be many more Tibetans from Tibet than before. The foreigners looked more well-heeled and older. Before, the visitors had been young backpackers who didn't mind braving the difficult journey or the funky, drafty cold-water guesthouses. Now I saw Western couples with small children in tow. There had always been Europeans, but now Asian visitors were also in attendance in substantial numbers.

After about fifteen or twenty minutes, I spotted Mrs. Namseling. She looked exactly the same, except her hair was grayer. I maneuvered through the crowd, tracking her. About thirty feet up the hill, I caught up to her.

"Mrs. Namseling!" I yelled. She turned, mid-sentence, mid-laughter, engaged in talking to a friend. She looked at me for a couple of seconds. Then, she kept moving, carried by the momentum of the thickly packed crowd. By the blank look on her face, I knew she hadn't recognized me. A young man straggled behind. Perhaps, I thought, he was with her party.

"Do you speak English?" I asked desperately, as the crowd pressed us forward.

"Yes," he replied.

I explained that I'd interviewed Mrs. Namseling years ago and was in town to talk to her, yelling over the din of hundreds of conversations and the roar of taxis. He looked at me warily and then left to find her again. I'd had four lengthy sessions with her. I knew she'd remember me.

I kept track of her short figure, her gray-haired head as it floated uphill with the tide of humanity. He came back. "Now she remembers you," he said. "You came over with His Holiness's niece."

Great! I thought, elated.

"She is busy with the teachings," he concluded.

"Yes," I said. "I know that. Could I meet her some evening? *After* the teachings?"

Mrs. Namseling proceeded uphill with her friend, not even stopping to look at me. A bad sign, I thought; it was easier to turn someone down if the person wasn't in your sight. He ran off to catch up to her and came back a few minutes later.

"In the evenings she has to do prayers," he called back. "After the teachings are over, she'll see you."

My heart sank. I was scheduled to leave four days before the teachings ended.

"But I have come here *to see her*," I declared loudly into his ear. "I have come from America to see her. I will only be in town a few days. I am writing a book about Tibetan women." I was on the edge of panic. The stress of everything I'd been through the last couple of weeks started to unravel my nerves. He was stone-faced, looking a tad annoyed. He shuttled back to her—his grandaunt, he said—his head melting into the crowd. He came back a few minutes later.

"Okay, come the day after tomorrow."

"What time?" I yelled.

"After the teachings."

"Yes, I know. But what time is good?"

"After the teachings."

"What's the best time?" I persisted. There was a lot of time after the teachings, and I thought she might want to do her prayers before having a visitor.

"Anytime," he said.

"She is living in the same place?"

He nodded. I thanked him, and he disappeared back into the crowd.

What luck, I thought. Mere hours in town and I have lined up one interview. How lucky could I be? Mrs. Namseling looked happy, active, healthy. Her mind was intact. I felt jubilant.

Fortified by this lucky turn, I lingered at the road junction—this was where things were happening. Monks and nuns by the hundreds passed through. I was keeping an eye out for Lobsang or for people who looked like they might know Lobsang. After more than half an hour, the crowd thinned considerably; I saw about three or four nuns talking among themselves. They looked like they'd know my friend; it was just the way they carried themselves, an air of confidence. They'd been raised in India, I guessed.

"Excuse me," I said. "Do you speak English?"

"Little," they said.

"I am looking for Lobsang Dachen. Do you know her?"

"Yes! We know Lobsang Dachen!" they answered excitedly. "Come. . ." We walked down another road to Geden Choeling Nunnery, about ten minutes away, and into the hillside complex, where they pointed to a door inside a wooden building. The building looked familiar. "That's her room," they told me. Within fifteen minutes or so, Lobsang's roommate came home and then Lobsang herself.

My old friend looked the same save that her frame had filled out and her face had taken on an air of strength and authority. When I'd first met her twenty-one years before, she'd been so shy that she often blushed if she spoke English in front of unfamiliar Westerners. Now she was codirector of the Tibetan Nuns Project and traveled all over the world doing fund-raising.

"Do you remember this place? It used to be the kitchen," she said.

Indeed, I suddenly remembered the two long, wood-burning stoves in here, a very rustic setup and quite dark; there hadn't been adequate light for the cooks to work. That was early 1990. The nuns had a new kitchen now, she said, and had recently added a new dining hall and more buildings. The place was thriving. When I had first visited here in 1986, Geden Choeling was a neglected, slightly rundown small nunnery, so I was heartened to hear of these improvements.

Lobsang said she normally lived down the valley at Dolma Ling Nunnery, forty-five minutes away, but was staying up in town during the teachings.

She told me that Sonam Choedron and her son were living in Australia. I asked why Sonam had moved there. Australia apparently had a program to resettle a certain number of former political prisoners from Tibet each year, Lobsang explained. Sonam hadn't been interested at all, but the Australians had extended a special invitation, something to do with medical care. So she had decided to go.

I walked around town later. The place was packed. Originally, these had been just pedestrian lanes—rarely did one see a car here. When vehicles arrived in the early 1990s, pedestrians used the same paths, but since there were still no sidewalks, trucks, cars, and motorcycles now honked at

Posters calling for a protest march on March 10, 2007, marking the day in 1959
when the Tibetans in Lhasa resisted the People's Liberation Army. Such protests take
place in Tibetan communities in India, whereas the slightest reference to Tibetan
independence in Chinese-occupied Tibet is met with swift repression.

the heels of people on foot and squeezed them up against the storefronts.
With evening falling, the town's two narrow roads looked like a crowded
carnival scene, thick with people. Red-robed monks trawled the streets in
packs, strings of colorful lights adorned storefronts, and a roar of noise
buzzed from the cacophony of music, motors, and mutterings. Everywhere
I went—cafés, Internet shops, tea stalls—and everywhere I turned, I was
in someone's way or they were in mine.

The next morning, the guesthouse proprietor, Jigme, a Tibetan man in his
sixties, asked me to formally register. The day before, I'd just stuffed some
rupees into his hand and headed down to the teachings. I hadn't even given
him my name. He brought a big ledger to the sitting area on the third-floor
balcony outside my room. The perch had a beautiful view of the mountains.
We sat on the weatherworn old couch, and I handed him my passport.

As he copied information from my Indian visa into the ledger, he remarked on my transit visa. I told him I'd had to make magic to get it in Nepal on the same day I'd applied. The official had kept telling me that he would not issue a transit visa since I was going to Dharamsala. The transit visa allowed a foreigner to stay in India for fifteen days. Foreigners generally traveled with tourist visas.

"Wow, you have good karma," Jigme exclaimed. "To have gotten an Indian visa in one day!"

We got to chatting a bit, and I told him that I'd also had to scramble in Lhasa to get the Nepalese to cough up my passport the same afternoon I had dropped it off so that I could catch a last-minute ride to the border.

He was a learned man, a longtime local, not one of the young entrepreneur types who were just interested in making a quick buck. Those types had jacked up their prices four times the usual rate during the teachings. I told him about the shocking changes to Lhasa, about how local people were being squeezed almost beyond their tolerance, how they staved off poverty and homelessness in the face of China's policies, how they prayed constantly, almost desperately, to His Holiness, put every ounce of faith in him. I remembered how much Auntie had worried that she wouldn't see the Dalai Lama before she died. She couldn't leave the country to visit him in India; ordinary Tibetans could not leave China.

I explained that I was in town to talk to a couple of people who were here during the teachings. Plus, I added as an afterthought, I had to deliver a package to the Dalai Lama for the family. I groaned. It wasn't going to be an easy job. The only person I still knew here was his private secretary, whom I'd been friendly with since we met in 1986. Everyone else I knew had been posted abroad. I was feeling grumpy about it. I had so much on my plate already. It was daunting just thinking about it.

"You have been chosen because your heart is . . ." He put his right hand in a prayer position against his chest and tilted the fingers forward in a quick motion like a salute. "I can see that by the way you talk about the people in Lhasa. You have the right . . . understanding, the right . . . feeling, and you can tell Kundun what they feel."

Whenever I thought I might just drop the package off at the office and no one would know the difference, I remembered the relative who had safeguarded the robes for fifty years. I remembered how much the family had done for me—cared for me, included me, considered me. On this visit and my other ones. I'd promised them I would do my best. They couldn't leave the country themselves to give him the gift. They were under house arrest. Nationwide house arrest.

"Ahh," he said, "you know, I believe very much in karma. In karmic force, energy. To have gotten an Indian visa in one day and a Nepalese visa in hours . . . this is *really* something," he said with a soft whistle. "You are the medium the people in Tibet have chosen to bring these things to His Holiness."

I took a moment to ponder his words. I was talking to an older traditional Tibetan. They understood the intricacies of karma. This was the real deal, not some charlatan New Ager in the West. As he spoke, something a psychic had told me about twenty years ago popped into my mind. She said that I was a conduit for Tibet in the West.

Jigme said that Tenzin Geyche, the private secretary, lived near the Pema Thang Hotel. Up Bhagsu Road. I could try and find him there.

Later that night, I thought about our talk. Maybe it's true, I thought. Things had happened to me around the Tibetans these last twenty years that I never could have imagined or predicted. Doors opened, one thing led to another. That's how I knew I was on the right path. The synchronicity.

Besides, Amala had never asked anything of me. In Lhasa, I had attended many social events with the family, met many people, and I had come to realize that Amala was exceptionally charming. Not that she stole the show, or was effusively talkative, but where others might be ill at ease, she was outgoing and welcoming. Where others could be cruel or selfish—like one relative who kept a ten-year-old as a maid and then made her the butt of jokes—Amala was humane. And far from being self-centered, Amala was continuously thinking of others. At night, she organized all of Pala's traditional Tibetan medicines and treatments for him. She loaded snacks and drinks into the pockets of her grandchildren when they left on a trip. She had seen to it that a hot-water bottle heated up my bedding at night in the freezing-cold temperatures. When we visited less well-off relatives I observed her slipping bills into their hands in private.

Tashi told me that when her mother had visited her in Canada, they were driving away from the house one day, and all the neighbors on the street waved to Amala as they passed by. "There are people I've never said one word to in all the years I've lived here," Tashi exclaimed. In just a few days, Amala had made friends with them, and she didn't even speak English!

The last time I was in Lhasa, for a very brief visit in 1994, she chided me for paying so much for a guesthouse room and urged me to stay at the family home. Then she asked me to bring over my dirty laundry right away so she could wash it. And before I left, she asked me to try on a magnificent magenta silk *chuba*. She had guessed my measurements and sewed it by hand, keeping it neatly pressed in the bureau drawer until I returned. It had been stored in the drawer for eight years! She'd made one for each daughter and me. One of my American traveling companions, a travel writer, said that it was the most beautiful gift he'd ever seen someone give a Westerner in the twenty years he'd been traveling in Asia. Now with these same hands, Amala had sewn a robe for the Dalai Lama.

Before, delivering the present to His Holiness had felt like a chore, an obligation. After I talked with Jigme, my attitude completely turned around. Getting the package to His Holiness was part of my mission. An important service. Even part of my spiritual practice. But still, during this insanely busy time for the Dalai Lama, it would be a logistical challenge.

Early the next morning, I set out for Bhagsu to find the Pema Thang Hotel. I turned left toward the edge of town in the direction of Bhagsu waterfall. After fifteen minutes, I reached another developed area with a couple of hotels and shops, but scarcely any people. An Indian man asked me what I was looking for, and when I told him, he said the Pema Thang Hotel was by the Hotel Bhagsu, in the center of town up on the hill. I knew the area; it was where the older, high-end hotels were located. I hadn't understood Jigme correctly, and, having not been here in more than a dozen years, I'd lost my bearings and gone in the entirely wrong direction.

I turned around and walked all the way back to town, past my hotel and past the Security Office. Since I was here, I decided to get a security badge. The office had run out of application forms, so it took an hour and a half to get a pass even though I was at the front of the line.

I climbed up the hill to find the Pema Thang Hotel. In the low-slung lodge perched on a quiet hillside, I asked the front desk clerk where Tenzin Geyche's house was. The clerk said he'd call the house for me later, that I should ring him back that night. I wrote a long note to Tenzin Geyche; he and I had made a nice connection in 1986, and it was he who'd invited me to the private audience with His Holiness. I'd seen him a few other times through the years as well. I explained in the note that I was in town and asked if it would be possible to present something in person to His Holiness.

By now, I was late for the morning session of the teachings. It wouldn't look right to step in late, I thought. I was halfway to the library and the government administration area where I'd lived before. I decided to head there for a quick visit and come for the afternoon session of teachings.

Half an hour later, mere feet away from my former home—a three-story building of fifteen studio units situated a stone's throw from the library— I saw a similar three-story structure, built in what had been open space. Throughout the area, buildings had been built in the spaces between buildings. It felt so cramped. I took a couple of photographs and hustled back up the mountain.

I ran into my old landlord and asked if he knew Sonam Choedron. Had he seen her? He wasn't sure who she was, he said, but he'd seen a large, "royal-looking woman" in town flanked by two daughters and thought that might have been her. He said the best way to find her was to stand at the junction.

I stood at the intersection outside the temple, eyeing the faces of all the older Tibetan women in the crowd. The left entrance was designated for foreigners, and the right for the Tibetan public. I wandered down the lane for Tibetans and, to my surprise, found a whole other encampment with a long lane of tea stalls, food stands, and information booths. I found a little perch off to the side and watched from there a long time, looking for Sonam.

When it was time to reassemble for the afternoon session, I noticed that men and women each had their own extremely long line for the security check. How perfect, I thought. All I had to do was check everyone in the women's line. I walked up the long incline past about seventy women.

Near the head of the line, a security guy in his early thirties, seeing me approach, yelled, "Get in line, get in line!"

"I'm just looking for someone, don't worry," I said, trying to reassure him I wasn't cutting in line. I marched back down the incline slowly, scanning each face.

I didn't see Sonam anywhere, and almost everyone was inside. I thought I'd sit in the Tibetan section, where I'd have a chance to spot her. As I stood in line, I saw a bulletin posted on the building that said no cameras were allowed. I had my camera with me because I'd taken pictures earlier. At the Security Office that morning, there'd been no notice posted about contraband items. After half an hour, I got to the front of the line. Two women frisked me roughly, while two men barked orders. One guy yelled in English to the others: "She's Chinese!"

They found the camera. I said I had the camera because I'd taken pictures that morning but wouldn't take pictures inside. I had just seen the notice. I'd stood in line at the office for an hour and a half that morning—there'd been no posting. I even offered to give him the camera.

"Get out!" he yelled in a hard voice. "I don't want your camera!"

My hotel was a good twenty-five-minute walk up the mountain, and I was worried that my being late would be frowned on, seen as disrespectful. Little did I know that no one in the audience would have cared. After walking around a few minutes and considering two or three options, I hid the camera behind a screened-off area of the temple parking lot, after checking that no one had seen me.

I went back inside the temple grounds and back into the security line.

The security staff bounced me out of the line a second time, telling me harshly that I couldn't come in this way, I had to go to the foreigners' line.

Near the foreigners' line on the other side of the building, hundreds of Zippo lighters and cigarette cartons, along with a few penknives, lay on the ground by the security checkpoint. These were all contraband as well, but since there had been no notice at the Security Office this morning, people had showed up with them.

Inside, His Holiness talked about the fact that we were dominated by afflictive emotions—attachment, greed, hatred, pride, jealousy, and the like—and that most of our actions were motivated by these emotions. We had to find the determination to overcome them and instead to cultivate virtuous emotions, or *bodhicitta*, called "loving kindness," the wish that all beings find happiness. This determination was known as renunciation. Anger overwhelmed and obscured the natural, clear state of the mind. We should try, he counseled, to never give in to the power of anger. We should hold the Bodhisattva vows and engage in the Seven-Limb Practice—disclose the wrongdoing, commit no more offenses, make an offering to the Buddha, and so on—in order to live a life with a minimum of afflictive emotions. If we accomplished this, our lives would be peaceful.

After the teaching, I stationed myself at the top of the stairs to the Security Office. I hung there on the outer edge of the landing, scanning the thousands of people leaving the Tibetan section, looking for Sonam Choedron. I had in mind to go inside later and ask after Tenzin Geyche, but the crowd gathered to get inside got bigger, rowdier, and pushier instead of smaller. About a dozen monks, yelling and jamming up at the door, started to push me off the small landing. After fifteen minutes, I was hanging in the air off the side of it, arm extended, fingers hanging onto the door frame and toes gripping the edge of the top stair. I didn't see Sonam in the half hour I was there.

I walked back out to the parking lot to retrieve my camera. My bag was gone. It couldn't be. I searched everywhere in the vicinity but found nothing. I got a queasy feeling in my stomach, and my pulse started to race.

Shocked and shaken, I sought out Kunsang at her cousin's place. Her relatives thought we should report it. She and I walked over to the car park where I'd left the camera behind a screened-in corner. We searched for it again. Kunsang talked to a staffer from the Security Office who was walking through the junction. He exploded, yelling in Tibetan, accusing me of hiding it unwisely. I tried to explain that the security staff had refused to let me in with the camera, that I'd even offered to give them my camera. He didn't listen, just raised his voice in Chinese-accented English. I saw from his name tag that he was a Tibetan from China. He and Kunsang switched to speaking Tibetan.

After a few minutes, an Indian constable wearing a khaki uniform and beret and carrying a nightstick came over. Kunsang spoke to him in Hindi. He started yelling in Hindi over the security guy's Tibetan, and then they all switched to English. I tried to assert myself. I'd seen a taxi driver watching me when I'd left the lot and wanted to trace him through his taxi company. Was there a phone book or something? No one heard me. Kunsang raised her voice to match the hollering of the two men. I tried a couple more times to be heard, but it became a screaming match. A crowd of onlookers sprouted around us. The swirl of people and tangle of angry voices in so many languages, on top of the shock of what had already happened, was too much. I wandered away into the parking lot, crying.

What was I going to do? I needed a camera to take pictures of the women. How could anyone steal during a teaching by the Dalai Lama?!

I remembered the first time I'd attended the Dalai Lama's teachings. It had been so relaxed, so beautiful, walking out in the foggy dawn to the edge of Bodh Gaya, the site of the Buddha's enlightenment in India, carrying our meditation cushions. My companion, a potter, commented that the ground on which we walked contained good clay for pots. It felt timeless, like we were part of a stream of pilgrims who had walked along these paths for centuries, participating in something people had been doing since the beginning of humanity: gathering from far and wide to hear ancient wisdom teachings. There had been less than a hundred Westerners then, in January 1987; we strolled in every morning and plopped on the ground to hear the Dalai Lama teach the graduated path to enlightenment. No badges, no lines, no crowds.

Now nearly 2,400 foreigners had marked their spots with big signs and their names inked in capital letters with fat felt markers. People got territorial about their seats. Not only that, but you were searched, frisked, carded, roughed up by rude officials, and had to endure long lines to get in, for the bathroom, for food, to get a badge. Things were not getting easier or simpler, but more stressful and full of hassles.

That night, I phoned the front desk man at the Pema Thang Hotel. He said he'd called the private secretary's house, and Tenzin Geyche's wife had said he still wasn't home and that I should try and reach him at the office.

Late that night, I had to check in with Lobsang. Although I was emotionally spent, I walked across town and down the mountain to the nunnery.

"I found Sonam Choedron!" Lobsang announced as soon as she saw me. "I was just coming into Hotel Tibet as she was coming out. She told me where she was staying at the temple. We can meet her the day after tomorrow."

The next day, the Indian constable stationed at the junction nodded hello and came over, looking sympathetic. He wanted to know where I was staying. What room number? he asked. Maybe if he came up with a lead, I thought, he'd let me know.

That evening, after the teaching, I visited Mrs. Namseling. Kunsang agreed to help translate. We climbed up to Mrs. Namseling's third-floor walk-up on the main street. We found her sitting on the bed, prayer book in her lap, wearing wire-rim glasses and a gray wool sweater over a dark tan *chuba*. Her living space was a third of its former size; the landlord had subdivided the large studio. I introduced Kunsang, who sat down at the far end of the couch, a respectful distance from Mrs. Namseling.

Mrs. Namseling—looking much the same as she had thirteen years ago, just with more gray hair and a few more lines—sat up and pretended to pull her sweater together.

"Is this a book or a film?" she joked. "Should I get ready?" She laughed, an infectious, musical laugh that reminded me how lively and playful she was. I explained that I had been working on the book all these years since I'd seen her, and that of thirty-six interviews now only four were left in the book, one of them being hers. I wanted to follow up with her because so much had changed in Dharamsala, in Tibet, and in China in the dozen-plus years since we'd last talked. Afternoon sun from a large window behind her warmed the room, the walls of which were painted fuchsia, matching one of the colors in the curtains.

I said that I considered her interview of prime importance because she had witnessed the bombing of Lhasa, what the older Tibetans called "The

War." Even though China had claimed Tibet earlier and had maintained
a military presence in Tibet since the early 1950s, I considered the violent
military invasion of 1959 a decisive turning point. She had a valuable insider's perspective on this as a Cabinet minister's wife. Also, she had lived in
Tibet when it was free.

I reminded her that when we had last talked, she had told me that while
she was in prison for nearly a decade, she always prayed for three things: to
see her children again, to see His Holiness again, and to see a free Tibet.
Her first two wishes had long ago come true. What did she think now of
the third wish? And where were her children?

She said that her son, the former *rinpoche*, lived in Washington, D.C.,
and had a job working with Tibetan carpets. One daughter was married
to the prince of Gangtok. Three daughters lived in Switzerland, and one
daughter resided in the States.

As for the question of Tibet, she said that in fall 2006 she had visited
Tibet for the first time since 1981.

"There's more food, more things to buy, more freedom of movement.
On the surface, these things are true. But in reality, the Chinese government keeps tight control. Tibetans always have to be careful. There's a hotel
where the older Tibetans gather every day. I spent a lot of time there. They
couldn't talk about anything that really concerned them, about what was
really going on in Lhasa. They could only talk superficially. You can't speak
certain words, can't go certain places. You can be taken in, 'disappeared.'
Anything could happen at any time. The Chinese still hold the keys."

She added: "They are grateful that the Dalai Lama is looking after the
situation. I still hope to see a free Tibet one day. I still hope we will gain
our freedom."

I found it interesting that she used the metaphor of keys for retaining
control. She'd been in prison for nine years, some years locked in a cell night
and day. The implication was that the Tibetans were locked up.

I said I had heard that she had just spent time in Switzerland with her
children and grandchildren. Had she found that the Tibetan Swiss were
keeping their Tibetan identity, or was it drifting away?

"At school, the children speak German, but at home, they speak Tibetan.
They try to keep the Tibetan ways," she replied.

In the Kathmandu airport, I told her, I sat next to a woman from Paris who said there were four hundred Tibetans in France. I met a Tibetan who had been living in Sweden for the last thirty years. Many more were emigrating to Australia.

"When people live in other cultures, it is hard to keep all the old ways," I said. "What do you think is essential to preserve in order to stay Tibetan?"

"Wherever you go, you are always Tibetan. It's important to keep your own culture. Like if you have children, it's important to teach your child whatever you think is important to keep the culture alive."

"Do you see Tibetan culture taking new forms in Dharamsala and other places?"

"Here in Dharamsala," she answered, "this new generation is trying to keep the culture because His Holiness constantly reminds them to study Tibetan language, keep the reading and writing, practice the traditions. Even the hip-hop kids, in a corner of their hearts, they're trying to stay Tibetan.

"I'm more afraid," she continued, "about people in Tibet losing the culture than the people here. In Tibet, the Tibetans drink a lot. There are no restrictions on selling, drinking, drunkenness, or anything because the Chinese *want* the Tibetans to lose consciousness, they *want* them not to think.

"There's a lot of illegal activity there, but the Chinese ignore it, pretend it's not happening. It's like they want to encourage the breakdown of the society. For thieves, smugglers, drug dealers, and so on, they turn the other cheek, but if Tibetans say two words of anything remotely political, the government strikes down fast and hard on them."

When we last met, a dozen or so years ago, Mrs. Namseling was very upset about the change in the mentality of the local Tibetan community in Dharamsala: they were becoming preoccupied with material desire and less interested in traditional, spiritual values, she thought. Dharamsala at the time was experiencing a glut of construction—new hotels mainly, due to the tourist boom—and also a marked increase in automobiles.

"Now it's even *more* developed here in McLeod Ganj," I added. McLeod Ganj was the upper portion of Dharamsala where the Tibetans lived. "And in the whole of India. And in China. What do you think now?" I thought she was likely to have an opinion on this since she'd recently been in the States, Europe, and Chinese-occupied Tibet; she had some perspective.

"Nowadays, not only Tibetans—not just people in Tibet—but the *whole world* pursues material things and material development. So I guess . . ." she shrugged, "it's normal. I don't really know what to say about it."

"In 1994," I said, taking a different tack, "you were very involved with your spiritual practice, and I see that this is still true. I know that before, in Tibet, you had no practice. Do you find that your desire to practice gets stronger as you get older?"

"As you get older," she answered, "the mind is naturally inclined to want to do the practice. I wasted time when I was young."

"The man at the security bureau who registers foreigners told me this morning that over 2,300 foreigners have registered to attend the teachings, from as far away as Moscow and Malaysia. What do you think of the dharma spreading to foreigners? Do you think it is positive for Tibetan culture?"

"It doesn't matter if you're Western or Tibetan," she responded, "if a person wants to practice, it's a good thing. I'm sure they are sincere, otherwise they wouldn't waste their time. They could be visiting somewhere sunny and comfortable, not coming up here to sit in this freezing weather!"

"You've lived through so many eras and so much change: when Tibet was peaceful and free, when the Chinese invaded and the culture was destroyed, spent many years of prison. Then here in exile when this was a quiet, intact community of Tibetans and now that it's become an international tourist destination, very crowded and full of foreigners. How do you look back on the meaning of your life?"

"Before, I had so many material things, but they had no meaning," Kunsang translated. "I wasted my time. Before in Lhasa, I couldn't say what I really felt like saying; I had to comport myself a certain way, being a high official's wife. Now I don't have much," she looked around the small room; along with the two beds we sat on, the only other furnishings were a coffee table, a small fridge, a tiny television, and a two-burner stovetop where a young helper had prepared tea for us. "Even that altar," she said, nodding at a cabinet in the corner, "belongs to the landlord. When I see people with a lot of things, I don't feel envy. I think less is better. I don't need anything beyond what I have."

I knew that in her former life, she had had to manage household staffs, something she never relished but had to do owing to her husband's station in life. Now she had more freedom to do as she pleased.

Mrs. Namseling, around twenty-five years old, at her home in Lhasa, mid-1950s. As a Cabinet minister's wife, she was part of the Lhasa aristocracy. The elaborate headdress and jewelry were worn for Tibetan New Year and other special occasions. Photo courtesy of the Namseling family.

"Now, here, I get to listen to teachings from His Holiness. My children send me financial support. I have no worries. Everything has worked out for me. I feel very lucky. I am quite happy. I feel free."

I remembered that Mrs. Namseling had expressed this attitude when I'd talked with her years before. She had told me that before the takeover, she found herself caught up in things like procuring more beautiful dresses or jewelry. It was what women of her class occupied themselves with. In Buddhism, one would say it was entanglement with the afflictive emotions of envy and greed. In feminism, one might say that since women weren't allowed meaningful occupations, in business, religion, or government life, their talents and energies were necessarily confined to the sphere of domestic and personal concerns. This was particularly true of Mrs. Namseling's social class because she hadn't even done household chores herself. But the forced simplification caused by the invasion—the loss of home, marriage, country, even her personal freedom for nine years—had stripped her life down to an essence.

Mrs. Namseling in her home in Dharamsala, 2007.
Photo by Shannon Thompson.

I woke up the next morning inspired. Things were going well. I was glad to have found Mrs. Namseling happy and spry, healthy, and as lively as ever. I wondered if I should go in early to look for Tenzin Geyche. I'd tried his home and his office; I had tried after the teaching, but the office had been mobbed. What about early?

I walked down to the temple, enjoying the quiet and peace of the town at this early hour, half past seven, before car horns blasted and shop music blared. I arrived at the reception office, and the staffer behind the desk said I was too early. Tenzin Geyche hadn't come in yet. Try back in an hour, he suggested. I wrote a polite note, enclosing a picture of myself from an old flyer.

I came back at 8:45. The only other person in the waiting room was an Asian woman in her sixties. "I want His Holiness to give my daughter a blessing," she said in an imperious tone to the young man behind the desk, a different fellow from the one I'd spoken with earlier.

"Sorry, too late," the staffer said to me when it was my turn and I had explained my case, "Tenzin Geyche's here, but he's already gone inside to the palace."

I must have convinced him sufficiently of my credibility, or maybe I just appeared sincerely desperate, but after a few minutes of chatting, he piped, "I will give you his mobile number," and proceeded to write the private secretary's cell phone number on a small slip of paper. He retired to the adjacent Security Office. Heartened that I'd made some measure of progress and finding the waiting area cool and comfortable, I lingered a while; I was in no rush to go back into the crush outside.

I picked up some literature from the table, current reports from human rights organizations and various offices of the Tibetan government-in-exile. It was always mind-blowing to be in Dharamsala after being Tibet—like traveling overnight to the Age of Enlightenment from the Dark Ages. In Tibet, information even hinting at China's oppression, past or present, was suppressed, and the Internet was blocked. In Dharamsala, it was the opposite: information flowed—even more so in the last ten years because the West, newly interested in Tibet, thirsted for information and needed it in English.

I read that the once pristine river in Lhasa, the Kyichu—which I had been so distressed to see two weeks earlier, dried up, stagnant, and dirty brown—had been polluted by 41.9 million tons of industrial chemical waste about ten years ago. There was no telling what had been dumped in it since then.

I read about the Kongpo area, where Tashi's friend lived, the one who mourned the disappearance of the forests there. Ten or twenty years ago, Tibet watchers had known that logs from the mountains in Kham, eastern Tibet, floated downriver night and day to fuel China's building boom. At last check, years ago, it was $52 billion worth of timber. This report said that the famed Kongpo forest had lost a majority of its tree cover. Central Tibet's forests, with trees more than two hundred years old, had been known for having the world's highest stock density of conifers. Reckless and rampant deforestation had left hills and valley barren. Bears, mountain sheep, and musk deer had vanished. I read hungrily, eagerly, my interest piqued. This substantiated what Tashi's friend had talked about. Between 1949 and 1985, nearly half of the ancient old-growth forest in Tibet, primarily montane, had been destroyed. Huge convoys of trucks transported the logs, but now the railroad would make the logging operation more efficient.

China had earned billions, I read, from mining more than three dozen precious metals in Tibet, and open-pit mines sometimes left holes in the ground as deep as a five-story building. Mineral reserves in central Tibet were estimated to be worth in excess of $80 billion. It would all be moved out by railroad. I fell on the readings, devoured them. Here was everything Tashi's friends had talked about, substantiated by documents and reports.

Buddhist teachings stress the concept of contentment and discourage overconsumption. As early as 1642, the fifth Dalai Lama issued his "Decree for Protection of Animals and the Environment." Hunting, mining, and other activities exploiting the environment were forbidden. Thus, to the Chinese government, Tibet was literally the Western Treasure House, an astonishing wealth of untapped natural resources.

Jiang Zemin, former president of the People's Republic, said this about the railroad in early 2001: "Some people advised me not to go ahead with this project because it was not commercially viable. I said this was a political decision; we will make it succeed at all costs, even if there is a commercial loss."

The railroad, according to the Tibetan government-in-exile, was indeed a political undertaking, a tool of cultural genocide, designed to wipe out the Tibetan identity through the huge demographic transformation, which amounted to ethnic cleansing, through changing the face of the Tibetan landscape, and through giving China greater political, military, and economic hegemony.

I read that the campaign to denounce the Dalai Lama, called "Patriotic Red," began in 2006 when a new party secretary took over the TAR. Monks and nuns were forced to put aside religious study and undergo full-time political indoctrination, or "patriotic reeducation," by studying six books, including one on the crushing of separatism. The campaign even went into elementary schools, where soldiers in uniform encouraged children to trample photos of the Dalai Lama.

Suddenly, the security man whipped through the waiting area, calling to me as he bounded toward the front door:

"Come!" he said. "Tenzin Geyche is coming now!"

I leaped up and sprinted behind him outside. A large entourage of Tibetan officials swept by, headed toward the front of the grounds. I saw Tenzin Geyche among them in a gray-green *chuba*.

"Tenzin Geyche," I said.

He looked at me, startled. He'd gotten grayer.

"Oh! Yes, hello!" He stopped and smiled. The group of officials walked on. "I read your note." He looked torn between wanting to talk and needing to go. "I've given the matter to Chhime-la," he said. "I'm sorry . . . I've got to go." He nodded and hurried to catch up with the others.

Great! I exulted. He read my note!

In the next moment, I thought, Who is Chhime-la?

Chhime, another staffer explained back inside the office, was the assistant private secretary. Tenzin Geyche had retired a few years ago, but the Dalai Lama prevailed on him to break in a replacement. A team of three now handled Tenzin Geyche's job, and Chhime was one of them. It proved impossible to find out the best time to reach Chhime, however, since his schedule was woven around the teachings.

The staff was also busy preparing for Saturday, March 10, Tibetan National Uprising Day. The occasion brought a full day of commemorative ceremonies; the teachings were halted, and His Holiness delivered his annual state of the nation address. I felt bad to have to press myself on the Private Office at this exceptionally busy time. Many dignitaries were in town—*geshes* from southern India, Indian officials from Delhi—and His Holiness was probably working on his speech. Ten thousand people from dozens of countries all over the world were packed into this tiny town, and many of them no doubt wanted an audience. I thought of the lady in the office this morning. I needed only five minutes to present the gift, but I had to speak to Chhime to do it. I wrote a long note for him and left.

In 1986, this had been a sleepy town. All the Tibetans wore *chubas*. There were no cars. No tourists. Just Tibetans, a sprinkling of Indians, and a few dozen Westerners. The prominent feature of the main street was the bank of prayer wheels. The receptionist at the library was friendly and graceful.

Four years later, in 1990, young Tibetans, breaking with the tradition of wearing *chubas,* walked along on one side of the street wearing Patagonia™ jackets, while on the other side strolled Westerners wearing Indian cotton drawstring pants and striped Nepali jackets. The East was fascinated by the West and the West by the East. The receptionist at the library started to look weary from greeting so many foreigners. We lit dozens of candles in our guesthouse room for heat and shared toilet pit bathrooms.

After another four years, in 1994, the streets teemed. Bejeweled foreign tourists browsed in Indian-owned shops with halogen track lights, blithely bought exorbitantly priced religious souvenirs, and took them back to hotel rooms with private bathrooms and hot running water. I was so put off that I started walking back to my guesthouse via a forest path below town so I could avoid the main street. Interest in Tibet and Tibetan Buddhism had exploded following the Dalai Lama's 1989 Nobel Peace Prize. My Swiss Tibetan friend captured it perfectly in his expressive English: "Everyone in Dharamsala is *hunting.*" The foreigners hunted for a novel experience with a Tibetan, and the locals hunted for a potential Western sponsor or benefactor. The receptionist at the library looked like a zombie, opening and closing her mouth to speak but with no emotional affect, worn down by the onslaught of foreigners opining on everything from what to do to free Tibet to how the local government should clean up the trash-strewn streets. There was little trace of the sleepy, friendly feeling the town had had before.

Twenty years ago, when the public didn't know the first thing about Tibet, we used to pray and dream that somehow Tibet would become a household word. If people knew the truth, we believed, they would come forth and intervene. Tibet would be saved. Now Tibet was indeed a household word, but China had imposed its will, transformed it. Beyond our worst nightmares.

I met up with Lobsang at the lunch break, and we searched for Sonam's room in the hillside housing block behind the Central Temple. There was a mix-up with the room numbers and quite a bit of confusion, as we knocked on various doors and ran around asking people where she might be. After a long time, we found her studio apartment on the second floor of one of the buildings. I was thrilled to see her after all this effort. She greeted us warmly, as engaging and spirited as ever. She looked very much the same, save a bit heavier.

Lobsang and I sat on the couch bed. Compared to the place in Dharamsala where she'd lived years ago, the room had a temporary feel to it, with nondescript basic furniture and few personal belongings. I said I was surprised to hear she had moved to Australia.

"What brought you to *Australia*?" I asked.

She laughed.

"All the time I was in prison," she said, "I tried to get sick! You can go to Lhasa if you get sick. I *tried* to get sick, but I couldn't!" She leaned forward. "Now that I'm free . . ." she held the moment with perfect comic timing, "*I'm sick*!" She slapped her knee and erupted into laughter. She rocked back and forth in waves of laughter. Lobsang joined in.

Sonam explained that the Australian government gave political asylum to a hundred Tibetan former political prisoners every year. They chose people by lottery. She had never been interested, so she'd never applied. Besides, she was over the fifty-year-old age limit. The Australian government contacted her. Apparently many other former political prisoners in the program had recommended her. By then, she was having problems with her legs, a kind of arthritis—Lobsang didn't know the English word. She had pain in her knees and down her legs from living in the underground cell when she was in solitary confinement. It had been constantly cold and damp down there.

She had received a letter from the Australian Embassy through the Security Office personally inviting her to immigrate. When she told the Security Office she wasn't interested, the Security Office said she had to tell the Australians herself.

She met with the Australian Embassy officer, who asked why she didn't apply. She explained that she hadn't applied because she was too old and she couldn't walk well. Plus, she hadn't been among the one hundred chosen for that year, so she would be taking somebody else's spot. The officer promised her medical attention for her legs, including surgery. First-class Western health care. At no cost. He urged her to reconsider.

After thinking about it, she'd decided that since the Australian government had taken such a personal interest in her and since the health care would be better there than in India, she would go. Her son, formerly a monk at the Central Temple, was already living there.

It was already time for the afternoon session. We arranged to talk another day when we'd have more time.

Later that evening, after the teachings, I saw the Indian constable at the junction. That was his beat. He smiled at me. He looked sympathetic.

"Come, have a cup of tea," he said. I thought there would be no harm in talking to him and keeping the theft of my camera in the front of his mind, in case he heard anything. We sat down on an old rickety wooden bench in front of a tea stall.

He asked me where I lived. When I answered, he asked if I was married. He looked directly at me. Yes, I lied, tapping my gold band from my high school graduation on my right hand.

"What job have you in the U.S.?" he asked. Cups of hot chai were placed in front of us. "How much salary?"

The conversation quickly took an unexpected turn I didn't like. He complained that he made a very low salary.

"I love you," he said about three minutes in, gazing at me with puppy dog eyes.

Luckily I had my teacup in front of my mouth to hide my reaction. "I can visit you in America? I love you," he intoned.

"Uh . . . aren't you *married?*" I asked, trying to shame him. I'd barely had two sips of tea.

"Yes," he said.

"With children?"

He did that head tilt, which the Indians here did, a half swivel and a little shake, tossing off my objection.

"I love you," he said a third time.

"I loved my camera," I responded. "Have you heard anything about it?"

The tension got thick. I had the distinct impression that he was about to touch me. I thanked him for the tea and left.

"Miss!" he called out.

I told Jigme, the proprietor of my guesthouse, about the theft.

"It is one of my people," he said immediately.

I must have looked shocked.

"Definitely," he said flatly. "I'm sure of it. They saw you put it there."

I had noticed a lot more rough-looking types of Tibetans in Dharamsala, especially groups of young men who hung around in small packs. They reminded me of hungry wolves. Years before, the vibrations in Dharamsala had conveyed a certain gentility. Not wealth, but gentility. The Tibetans had been brought up in the local Tibetan schools, but many of those people had since left. Tibetans from Chinese-occupied Tibet had started moving here in the 1990s. When I asked Lobsang about these guys, she said they were from Tibet, mostly Kham, and had lived their whole lives under Chinese oppression. "All they know how to do is fight," she said.

Lobsang and I visited Sonam again the next day, after the teachings. I told her that it was a real privilege to meet her again and that her story was one of true heroism. She had shown tremendous courage and dedication in all the work she'd done through the years to regain Tibet's independence. She had stood up to prison officials, often defying them, lobbying for herself or on behalf of others and sometimes even dressing down guards. And she had lost her husband, granddaughter, and son.

I asked her what it was like for her to live in Australia.

"It has good facilities and everything, but it's not our country," she answered. "I feel uneasy, unsettled . . . like it's merely a rental place to stay."

She said there were about three hundred Tibetans living in Sydney, all former political prisoners. Her daughters, with whom she had lived in Dharamsala before, had emigrated four years ago to France. An agency had sponsored them, but unfortunately the younger daughter was in poor health. The adorable granddaughter who had been just a baby when I interviewed Sonam more than a dozen years ago was about to graduate from TCV.

As for her own health—her key reason for leaving Asia and moving to Australia—the Australian doctors had proposed surgery for her knees. I got the impression that they wanted to do a knee replacement using an artificial part, because some part of the knee was worn out and rubbing against another part. (The English translation got sketchy here because of the anatomical vocabulary.) She had consulted with some other sources and decided against the operation. She took painkillers, she said, for what sounded like constant and considerable pain.

Sonam had told her relatives in Lhasa that she was going to get citizenship, which took two years, and then would return to Tibet as an Australian citizen. All this time, Chinese authorities had been coming around, ready to arrest her upon her return to Tibet. She'd be protected then, she thought. Her relatives disagreed: "The Chinese won't recognize you as an Australian citizen—they'll put you in prison anyway."

One day in Sydney, she said, a man in a car starting waving and calling out in her direction in a rather emphatic manner. She thought he had recognized someone else, so she ignored him. He kept it up, and finally she stopped and approached him. He was about thirty years old, she said, from China. He had spotted her *chuba* and apron and knew she was Tibetan. He asked what had brought her to live in Australia.

"Our country was taken by China!" she told him. "That's why I'm here! You took our country! You took our country . . . so I'm exiled here!" She couldn't believe that he had no idea what she was talking about. "Didn't you know that China invaded Tibet?" she cried.

He didn't know anything. He offered her a ride home, and she accepted. She told him that China had taken Tibet and killed more than a million Tibetan people. He was dumbfounded. She said she told him—with her characteristic passion, it appeared—that the Chinese army took Tibet by force, bombed and killed the townspeople, destroyed all the temples, imprisoned people and tortured and enslaved them, and was felling the forests and mining the minerals. She unloaded a blitz. He was aghast.

She learned that he was also opposed to the Communist government. At one point, before they parted ways, he said very humbly, "On behalf of the Chinese people, I apologize."

She said he'd wanted her address. It sounded as if he might want to look her up again. She put him off, claiming not to know the address in English. "It's the place near the petrol pump and a half block from the Indian restaurant—the place with the *big Tibetan flag* on the door," she told him.

She told us she'd confronted a dilemma when filling out the papers for her Australian passport. For place of birth, she'd said "Tibet." The person helping her had responded, "We should put down China." "I will not!" she'd answered. "Tibet is an independent country. I was born in Tibet. Not China."

The problem was that if her passport listed Tibet, then every time she traveled to Tibet, it would draw attention and make the Chinese authorities suspicious. It would be equivalent to making the political statement that Tibet was not part of China. But if she put China as her birthplace, it meant she accepted the Chinese claim that Tibet was part of China.

"Either way had many problems," she said. I could see it had been a painful decision. She didn't mention her ultimate course of action, and I didn't want to ask.

In her English as a second language class one day, the class had been talking about food. The teacher, leading a conversation on fruit, asked the Tibetan students, "Are there bananas in Tibet?"

A Chinese man, a former security officer with the Beijing government, answered, "No, there were no bananas."

At this, Sonam bristled. She asked him pointedly, "Have you ever *been* to Tibet?" When he said that he had not, she asked, "Then how do you know if you've never been there?" She continued: "China has taken all the precious metals from Tibet. They have taken all the trees, all the forests, all the valuable religious objects. They have stolen the land from people and polluted the air and water." She then laid out a thumbnail history of Chinese aggressions in Tibet over the last forty-odd years. When she was finished, he was speechless.

She told us she had traveled to China in 1969.

"It was *very* poor at the time; they didn't even have wood for coffins. Now they have taken all the virgin forests from Tibet, cut down all the trees in Kham.

"They use them to construct buildings," she said. "They've taken iron ore, silver, gold from Tibet. China has become very wealthy since then. Before, if there was gold in the ground and someone wanted to extract it, the local villagers would run them off. Now when they find valuable minerals, the Chinese authorities move whole villages out so they can open a mine. They did this in Amdo. They used to use trucks to take it away," she said, "but now with the train, it's even easier to take it off to China. One day, at this rate, Tibet will be empty."

(Many months later, back in the States, I read a newspaper article that made me recall this conversation: a group of mine owners in central China, Amdo, had traveled to Beijing and each paid $100,000 in cash to buy a Hummer. Then they drove home in a ten-car convoy to show off. These were the same mine operators who used slave labor, or near-slave labor, often Tibetans, to work the mines.)

"Also, Tibet has become very hot," Sonam said. "They've taken the trees out, and with climate change, that's changed the weather pattern."

I asked her if she had any hope that the next generation of Chinese leaders would be more enlightened about Tibet. I had met many young Chinese with a very sincere and keen interest in Tibet. The problem was that they also had no clue whatsoever about their government's invasion and occupation over the last fifty years.

She said she didn't have hope in the younger generation of leaders. "It's becoming like 1959," she declared. The Chinese government back then made the Tibetans set up three pictures on the household altar—Chairman Mao, Zhou Enlai, and another man whose name she couldn't remember. When TV cameras rolled, the villagers were compelled to say: "We're so grateful for the leadership of Chairman Mao, Zhou Enlai, and so-and-so. We're so thankful for the liberation." All this while no pictures of Kundun, their real leader, the Dalai Lama, were allowed. I sensed she was saying it had been a harshly repressive time.

"How do you hope to keep the Tibetan struggle alive in Australia?" I asked. "Do you think there is more power working outside of Tibet than inside?"

"Now wherever there's a Tibetan event in Australia, wherever I can get involved, I'm ready to join," she said. "In Australia, a major difference is that people can shout and demonstrate at the Chinese Embassy, say anything they want, without harassment from officials. Chinese people themselves, Falun Gong practitioners, for instance, stage protests against the PRC government."

The most effective thing, she thought, was when Tibetans inside Tibet got international media attention. Even if it was a relatively minor thing, if it got international news coverage, that was the best. She cited an incident a few months earlier at Nangpa Pass. Near Mount Cho Oyu base camp in Tibet, the Chinese border patrol shot at a group of Tibetans escaping to Nepal at Nangpa Pass. Video footage shot by a European mountaineering team shows a line of figures climbing a steep, snow-covered mountain trail in single file when shots ring out and people fall to the ground. The Chinese government claimed the soldiers had acted in self-defense, but the Western witnesses testified that the Tibetans were actually running uphill, away from the shooters, and that they were unarmed and defenseless. "They were shooting the Tibetans like dogs," said one of the witnesses. The murdered victim was a nun; several others were injured. The footage was broadcast in the West and drew international criticism.

I asked if any particular spiritual practice helped her stay hopeful and optimistic.

"I believe in Buddhist philosophy. I took lay vows, Lam Rim vows, when I was forty-eight. My granddaughter died while I was in prison, my husband died, my son died. I think they all died for the sake of the country. I don't despair because His Holiness says he prays for all who died for the sake of Tibet. So I think they will have a good rebirth in a better place. My neighbors in Tibet used to say to me, 'You really manage well. If I were in your shoes, I'd go mad.'

"I'm not that worried," she continued. "Because when I first arrived, I had an audience with His Holiness. At another point, I requested a second audience and saw him a second time. All my family has worked for the Tibetan cause. He said he's grateful for all that my family has done. He's always very, very kind. Even yesterday, seeing me in the teachings as he walked in, he waved to me. Having received his blessing, I think that, whatever has happened to me or to my family, we have earned good merit."

I asked what she thought of the idea of autonomy. His Holiness advocated a kind of domestic autonomy within the larger Chinese nation.

"Whatever His Holiness says, I support. Because he is broad-minded, he sees long term. And he thinks not just for the benefit of Tibetan people but of Chinese people. There's not another world leader who is as broad-minded as he, who thinks of the welfare, the benefit of all people."

I asked what her best vision and her worst visions were of Tibet in the next fifteen or twenty years, given that China has hyperaccelerated its development and continues to push for rapid growth.

"I think one of these days there will be changes in the Chinese government, because many foreign countries recognize His Holiness as the leader of Tibet. They know the real situation between Tibet and China. Also many of the Chinese expatriates living outside of China are against the current government.

"The Chinese plan is to wait out the lifespan of His Holiness. Wait for him to pass away, then they will really finish off Tibet. When he dies, the situation in Tibet might get violent, like in Kham. Now the Dalai Lama advocates peaceful negotiation; that's why Tibetans are not using violence. If it weren't for him setting the course, people might engage in violence. If he was not around, they wouldn't listen to anyone. Many people would be killed. Tibetans and innocent Chinese in Tibet."

I confirmed with her that I would use the pseudonym Tsichoe Drolma for her in the book. We had agreed on it years back.

"Oh, you can write 'Sonam Choedron,'" she said.

I was taken aback.

"You can use my real name," she said. "I'm not going back to Tibet; I'm living in Australia."

I was shocked to hear those words coming from her mouth: "I'm not going back to Tibet." A dozen years ago, only the threat of death or prison had kept her from returning home.

"It's safe to use my real name now," she said.

So much had changed in these last few years, I thought.

Lobsang and I stood up and said good-bye. Shaking my hand good-bye, Sonam said, "Whatever you do for Tibet, I'll pray that it meets with success. You have been working so long, for so many years, for us Tibetans. It's very admirable. We owe you a great deal of thanks."

I was very touched. She said she'd like to get together again before I left town.

Former political prisoner Sonam Choedron, Dharamsala, 2007. In 1994, she had used a pseudonym and wanted no photos of herself taken, but after she emigrated legally from China, she authorized the use of her real name and photograph.

Lobsang and I walked to town and ordered some noodles in one of the greasy spoons tucked away off the street. You'd never know it was there. It was packed with locals, probably half of them monastics, and not a single *inji*, even though the town swarmed with them. Lobsang and I parted ways after our meal.

As I headed up the path, the piercing racket along the short, main street funneling through the tall buildings on each side rattled my nerves: booming disco from video parlors, caterwauling Hindi pop songs from shops, the blasting of truck horns, hammering, whining power tools, the screaming whistle of pressure cookers, humming generators, not to mention shouting voices. I was glad to get back to my guesthouse, though it wasn't quiet there either, as the building was right on the road. Below my room, vehicles and motorcycles constantly honked their horns to move pedestrians off their path. One heard traffic all day and night.

The trajectory of the Tibetan diaspora shot out all over the globe now, I thought. It used to be that Tibetans lived mostly in India and Nepal; then they'd settled in Switzerland starting around 1960. Canada and the States had populations as well. Though it seemed obvious that outspoken politically active Tibetans had to leave to avoid being killed or silenced, it was unnerving and sad to see Sonam exiled so far away. The country originally settled by prisoners now offered refuge to Tibet's political prisoners. When stalwarts like Sonam lived halfway around the world, then Tibetans had indeed, as the thirteenth Dalai Lama had prophesized, "scattered all over the world like ants."

Jigme and I had another talk out on the balcony. He was listening to the teachings every day on the radio, following along in the *paija*, the loose-leaf scripture book, rather than going to the temple.

"Ninety percent of the people here now," he said, "just care about easy pleasure." We looked out over town from the third-story balcony. "They have young minds. Young hearts. They could be developing more peaceful, secure minds, but they're not. The whole environment of the place has changed. The community is corroding from the inside."

He said that two foreigners had been killed this year, and a woman raped. Doing *kora* alone put you at risk of armed robbery; it had happened several times already. He called it "cultural pollution."

"Pollution of the mind . . . of the values. It came from tourism, from the greed from tourism. Drugs, crime, smuggling, political games. We are ripe here for organized crime.

"Pollution is growing—both in the environment, from all the motorbikes and taxis and cars—but also in people's natures. It's alarming. It's destroying our life. The majority of people have a strong sense of patriotism, of cultural identity, but the young people are distracted with the idea of going to the West. The place has changed so much. It's very heartbreaking. I feel helpless, embarrassed. I'm ashamed to say it, but it's true.

"We must study, we must educate our people. It is the only tool we have to gain back our country. Now they listen to the Dalai Lama give teachings, but it's just in one ear and out the other. Making money—like everyone's doing with more hotels and shops—is not going to bring back our country."

In his teachings, His Holiness had mentioned frivolous amusements, though not in those exact words. He said we had to use our precious human intelligence and consider the short- and long-term benefits of our actions. With this discernment, we'd then reject activities and pastimes that might have short-term benefits, but were actually harmful, and instead choose right actions springing from healthy desires, which carried long-term benefits.

"This generation can connect fast—with e-mail, with the Web," Jigme said. "They have more modern technology—video games, laptops, digital things—but those do not make a person happy. In fact, people have more inner confusion, more discontent. They have more computer know-how, but not deeper human understanding or judgment. This generation needs self-discipline, wisdom." The orange light drained from the sky.

"We must do something, because I feel that the time is coming for our collective karma to ripen."

I met with Sonam Choedron again a couple of days later, with Lobsang accompanying to translate. I had no questions, no agenda; it was a social visit. I brought her some pictures of Lhasa, about which she said little.

Over tea and pastries, she recalled the first time she had worn pants in Australia. She almost fell down, she said with a laugh. She stiffly swiveled her hips back and forth, imitating how she had toddled. She wanted to wear *chubas* in Australia, she recalled, but her son, who worked at a university in food service, warned that she would stand out too much. "You should wear pants," he told her.

He brought home a pair of pants for her one day, and she withdrew to another room to try them on. She felt very shy about being seen in them. After a long time, her son finally called out, "Come out and let me see!"

"I could hardly walk," she recalled with a laugh.

After she'd been in Australia a year, she told us, she and her son took a celebratory boat ride in Sydney Harbour. Gazing out on the water, in a reflective mood on her first anniversary there, he asked, "Are you happy here?"

"No . . . not really," she answered. "Are *you* happy?"

"No, not really," he replied.

"Isn't everything clean?" he asked, and she agreed that it was. "Very modern?" Again, she had agreed. "Everything works how it's supposed to? There is plenty of food and goods?" Yes to both.

"I don't know what exactly it is," he said, "but there is something missing living here."

"Hmm . . . ," she agreed. "I feel the same. There's just something . . . not quite . . . right."

She passes the time in Australia watching Chinese videos, she said. She likes the films with a moral message, the old ones, from before the Communists. She can watch hours of Chinese films, she said.

Her son teases her about it: "Our whole family was tortured by these people, and you want to watch their movies all day?!"

Lobsang and I laughed. I enjoyed Sonam's self-deprecating sense of humor.

I started to notice that Sonam could talk a blue streak. She was never at a loss for something to say. Our previous visits had been more formal because I had been interviewing her. Now she spoke naturally and, it seemed, almost ceaselessly. I had to interrupt to ask Lobsang to translate every few minutes. I also noticed she had perfect comic delivery.

Her son is a very compassionate person, she went on, but "not emotional," whereas she always spoke her mind. Sometimes her son urged: "Mother, don't say that. People will get upset." I wasn't sure here about Lobsang's translation of the word "emotional," but I got the general idea.

Once, in her ESL class, they had planned a big party. The students were supposed to bring foods from their native countries to share with everybody. Her classmates originated from Japan, Korea, China, Tibet, and other parts of the world. They were going to decorate the walls of the classroom with flags from all of their home nations. A Tibetan youth in her class said that he would hang the Tibetan flag. As the time for the event approached, he wavered. "The Chinese might get angry," he said.

"This is Australia, the Chinese don't have authority here!" she scolded him. "We're in a free country! We should tell people the *truth*! They should know that Tibet is an independent country!"

He was still afraid. She was the oldest Tibetan, and oldest student, in the class. She said she had rebuked this youth, an Amdo boy, before because he was always slouching, drinking beverages, being distracted when the teacher talked. She had insisted that he treat the teacher with more respect. When she said this, I could really see her as the mama of the others in her prison cell. Sonam had threatened that if he didn't hang the Tibetan flag, she would. Good to her word, she brought a Tibetan flag the day of the party and prevailed upon someone to hang it high up on the wall.

She joked about the new cultural forces in her life: "The next time you see me, I may speak English with an Australian accent." Lobsang cracked up.

"I'll have cut my hair short." More laughter. Traditionally, Tibetan women wore their hair very long. She tilted her torso side to side as if taking dainty steps. "I'll carry around a tiny little handbag!" Tibetan women carried big cloth shoulder bags. Lobsang and I both howled.

I noticed her charisma and charm for the first time. It was in her humor and keen powers of observation. I saw how she could draw people to her, influence others—her family members, the Chinese she came in contact with, the other Tibetan dissidents.

Lobsang told her I was finished with my work in town, except for delivering a package to His Holiness. She explained the trouble I was having finding a way to give the items directly to His Holiness as I'd promised the family.

Sonam had an idea: "He walks right by where I'm sitting. Sit with me there, and you can hand it to him."

"What about his bodyguards?" I asked. "They won't allow that."

Lobsang said, "If he himself stops to talk to you, they won't interfere."

I don't know, I thought. Tomorrow, Thursday, I was going to try and snag Chhime in the evening after the teachings. But even if I did manage by some miracle to talk to him, and he squeezed me into the schedule, it would have to be on Friday, because I was leaving Saturday. I'd have to see His Holiness on Friday evening after the teaching, a narrow frame of opportunity. But Friday evening would also be my last chance to get photos of Mrs. Namseling and Sonam Choedron, using some volunteer photographers I'd recruited.

"Meet me tomorrow morning at the temple at eight," Sonam said.

"This way," Lobsang added, "you don't need to ask the Private Office for an audience. Just tell them you're going to give him the gift as he walks by."

It sounded like a long shot to me, but I agreed.

The next morning, a few minutes after eight, I arrived at the temple. The Tibetan section was already full, with thousands of people seated on the ground. Sonam Choedron—in a spot about sixty feet from His Holiness's throne, near the center-left railing—was standing up facing the back, where the Westerners entered, so I'd be able to see her easily. Mrs. Namseling was right next to her on the aisle side of the railing.

I was amazed. I hadn't even known they knew each other, and now here were two of my favorite women together. I wished I had my camera. They greeted me very animatedly, delighted to see me. Mrs. Namseling told me to sit right in front of her, so that I'd be right on the pathway where His Holiness walked. I sat down and tucked my legs in close.

I reached into my black shoulder bag and took out Amala's gift, a tan plastic bag with cut-outs for a handle. The garments were neatly folded inside, wrapped in white paper. I demonstrated how I would hand it to His Holiness—extending it out to him holding the plastic bag by its handle. A roar of exclamations, hand slaps, and mock shameful looks erupted.

"Mindu, mindu," they shook their heads. No! That's not right! That's not the way to do it!

Mrs. Namseling took the bag. She peeked inside and carefully tugged on the garments. She stacked them like stairsteps: the goldenrod one on top; the orange one under it, a little farther out; and the plum-colored one, a heavier piece, on the bottom. It was the first time I'd ever seen Amala's gift—the vivid colors and shimmering textures were absolutely stunning. They certainly would catch his eye. Sonam commented and coached the whole time. Mrs. Namseling put the letter from Pala, folded in thirds, on top of the garments, sticking out of the front edge of the bag about three inches. Bowing her head slightly, she lifted the package in her upturned palms in front of her.

"Yes, that's it," Sonam said, nodding encouragingly. She raised her hands up and tilted her chin down the same way, holding the posture a long, still moment. She gestured in front of her mouth, fingers spraying forward.

"Inji, inji," she said. "English. Speak English," she meant. She nodded at me and repeated the gesture, her fingers flicking like a flower bursting open.

"La, la," Mrs. Namseling chimed in, in agreement. "Inji. Inji."

I took the package and mimicked what she'd done. "That's right," they both said. All the people around us looked on. The point was to get his attention, and calling out in English from a section of mostly elderly Tibetans would do just that.

"And now . . . inji. Inji," they called.

"Okay, okay," I said. I'll work on that, I thought.

I waited with the package in my lap. Every minute or so, I'd practice raising it up in front of me and simultaneously tucking my chin down. "This is from the Nyima family in Lhasa," I rehearsed in my head, "who saved your robes from the Norbulingka for fifty years." Everything I was supposed to say I had to condense into a few seconds.

"No, no," they exclaimed behind me. Mrs. Namseling, who was closest to me, took the package again. She held it against her chest with both hands, like a student with books or a mother clasping a newborn. "When Kundun comes, then lift it up."

"Okay," I said, watching carefully and noting her movements.

Sonam nodded emphatically, in full agreement. They gestured with their fingers near their mouth: "Inji, inji," they said. I always forgot. I had to yell out in English.

Security guards came by and gruffly pressed the crowd back against the railing to restore a clear aisle, maybe six feet wide. Now I was practically sitting in Mrs. Namseling's lap. She was a tiny woman—I was afraid I'd crush her bones, but she said it was fine.

We had a good hour until the teachings started. An auburn-haired European woman in the Tibetan section said prayers loudly in Russian-accented Tibetan.

"Excuse me! *Excuse* me! Hal-*lo*! Excuse me!" I practiced using different inflections of my voice to flag him down. Then I'd say, "This is from the Nyima family in Lhasa who saved your robes from the Norbulingka for fifty years. You met them in Toronto in 2003"—everything Tashi had told me to say.

I could cut out the fifty years—he knows how many years it's been, I thought. I started again: "This is from the . . . you met them in . . . 2003." Oh, what the heck, I could cut out all references to time. "This is from the Nyima family in Lhasa who saved your robes."

No, he'll *see* the robes, I thought; I didn't have to say "robes." "A Lhasa family saved these from the Norbulingka. You met them in Toronto."

After forty minutes had passed, I saw two men at the far end of the aisle, by the Palace, the residence of the Dalai Lama, bent over a log-shaped object. When they got nearer, I saw that they were rolling a red carpet down the aisle, and a minute later, they rolled it right in front of me.

My stomach turned somersaults as the time neared. It churned and flipped, rumbled and flipped some more, alive with nervousness.

A few minutes before nine thirty, security officials came down the aisle. I was clutching the bag to my chest.

"Put that away!" a security man growled in English.

I stuffed the gift into my black shoulder bag. When he was out of sight, I turned around and gave my friends a look: "Now what?"

Sonam and Namseling whispered, raising their upturned hands like before.

"Hold it out! Do like before!" Sonam straightened her spine and puffed out her chest, coaching me to speak out, to be bold. They nodded vigorously, like third-base coaches boosting the winning run on third. "Inji!" they hissed loudly.

I nodded. I knew the plan, but I couldn't just flag him down like a cabbie: "Yo! Dalai!"

Suddenly, he emerged. He was walking fast toward us. I bowed my head into my chest. That only seemed to push my voice farther down my throat. I think it was down near my belly button. The entire audience of ten thousand people sat motionless, reverent, silent. I tried to bring up a sound. But the closer he came, the farther away my voice sank. I think it was down near my kneecaps.

He swept down the aisle, his posture slightly more hunched than when I'd seen him two years ago. He moved at a good clip, security men winging him. He smiled and acknowledged people on both sides with a small wave. Then he was gone.

Suddenly, there was a tremendous commotion. The woman on my left tapped me on the knee. She pointed up the aisle toward the front. Dozens of people hastened along the carpet, moving closer to the front and sitting down. None of those around me seemed to be moving, but I made a split-second decision: I grabbed my things and ran forward.

I looked back but couldn't see my ladies. Sonam was on the other side of the railing and couldn't move, and Mrs. Namseling was not that mobile. I settled in quickly because the Dalai Lama was already speaking from his tall throne chair about forty feet in front of me. His lecture centered on the subjects of patience and anger.

Try never to give in to the power of anger, he said, in every action, small or large. Otherwise, the natural clear state of the mind could be obscured. One's wholesome deeds over thousands of eons could be destroyed in a moment of anger. There was no transgression like anger, no virtue like patience.

Later, he referred to the fourteen Tibetans whom the Chinese had recently arrested in Lhasa during Losar. They had apparently been set up and were hauled away by the Public Security Bureau. I hadn't heard about it. He said we had to make supplications to Avalokiteshvara to generate the motivation to release all afflictive emotions around the incident. We had to distinguish between the actor and the actions. When you lead a life free of afflictive emotions, he said, your life will be peaceful.

An hour or more into the teachings, my mind felt spacious and forgiving. I imagined that the thief needed my camera to feed the hungry mouths of his large family; I wished that he would not accumulate too much bad karma for his actions. The power of the teaching had led me into a completely different state of mind—peaceful, grateful, open-hearted.

We were saying closing prayers before breaking for lunch when, all of a sudden, as if on cue, the people around me scattered. The aisle cleared instantaneously; I'd never seen Tibetans move so fast. I was practically alone on the red carpet. I jammed the radio into a pocket, shut my pencil in my notebook, stuffed the notebook into my shoulder bag, and swiped the scarf and jacket I'd been sitting on off the ground. I had to chase after my water bottle, which had been kicked and had rolled a distance behind me. I sprinted down the red carpet, half my stuff in my hands, the earphone dangling from my ear.

Solid crowds lined both sides of the aisle. I scurried thirty feet back to where the railing stopped and the *injis* were sitting. When I tried to pull over, an outcry rose. I scuttled back a few feet more and stopped again, but another collective cry burst out. His Holiness was coming. I had to get out of the way. My belongings were dripping from my arms, my ear, my shoulder bag. I felt like Pigpen. I hastened along down the aisle. Every time I so much as paused to *think* about stopping and getting myself together, a hailstorm of protest in dozens of languages and accents erupted. The tone said it all: Down in front! No room here! Move on! Get back!

I sprang back another few feet. A large wrought iron gate opened out so that the crowd on the right was sitting behind it. I slid behind it. Still, every bit of ground was occupied. About six or seven feet back, nearly at the building, I saw a patch of worn asphalt. An old Tibetan man sat leaning against the wall, *mala* wrapped around his hand, deeply peaceful, almost as if in a trance. He gestured at the tiny spot with his rosary-wrapped hand. "Here. Sit here."

Before I could even bend my knees, a crowd of people swarmed by on the other side of the gate. Red-robed older monks, Tibetan officials, a few well-tailored Indians, the women in colorful saris, and a few Tibetan women in fine *chubas* scurried through the gates.

Then, *whoosh*—the gate snapped closed.

The crowd stirred noisily, as if people had been holding their breath before and now finally released it. No wonder the mood of the crowd was so tense. His Holiness was mere steps behind me. I looked through the gate up the path inside the palace, but there was no trace of his figure, just a couple dozen people milling about.

Then I saw him! Saw his profile. He turned away, looking toward the palace, his back to me. He was alone for a split second, not in conversation, not moving. No one was around him. He wore a charcoal gray *chuba* on his medium frame. It was Tenzin Geyche! Three feet away.

"Tenzin Geyche," I called through the iron gate.

He turned.

"Oh hello!" he responded, surprised, and then pleased.

"Hello! Tashi delek," I said, smiling. He looked very well, albeit older. As I saw him, I remembered how much I liked and respected him. I held out the package.

"Here is the present," I said, opening the bag and showing him the richly colored robes inside.

I pulled out Pala's letter. I unfolded it, and held it on top of the package facing him. He began to read. Pala's Tibetan script on the page was gorgeous, like flowing water. He looked up.

"Yes, I'm sorry," he said. I gathered he was apologizing for not being able to get back to me personally.

"That's okay," I said.

I passed the whole package through the wide gap in the gate's curlicued design.

I explained about the Nyima family: the aunt who had saved the robes, the antique silk robe perhaps of the thirteenth Dalai Lama, and about Amala sewing him a new shirt. I groped around for a snapshot of the family I had put in my jacket pocket that morning. I had taken the picture in Lhasa last month.

"Here they are," I said, looking at the photo, bathed in warm orange tones, my favorite picture of the family. They were seated on the balcony in front of one of Pala's door carvings. Middle sister was wearing the traditional fox fur hat, as it had been cold that morning, the morning we set the new prayer flags on the roof.

"These two daughters are in Canada." I explained. "This one teaches Tibetan language at a university. This one works in health care."

Tenzin Geyche nodded and murmured approvingly.

"They met His Holiness in Toronto in 2003."

He took the photograph and put it on top of the letter. We chatted a bit.

"I'm going in now; I'll take it to him."

"Oh!" I said, suddenly remembering. "Could I get a receipt?"

He nodded.

I pulled out the note I had written him earlier. It didn't have my address so I hurriedly jotted it down. "Oh! And two prayer beads," I added, explaining briefly about Pala's illness and the extra bead for the aunt.

"Sure, sure," he said, his manner as gracious and warm as I'd remembered it to be. "I'm sorry," he said again, about the audience.

"I understand. I do. Thank you."

"No. Thank *you*," he said.

I could feel he had to leave and didn't want to detain him. "It's wonderful to see you," I said.

He lifted the package toward the palace behind him. "I'm going right now," he smiled.

"Good-bye."

"Good-bye."

What an amazing turn of events, I thought, walking home, back to town. I felt dazed and lighter than I had in days—no, *weeks*. I hadn't been successful with all the attempts I'd made in four days—going to his residence, to the reception office, to the Security Office, going at night, in the afternoon, in the morning—and then suddenly, I was in the right place at the right time to see the exact man I needed to talk to.

All my tasks in Dharamsala were accomplished.

An American from Maine whom I had met earlier in the week helped take photos of Mrs. Namseling for me that evening. She snapped some images while I told Mrs. Namseling the exciting conclusion of our scheme that morning, using mime and the few Tibetan words I knew—terms like *joo-kiyin*, which means "going"; *mindu*, meaning "is not" or "doesn't exist"; and *ma rey*, meaning "don't have."

I walked diagonally across her small studio, imitating His Holiness hurtling up the aisle. I didn't know how to say: "He walked by so fast I didn't have time to get his attention," so I just said, "Kali mindu"—Slowly it was not. Mrs. Namseling howled with laughter.

A Tibetan friend from the Bay Area took pictures of Sonam Choedron for me. Sonam gave me some blessing pills—Tibetan herbal medicine that had been blessed by the Dalai Lama—for my journey home. She gave me a 'Save Tibet' T-shirt. "I considered buying you a *chuba*," she said, "but thought it was too bulky to carry."

I was so glad to have had this delightful and unexpected experience with Sonam and Mrs. Namseling. It had given me a chance to see how much fun they both were, what good company, and get to know them beyond a formal interview.

That evening, looking at the soft golden light hitting the hills of the town, I thought that people could build a million guesthouses here and I'd always love this place, love the snow-shrouded, enduring presence of the mountains. I wondered, If the Tibetans didn't have this place, if India had not extended them hospitality, where would they be? I felt great gratitude to the government of India.

On my last day in town, the morning of March 10, thunder cracked the air and driving rain exploded from the skies. Winds howled and whipped through town. After six days of unusually exquisite weather—sunny blue skies—the weather suddenly and dramatically turned. I had to pack, clean, and take care of last-minute business, so I did not attend the ceremony at the temple.

I paid up my bill at the guesthouse and talked with Jigme again.

"I had a good visit," I said, "except for the camera theft."

"Canyon-la, this event removed obstacles from your path," he said.

"What do you mean?"

"There was an obstacle. An obstacle to your physical body or to your career aims or something, and this event cleared it away. This is how we Tibetans believe. For instance, if your bus had a problem, or something happened to a family member, or someone necessary to help you was not there—in these cases, having a camera would not help you."

"Yes? And so?"

"So you lost the camera to clear the obstacle."

He had to explain it three times before I understood. I figured it was a kind of switch out: We'll take this small sacrifice in exchange for smooth sailing. Something like the Chinese belief that, for instance, if you broke your jade piece, it didn't mean bad luck—the breakage protected you from a larger harm, because the jade took the hit.

"So you mean to say, this theft made my safety and success on my trip possible?"

"Exactly," he said.

I *had* been successful, I thought, and for that I was grateful. Long ago I had started this project with many questions: What were women's experiences, and how were they different than those of men? What role had faith played in their surviving the brutal circumstances of the last fifty years? What was our spiritual legacy from them?

I had learned that women, like all Tibetans, had suffered greatly through harrowing circumstances and long, bitter years that hundreds of thousands did not survive: driven to near death in labor camps, imprisoned in abysmal conditions, subjected to starvation, beatings, torture. But part of *how* they had suffered was particular to their being women, was linked to the status of women in their society.

Mrs. Namseling, merely a child when she was involuntarily married to a powerful man in government, had been left with their six children when he escaped. In this monastic-dominated society, men alone ran the government, and that government had left on a moment's notice under circumstances of such chaos, confusion, and peril that families, wives, and personal lives were ancillary. In the case of Mrs. Paljorkhyimsar, her entire experience after the invasion, the reason she had suffered for twenty years in the gulag, was formed by the fact that the *rinpoche*, whom her husband thought to save alongside his family, vigorously objected to traveling with women. A high monk trumped one's own wife.

But part of *how* they survived was also particular to their being women.

In prison, Sonam Choedron, coming off a year alone in an underground cell, rallied her cell mates. They talked and communicated even when they were forbidden to do so. They shouted out their convictions even when they suffered for it—left in wet clothes to freeze in the snow for days. They created their own inside jokes, kept their dharma practice alive, and taught one another to read.

This had been exactly the situation in the World War II concentration camps I'd read about. From studies of the gender-segregated groups in the camps, researchers learned about differences in how men and women survived. The women re-created family groups and gave mutual aid; they engaged in stealthy long-term resistance efforts that required patience and were often conducted behind the scenes. The men were not able to reach out emotionally in the same way; their acts of resistance tended toward splashy public acts that they hoped would yield quick results, blowing up the crematorium, for instance. These however created a backlash. In the Vietnam War, it was the same: Vietnamese women ferried supplies and weapons while posing as farmers going to market and gathered intelligence while posing as laundresses and maids in the U.S. military base.

Social scientists dubbed this response in women "tend and befriend," since they had found that "fight or flight" applied only to men. They also found that in times of disaster, a disproportionate burden fell on women.

In Hurricane Katrina, 75–80 percent of the survivors were women. In the 2004 tsunami in Southeast Asia, which cost more than three hundred thousand lives, the death rate for women averaged three to four times that of men. Of those killed in wars, 80 percent were women and children. The public invisibility of these lopsided numbers had to be attributed, wrote one researcher, to the predominantly male- and white-run media, which simply did not notice the gendered dimensions of these statistics, even for cases, like Katrina, in which the racial dimensions were obvious.

Had women suffered disproportionately in Tibet?

Some sources give indications of an answer. Of the approximately seventy thousand who fled Tibet for India in 1959–60, five thousand to seven thousand were monks, mostly high-ranking monks and scholars. And according to a high-level official in the government-in-exile, most of those who escaped in the first year or two were men; only in later years did intact family groups flee.

Another source, attempting to discuss the magnitude of loss of life among the all-male resistance forces in eastern Tibet, cites the disproportionate number of women seen plowing in eastern and northeastern Tibet in the 1970s, a traditionally male farming chore. Chinese government census figures of the time also show a large ratio of women to men in the population.

But verifiable numbers regarding the Tibetans in Chinese-occupied Tibet are impossible to obtain. When we do not even have accurate figures on how many protesters the government killed in Tiananmen Square in 1989, what were the chances of finding precise statistics, broken down by gender, about an extremely sensitive issue like Tibet, going back fifty years?

Around five thirty in the evening, I wheeled my luggage to the bus stand outside town to catch my overnight bus to Delhi. The storm had finally passed—the roads had dried and the skies had cleared. People had ventured out onto the street again. After a few minutes, Lobsang and Sonam Choedron arrived. They had come to see me off. They stood on the edge of the twisting mountain road, the tall dark pine trees of the forest behind them.

"How was the ceremony?" I asked Sonam.

She didn't answer for a moment.

"I cried," Sonam said. She drew her index finger from her lower eyelid down her cheek. "Because this is the day we lost our country." She blinked up at the trees. "And many Tibetans lost their lives."

She said when she had heard the student band from TCV play the Tibetan national anthem, the flutes and the drum corps led by a tiger-skin-clad drum major—she lurched forward suddenly as if taking a blow—that it had hit her "right in the stomach." She stood bent, one hand on her chest as if to keep from doubling over, the other hand protectively touching her stomach.

"It took great effort to hold myself up and stand through the end of the anthem. Otherwise I would have doubled over. I felt so incredibly sad, so anguished, so moved . . . So many things," she said.

"And seeing His Holiness standing there in front, with the anthem play-
ing . . ." She shook her head, at a loss for words. "I felt so much." After a
long moment, she glanced at the overcast sky above. "It was like the *whole
sky* cried, too."

I saw the rain dripping from the tree branches. I could feel it as she
recalled it: What is it called when you can see and hear the last vestiges of
your country as it slips through your fingers? When what remains brings
home the fact of how much you have lost? That His Holiness could bear
that and stand before them and continue to lead astonished me.

Lobsang and Sonam each laid a *khata* around my neck to say good-bye.
I stood with them at the edge of the narrow road as long as I could before I
had to board. From my berth in the bus, I looked back a few minutes later
and saw Sonam chewing out a skinny Indian youth standing next to her,
tucking her chin down and eyeing him sternly. I couldn't imagine where
he had come from or what he had done, but now he was going to hear from
the eternal matriarch about it. Not the nurturing earth mother, but the
fearless mother of tough love.

I missed McLeod Ganj mere hours after I left. Not the nerve-jangling,
crowded, noisy town, but the place it represented. The refuge it offered
Tibetans and Tibetan culture. I missed being with the Tibetans. Behind
all that mess, the Tibetan people still had the true Tibetan character—full
of generosity and heart.

I missed Tibet as I had first seen it and breathed it in 1986. Its soaring
peaks, massive sparkling blue skies, crisp pungent air, and luminous people. That Tibet, I thought, is *mindu. Ma rey* Is not. Don't have.

Lhasa was worse than ever, worse than I had even heard or read about.
Worse than I had imagined. And slated for more of the same. The Tibetan
struggle would continue, despite the mining, the burying of the Tibetans
beneath a mountain of Chinese people, despite China's bids for legitimi-
zation, with the Olympics and so on. The Tibetan struggle would continue
to gain the support and sympathy of the world. But as His Holiness said in
the teachings: What's done cannot be undone. What has happened cannot

be turned back. What is the use of holding hatred or holding attachment if, when we leave this world, we take nothing with us? *Mindu.*

For the rise of bodhicitta, the practice of patience is very important. Patience is the most powerful antidote to anger. Refuse to give any power to anger. Make a commitment: I will not allow myself to be defiled by mental pain and by the suffering of anger.

If you reflect on the thousands of causes and conditions underlying an event, you realize there is no target for blame and no possibility to undo what has happened. You will see that the offensive person is not to blame; it is the angry states that propelled him to act. Reacting in anger only contributes to the decline of our virtue.

There is nothing we can gain by dwelling on the event; our peace of mind can only be destroyed, our balance upset. Avoid casting the mind to the past, to memories. And avoid casting it to the future—to anticipation or expectation. Instead, counter negatives actions of others through skillful means and through compassion.

The act of refraining from injuring the heart of your enemies can result in favorable rebirth, long life, benefactors, and friends. The act of refraining from harming those who have harmed you can give rise to full enlightenment.

In my darkened berth on the jangling bus, riding through India at two in the morning, a torrent of thoughts poured through my mind: A memory rose up from many years ago, almost twenty years earlier. I had visited an astrologer. I was a full-time activist for Tibet, flush with both hope and uncertainty.

"Tibet is a place without borders," he said.

I didn't understand. Thinking he was referring to Tibet, the physical place, I asked him to clarify. Then asked again. And once more.

"Tibet," he repeated, "is a state of mind."

I finally grasped that "Tibet" (in quotation marks) is what he meant. Not Tibet the physical land or the political nation.

It dawned on me, after many days of sitting through His Holiness's teachings on bodhisattva training, that hospitality is the way Tibetans show their compassion for all beings. What human does not have thirst or hunger? A ninety-year-old woman with rheumy eyes and three teeth, who was starved and worked to within an inch of her life for two decades and really does not remember meeting me, can wheeze, "Choe," as I sit beside her. Drink. Have tea, eat well. The sisters in Lhasa had unfailingly kept my teacup and the cups of all their guests topped off. Even of the railroad head, the sister had said, "He is our guest, so we must be hospitable." Their culture taught them to treat others with dignity and respect, with courtesy and consideration.

I thought of my Tibetan friend from the Bay Area who had helped me take photographs of Sonam. He had been so excited to find knit caps in town with a "Free Tibet" image knit right into the fibers. When the cap was worn, the blue and red rays blazing from a yellow globe of sun beamed across the person's forehead, rising up behind a snowy mastiff. He wanted to buy a lot of them, he said, and take them back to the Bay Area to sell.

The phrase "Free Tibet" is, I think, both a call to action (if one reads "Free" as a verb) and a vision (if one reads "Free" as an adjective).

After six days of teachings, what I hear in the hundreds of verses is simply: Clean your heart. Keep your heart clean. Keep the vision. Be free.

With its insistence on refusing to injure others, or to harbor anger, the Tibetan struggle in the modern geopolitical landscape has moved at glacial slowness compared to most modern political struggles. But if the Dalai Lama could forgive the Chinese, if Sonam Choedron could joke about them after they had imprisoned her and killed her family, if Mrs. Namseling could become philosophical about changes to Dharamsala, then I could lay down my hatred of the Chinese leadership. And I could certainly forgive the thief who had taken my camera.

Two weeks later, at my artist's residency in the United States, I had a dream. I was raising a baby. She was Tibetan, and I was committed to raising her as an upstanding Tibetan, my way of contributing to a continuation of the culture. In my waking hours, I pondered how I might be able to fit a child into my life and how I could give her a culture that wasn't mine.

The next night, I dreamed again. The baby grew up, got older and older until I felt her energy as an adult. She had all the positive qualities I associated with a traditional Tibetan—present in mind and heart, good-humored, kind, patient, intelligent. I felt pleased with who she was, who she had become.

Wait, I thought, in the dream. That's who I am. At my best, I was that person. I didn't have to adopt a baby or spend two decades raising her, I just had to watch my own mind, maintain self-awareness.

Maybe the dream "baby," I thought, represented legacy. What is passed to me and what I leave to the world. The essence of what I had learned from the women's lives. My spiritual legacy. The baby represented the potential, and the adult the fulfillment.

For a long time, whenever I allowed myself to think about Lhasa, about what I had seen there, I was still horrified. Outraged and saddened. It was a nightmare. I reminded myself that I had to be the student. The disciple. Again and again, I had to tell myself: Clean your heart. Keep the vision. "Tibet" is a state of mind.

EPILOGUE

THE PRAYER BEADS. Two days into my artist's residency in Virginia, I received an e-mail from the Private Office of the Dalai Lama saying that the beads were at the Security Office for me to pick up. Since I was already back in the States, I asked the American who'd helped me take photos in Dharamsala to pick them up, knowing she was leaving India the next day and returning to Maine. I asked that she send them directly to Tashi in Canada by overnight mail. "Did you receive two beads?" I asked Tashi a few days later by phone, thinking we'd be lucky to have gotten one bead from the Dalai Lama's personal rosary. Maybe instead he had sent some symbolic beads, or a note saying we'll send you prayers, but no beads. I had thought it was a lot to ask him to take apart his mala. "You know what he sent?" Tashi replied. I could not tell from her tone if it was good news or bad news. "He sent his whole *mala*."

Sonam Choedron. A month after I'd seen her, Sonam Choedron wrote to me from Australia and said she had to go to France because her youngest daughter had passed away.

Mrs. Taring. Yangchen, the youngest daughter of Mrs. Taring, who now lives in Seattle, told me the circumstances of her mother's passing in July 2000, six years after the visit described in this book. Mrs. Taring waited years for the Tibetan translation of her book, *Daughter of Tibet*, which she had written in English. Unfortunately, she was disappointed with the results. She decided she had to take on the job of translating the lengthy text herself. She spent more than a year working on the Tibetan-language version and, a week after completing it, at age ninety, passed away of a heart attack. Her family, daughters, grandchildren, and great-grandchildren reside all over the world.

Lhasa. The year of my visit, 2007, four million Chinese tourists flowed into Tibet, mainly during the tourist season, from May to October.

A year later, in March 2008, riots broke out in Lhasa and spread throughout ethnic Tibet. Nearly a hundred protests took place over the next several weeks, and 80 percent of the protests occurred in eastern Tibet, outside the TAR, which China does not recognize as Tibet. Most involved rural communities of farmers and nomads. It was the worst unrest in Tibet in forty years. Chinese internal reports estimated that some thirty thousand Tibetans participated.

The Tibetan government-in-exile claims that 203 Tibetans were shot dead and estimates that from 2,200 to 5,700 were detained. In Lhasa, about a thousand Chinese-owned shops were set on fire. The PRC government expelled journalists and tourists, phone communication was cut, and Tibet again fell behind China's ice curtain. (Tashi and Lhakyi were unable to get through by phone to their family in Lhasa for months.) The Chinese government portrayed the riots as unprovoked attacks and killings of Chinese civilians by Tibetan nationalists.

Beijing Olympic Games. Various groups around the world used the occasion of the international torch run for the Beijing Summer Olympics to spotlight China's human rights record and its oppression in Tibet. After a tightly controlled torch relay passed through Lhasa, Tibetan Communist Party chief Zhang Qingli was quoted as saying: "To bring more glory to the Olympic spirit, we should firmly smash the plots to ruin the Beijing Olympic Games by the Dalai [Lama] clique and hostile foreign forces inside and outside of the nation." Human rights groups and government critics also accused Chinese authorities of exaggerating or fabricating threats to the Games in order to justify their repression.

Sky Train. China had planned to institute new luxury trains in summer 2008 along the Beijing-Lhasa route, replete with bilingual butler service, private suites, and a décor promising "to create a sense of harmony with the passing landscape" at the cost of $1,000 a day. Tibet tourism chief Wang Songping earlier had predicted an all-time high of five million visitors in 2008, but Beijing suspended all foreign tourism in Tibet after its March crackdown.

Mrs. Paljorkhyimsar. Mrs. Paljorkhyimsar passed away peacefully in November 2008. She was sitting upright—a very positive sign, according to Tibetans. After three days and nights of monks saying prayers for her in her home, she was taken for sky burial. It was snowing that day, also considered an auspicious sign.

Mrs. Namseling. Mrs. Namseling lives peacefully in Dharamsala.

United States and China. As this book goes into production, in spring 2009, the United States has a new president and its economy has gone into a tailspin of indeterminate length. China's economic engine, previously pushed to astonishing rates of annual growth and inextricably tied to the U.S. economy, has choked; 22 million workers have been laid off. With this dire state of world affairs, the United States urgently needs China's support and seeks to develop China as its most significant foreign partner. In February 2009, Hillary Clinton, visiting China in her first official trip as Secretary of State, stated that American concern over China's human rights violations would not stand in the way of fostering that partnership.

March 10th Uprising. Tibet marked fifty years in exile this spring, with the fiftieth anniversary of the March 10, 1959, Tibetan National Uprising Day, the event referred to at the beginning and end of this book. Tibetans declined to celebrate Losar in protest of the brutal handling of Tibetan demonstrators from last March, when hundreds were killed and thousands imprisoned. For the 50th anniversary, China clamped down on the entire Tibetan region, blanketing it with thousands of military troops and armored tanks, ordering a total news blackout, and banning journalists and tourists. The Dalai Lama in his annual state-of-the-union address couched the situation in uncharacteristically bleak terms, declaring that the Chinese government has made life "hell on Earth" for Tibetans during the last half-century and that the Tibetan religion, culture, language, and identity were "nearing extinction."

NOTES

INTRODUCTION

p. 3 *decisive and violent invasion* Jung Chang and Jon Holliday, *Mao: The Unknown Story* (New York: Knopf, 2005), 454.

p. 3 *eighty-seven thousand Tibetans were "eliminated"* From a booklet, marked "secret," about the aftermath of the Lhasa uprising, published in Lhasa on October 1, 1960, by the political department of the Tibetan Military District. Jamyang Norbu, *Resistance and Reform in Tibet*, ed. Robert Barnett (Bloomington: Indiana University Press, 1994), 189.

p. 4 *offerings from the community* Monasteries sustained themselves largely on offerings from the faithful. Tibetans, even those who were materially poor, offered respect to temples in the form of cash donations. Religion and culture were completely interwoven in pre-1950 society, and Tibetans believed that offering alms to monks and monasteries earned one spiritual merit. The three largest capital-based monasteries especially, Drepung, Sera, and Ganden, were extremely wealthy from the accumulation of offerings over centuries. Their resources were such that they were the largest source of loans to the public.

p. 5 *The 1960s and 1970s brought tremendous suffering* Almost the entire Tibetan army and many others were arrested and dispatched to labor camps in various parts of Tibet, where they worked building hydroelectric plants and in mining and logging. Besides being sources of cheap labor, the camps were also sites for ideological indoctrination. Hundreds died as a result of the extremely poor conditions. There are no exact figures for the number of dead; many Tibetans simply never returned home and became "disappeared." Tsering Shakya, *Dragon in the Land of Snows* (New York: Penguin, 1999), 245.

p. 5   *the Big Destruction*   June Chang and Jon Holliday, *Mao: The Unknown Story* (New York: Knopf, 2005), 456.

p. 5   *first Tibetan woman to speak and write English*   This biographical note is from the front flap of Mrs. Taring's book *Daughter of Tibet* (London: Wisdom Publications, 1986).

p. 7   *Demonstrations in 1987–89*   Robert Barnett, "Thunder from Tibet," review of *The Open Road,* by Pico Iyer, *New York Review of Books,* May 29, 2008.

p. 7   *Third Tibet Work Forum*   Melvyn Goldstein, *The Snow Lion and the Dragon* (Berkeley: University of California Press, 1997), 93. This is also translated by some scholars as the Third Tibet Work Conference.

p. 7   *in search of mineral, oil, and geothermal wealth*   John Avedon, *In Exile from the Land of Snows* (New York: Knopf, 1984), 326.

CHAPTER 1. SKY TRAIN

p. 13   *only a couple thousand foreigners had ever set eyes on the holy city of Lhasa*   The 1904 British-mounted invasion led by Francis Younghusband consisted of five officers and seven hundred troops. Tsepon W. D. Shakabpa, *Tibet: A Political History* (New York: Potala Publications, 1984), 206. Also see the chapter "Quest of the West" in anthropologist Françoise Pommaret's *Tibet: An Enduring Civilization* (London: Harry N. Abrams, 2002), 77–99. In the autumn of 1985, the Chinese government officially moved Tibet from the closed to the open list of tourist destinations, which allowed foreigners to visit with a tourist visa. Before that, special permits were required and few foreigners were allowed in. (The boss of an acquaintance visited Tibet around 1984 on an organized tour that cost $10,000. I also talked to someone who had sneaked in by hitchhiking with a Tibetan driver in August 1985; she had to hide under the seat every time they passed a Chinese army truck.)

p. 16   *brutal destruction of the culture and people*   Avedon may have worked with the numbers from the Tibetan government-in-exile. The Tibetan Parliament-in-exile, in its document "Gross Violation of Basic Human Rights under Illegal Occupation of P.R.C." (www.tibet.net), claims that more than a million Tibetans died from unnatural causes between 1951 and 1976 as a result of China's invasion and Chinese Communist Party (CCP) policies. The deaths are categorized by each of the three regions of Tibet—Central (U Tsang), Kham, and Amdo—and by mode of death: those killed in (resistance) fighting; those killed through torture, starvation, execution, and political "struggle"; and those driven to suicide. John Avedon, *In Exile from the Land of Snows* (New York: Knopf, 1984).

Robert Barnett claims, however, that verifiable figures do not exist. He cites a 2000 estimate from an Australian-Chinese demographer who estimated that the number of "missing" in the twenty-year period spanning the 1950s to the 1970s could be placed as high as 768,000, including the 70,000 or so who fled to India, or as low as 152,000. Robert Barnett, "Question 22: On the Number of Tibetans Killed," in *Authenticating Tibet: Answers to China's 100 Questions*, ed. Anne-Marie Blondeau and Katia Buffetrille (Berkeley: University of California Press, 2008), 89.

p. 22   *the Chinese treated the Tibetans "like enemies."*   June Chang and Jon Holliday, *Mao: The Unknown Story* (New York: Knopf, 2005), 456.

p. 22   *travel articles*   John Flinn, "High Train to Tibet," *San Francisco Chronicle*, travel section, November 5, 2006; Pankaj Mishra, "The Train to Tibet," *New Yorker*, April 16, 2007, 82; David Swanson, "New Tickets to Ride," *National Geographic Traveler*, July/August, 2005, 18.

p. 25   *images of Lhasa from the last time I'd been there*   The Chinese government imposed martial law in Tibet on March 8, 1989. On May 1, 1990, Premier Li Peng signed a state Council order ending fourteen months of military rule. A representative of the Dalai Lama in New Delhi welcomed the decision but called it more of a "public relations effort by the Chinese regime" in light of the eminent June 3 deadline for U.S. president George H. W. Bush to decide whether or not to renew China's most-favored-nation trading status. Anne S. Tyson, "Lifting of Martial Law in Tibet May Not Ease Persecution," *Christian Science Monitor*, May 2, 1990. Amnesty International wrote in a 1991 report that "police and security forces retained extensive powers of arbitrary arrest and detention without trial," such that martial law existed in all but name. The martial law decree is available at www.tibetjustice.org/materials/china/china7.html.

"All manifestation (i.e., demonstrations and political dissent) of dissatisfaction with Chinese rule, whether peacefully conducted or otherwise, are viewed by authorities as constituting 'illegal separatist activity,' and those who have led or participated in them have been punished with escalating force and severity. Merciless repression remains, in Tibet, the order of the day." "Merciless Repression: Human Rights in Tibet," *Asia Watch*, Washington, D.C., May 1990.

CHAPTER 2. MORNING ON THE CHANGTANG

p. 33 *the bridge structure had completely collapsed* By late July 2006, mere weeks after the train line had opened, the foundations of the support towers had already begun sinking into the permafrost. Railway minister Wang Yongping told Beijing News that sections of the track and supporting concrete pillars had already cracked. John Flinn, "High Train to Tibet," *San Francisco Chronicle*, travel section, November 5, 2006.

China's leading glaciologist, Yao Tangdong, warned that an "ecological catastrophe" was looming in Tibet because of global warming, based on the results of several surveys performed by U.S. and Chinese scientists over a forty-month period. Tibet's glaciers receded even more rapidly in the early 1990s. Yu Zhong, "Qinghai Tibet Glaciers Shrinking," *China Daily*, October 5, 2004.

Glaciologists at the Beijing Climate Center said in July 2007 that the Himalayas are experiencing global warming faster than any other place on earth. Robert Collier, "Warming of Glaciers Threatens Millions in China," *San Francisco Chronicle*, August 1, 2007, A8.

p. 35 *I had interviewed a nun* Interview with Ani Jampa Choezom, July 1994, translated by her niece, Ani Thubten "Tsen-la" Dekyong. Jampa Choezom, born 1924, was a member of NiChungri Nunnery in Lhasa.

p. 39 *the* rinpoche, *and another lama* I have omitted the name of the *rinpoche* at the family's request.

p. 41 *These I knew were* thamzig The Panchen Lama described them in the letter to Zhou Enlai in 1962. See *thamzig* in the glossary.

p. 42 *newly minted silver coins* Since Chinese currency was not valid in Tibet at the time, the Communists brought in large quantities of newly minted "silver dollars." They used these to pay the high wages of Tibetans on roadwork and work crews, to bribe government officials, and to cover their own food and lodging costs. Their use led to severe inflation. Jampa Panglung, "Question 17: On the Cause of the 1959 Uprising," in *Authenticating Tibet: Answers to China's 100 Questions*, ed. Anne-Marie Blondeau and Katia Buffetrille (Berkeley: University of California Press, 2008), 75.

p. 48 *people prayed to be reborn as men* Many Tibetan women from Tibet (especially pre-1950 Tibet) told me they believe that men have a better rebirth and pray to be reborn as men. In recent years, however, modern Tibetan Buddhist teachers in the West have been trying to downplay this belief, knowing that many Western practitioners are women, and strive to emphasize the genderless nature of enlightenment, that women are equally capable of becoming enlightened.

p. 51 *All Tibetan historians . . . were male* These were my thoughts in 1991 and refers to historians and writers whose work was widely available in the popular literature at that time. In the nearly twenty years that have passed, this has changed and women have emerged as Tibetan historians in academia.

p. 53 *railroad official had told a Hong Kong newspaper reporter* Chief operations director of the railroad speaking to the *Hong Kong Standard*. John Flinn, "High Train to Tibet," *San Francisco Chronicle*, travel section, November 5, 2006.

p. 53 *death toll averaged one worker per half mile* According to the Pakistani government, which issued a commemorative stamp of the Karakorum Highway, 892 people died building the road, mostly in landslides and falls. www.pakpost.gov.pk/philately/stamps2003/karakoram_highway.html.

In June 2006, China and Pakistan signed a memo of understanding to expand the width of the highway from thirty-three to a hundred feet, in order to triple transport capacity and allow heavier vehicles to use the thoroughfare. Some construe this as part of China's campaign to expand its military influence into the Pacific region.

p. 59 *People in the crowd yelled, "If anyone helps the Chinese . . ."* Right before I did this interview in 1994, I was able to read the first publications I'd ever seen on the Women's Uprising: "The Women's Struggle for the Freedom of Tibet," a pamphlet published by the Tibetan Women's Association, Dharamsala, 1994; and "The Tibetan Women's Uprising," by Philippa Russell and Sonam Lhamo Singeri, 51–60, published in *Chö Yang 5: The Voice of Tibetan Religion and Culture,*

p. 76 *BBC special on contemporary China* The documentary *China from the Inside* aired in January 2007 on PBS.

CHAPTER 3. LHASA

p. 88 *4,400 people arrived on the train every day* University of Colorado geography professor Emily T. Yeh, in her article "Tourism to Tibet: Context and Recent Trends," states that during the first month of operation, July 2006, a daily average of 4,400 people arrived via rail. The cost of a taxi ride went up by 50 percent, and the price of hotel rooms jumped by nearly 60 percent. She says the regional tourist bureau estimated the number of foreign tourists who visited Tibet in 2006 at 2.6 million people, almost double the number of the previous year and roughly equivalent to the entire population of the Tibet Autonomous Region (TAR). This compares to 1995, a year before tourism was declared a pillar industry, when 30,000 tourists visited the TAR. Yeh points out that China vigorously promotes tourism among its new middle class and offers Tibet as the primary exotic destination. Article available online at www.tibetjustice.org/trigyiphonya/num19.html (accessed January 7, 2008).

p. 90 *preserve eighth-century buildings in Bhutan* Lhakhang Karpo (Temple of the White Dove) in western Bhutan was undergoing restoration work in 2005. It was constructed in the eighth century.

p. 98 *the PSB, the Public Security Bureau* The Public Security Bureau administers criminal justice in the TAR. The Peoples' Armed Police, a paramilitary unit formed in 1983, is often used to quell disturbances through violent methods, especially around the Barkhor. There are also many plainclothes and undercover police. *Briefing Paper for Travelers to Tibet* (Dharamsala: Tibetan Centre for Human Rights and Democracy, 2003). Branches of Chinese security forces have been trained in the United States and Austria.

p. 98 *They had had experience with the Chinese before* Sonam Choedron's relatives were likely referring to the 1910 invasion of Tibet by the Chinese, in which several thousand Chinese troops fired on the Jokhang Temple and Potala Palace, seized the mint and national treasury, emptied the armory, looted monasteries, burned scriptures, and drove the thirteenth Dalai Lama to take refuge in India. Tsepon W. D. Shakabpa, *Tibet: A Political History* (New York: Potala Publications, 1984), 233–35.

p. 99 *Sonam remembered the 1959 Uprising* The Tibetans who took part in the uprising were unarmed, except for a few with small weapons. Tsering Shakya writes about the 1959 Uprising: "The streets were littered with corpses, some of which had been there for several days and been mauled by stray dogs." Between April and May, more than seven thousand Tibetans entered India seeking asylum. According to Chinese sources, four thousand people were arrested. Tsering Shakya, *Dragon in the Land of Snows* (New York: Penguin, 1999), 204, 207.

p. 99   *Mao's Great Leap Forward campaign*   Mao's collectivization campaign in 1959–62, intended to transform China overnight into a industrial giant, created harrowing social conditions for people throughout China and Tibet. Industrial and agricultural production dramatically declined, leading to a decrease in food production, a severe grain shortage, and a famine of proportions unprecedented in the twentieth century. The famine claimed twenty million lives between 1959 and 1962, half of them children. Jonathan Spence, *The Search for Modern China* (New York: W. W. Norton, 1990), 583. Western and Chinese writers have suggested that the total is closer to 40 or even 60 million, based on taking figures from the worst-hit areas and extrapolating them to the country as a whole. The PRC government officially acknowledged a death-toll of only 20 million (Hu Yaobang in 1980). Philip Short, *Mao: A Life* (New York: Henry Holt, 1999), 505.

p. 101   *she couldn't cry or show emotion*   Similarly, families with loved ones who were killed by government soldiers in Tiananmen Square in July 1989 are forbidden to mourn them in public. Pankaj Mishra, "Tiananmen's Wake," *New Yorker*, June 30, 2008, 74.

p. 113   *Three months in jail, minimum*   I heard later that one Lhasa resident accused of talking with a Western journalist was given a ten-year jail sentence.

p. 123   *Living well is the best revenge*   Economic development is the central thrust of China's current policies in Tibet, but it comes at the expense of local Tibetans, who rank among the world's poorest people, and with no regard for Tibetan culture or the fragile environment. Some believe that the CCP's narrow, Marxist, economically determinist view (i.e., that once economic deprivation is cured, ethnic nationalism will dissipate) is one of the reasons Beijing's policies have continued to fail in Tibet.

p. 127   *Nearly eight thousand monasteries demolished*   The Tibetan government-in-exile asserts that before the destructions of the 1959 invasion and the Cultural Revolution, there were eight thousand monasteries in all of Tibet. The International Campaign for Tibet quotes Chinese sources: in the TAR (central Tibet only) there were more than 2,463 monasteries in 1959, and 553 were active in 1966. International Campaign for Tibet, *Forbidden Freedoms* (Washington, D.C.: International Campaign for Tibet, 1990), 33. By 1976, only ten were still standing. Anne-Marie Blondeau, "Question 49: On the Destruction of Religion in Tibet," in *Authenticating Tibet: Answers to China's 100 Questions*, ed. Anne-Marie Blondeau and Katia

Buffetrille (Berkeley: University of California Press, 2008), 166. The Communist leadership viewed monasteries and monks as its main obstacles to Tibetan society's embrace of Communism. Thus it aimed to eradicate their influence. Blondeau also writes, "The Chinese [authors] dismiss the irreparable damage, not only to religious life, but to the Tibetan cultural heritage with which it was so closely associated: temples and monasteries were destroyed with all their contents—not only murals, paintings, statues, and religious objects but also libraries and xylographic print-ing blocks. According to an estimate of the Dalai Lama's government in exile, 80 percent of the Tibetan cultural heritage has vanished" (163).

Another Chinese source states that in 1958, in the TAR only, there were 2,711 monasteries and 114,000 monks and nuns. In 1960, this number had dropped to 370 monasteries and temples and 18,104 clerics. Zhang Yianlu, *Population Change in Tibet* (Beijing: Tibetan Studies Publishing House of China, 1989), 28.

p. 130   *coercing monastery members to denounce the Dalai Lama*   Campaigns to denounce the Dalai Lama have been part of CCP policy for years. Starting in 1994 at the Third Tibet Work Conference, when Beijing charted a new ideological course in Tibet, the Party has made the elimination of his influence part of its policy. This has included banning his photo, teachings, and books; denunciations; and aggres-sive promotion of "patriotic reeducation" programs in the monasteries. Tsering Shakya, *Dragon in the Land of Snows* (New York: Penguin, 1999), 440.

p. 133   *lowest population density in Asia*   One person per square kilometer (or roughly 1.5 persons per square mile) Albert Herrmann, *An Historical Atlas of China* (Chicago: Aldine Publishing, 1966), 56–57.

p. 142   *hysterical blindness*   Hysterical blindness is a psychological condition where emotional trauma causes a blockage of visual impulses from the eyes to the brain, resulting in functional blindness. The condition has been reported in sig-nificant rates among survivors of the Vietnam war, where clusters of Vietnamese women suddenly began to go blind, and of the World War II Holocaust. Cambodian women in Long Beach, California, are known as the largest group of hysterically blind people in the world, numbering over 150, and have been studied by medi-cal and psychological researchers. The women all had a trauma history which was extreme, witnessing horrendous events but also themselves experiencing beat-ings, starvation, forced labor, humiliations, separation from families, and rape for five to nearly twelve years under the Pol Pot regime. The condition would typically occur after they witnessed an event that their minds could not accept. (One woman watched her husband and three children taken away, never to return. She reported that she cried daily for four years, then she stopped crying and could no longer see. Another saw her four children and husband murdered in front of her, then lost her vision). The women also show signs of depression and post-traumatic stress disorder. The researchers found few men with the affliction. Alexandria Smith, "Cambodian Witnesses to Horror Cannot See," New York Times, Sept. 8, 1989. Lee Siegel, "Cambodians' Vision Loss Linked to War Trauma," *Los Angeles Times*, October 15, 1989.

p. 142 *woman who lost seven of her eight children* Lady Borton, *After Sorrow: An American among the Vietnamese* (New York: Kodansha International, 1996), 17.

p. 144 *There are so many people in Lhasa now* According to the Tibetan government-in-exile, in the first month of the train's operation, more than 5,000 visitors arrived every day and 2,000 stayed. This created a housing and job shortage and spikes in prices. The Chinese government claimed that 450,000 people took the train in the first two and a half months. www.tibet.net.

p. 145 *wages three times higher than in China* Salaries of Chinese who come to Tibet in what is called "spontaneous migration," that is, Chinese and Hui traders and service workers, are distinct from those of public sector or government workers. The former are small-business people, shoe menders, restaurateurs, tailors, sex workers, and even beggars, who come from other parts of China to Tibet to ply their trade. Specific monetary incentives are not necessarily offered these workers, although that is commonly perceived among local Tibetans. Instead, they are lured by the lucrative conditions in Tibet generated by the large government subsidies to the region since the mid 1990s, especially since the beginning of the PRC's Western Development Drive in 2000. A carpenter in Qinghai, for instance made wages of fifteen yuan a day, but could earn fifty yuan a day working on construction of the railroad. In this cash bonanza, Chinese migrants easily outcompeted Tibetans because of their higher skills, knowledge of Chinese language, more competitive attitudes, and better connections to sources of economic and political power.

In the group known as "staff and workers" in China, or public employees, the number of *Tibetan* workers was considerably reduced during this same time period from 2000 to 2002, at the exact time that wages for these positions were boosted. In Tibet in 2002, for instance, "staff and workers" received the highest wages in the entire PRC—higher even than in Shanghai or Beijing. This was followed the next year, 2003, by a re-expansion in state employment, even while the number of Tibetans in public employment was further cut.

The Tibetan losses and the Chinese gains have marginalized Tibetans from key sectors of dynamic economic growth, i.e., government administration and large-scale construction projects, such as the railroad.

"High TAR Wages Benefit the Privileged," *Tibet Information Network,* February 10, 2005, http://www.phayul.com/news/article.aspx?id=9033&t=1&c=1, accessed March 23, 2009. With additional information from Andrew M. Fischer (Institute of Social Sciences, The Hague, Netherlands), email correspondence with the author, March 23, 2009.

p. 152   *Mrs. Taring's book,* Daughter of Tibet   The edition mentioned is from Wisdom Publications, London (1986), and is no longer in print. The first edition of *Daughter of Tibet* was published by John Murray Publishers, London, in 1970.

p. 177   *We lose Tibet from the outside*   Wang Lixiong, a Chinese expert on Tibet, said something eerily similar: "The most important change the train will bring about is in Tibetan self-perceptions. Back during the Cultural Revolution the Red Guards smashed everything, but they left Tibetans' hearts unchanged. But now Tibetans' attitudes are being changed by . . . modernization and globalization." Pankaj Mishra, "The Train to Tibet," *New Yorker,* April 16, 2007, 96.

CHAPTER 5. DHARAMSALA

p. 211   *the Internet was blocked*   The main focus of Internet censorship is what's referred to as "the Three T's": Taiwan, Tiananmen, and Tibet.

p. 212   *polluted by 41.9 million tons of industrial chemical waste*   The Chinese government's 1996 TAR environmental report states that 41.9 million tons of liquid waste had been discharged into the Kyichu River in Lhasa. Office of Information and International Relations of the Tibetan Government-in-Exile; also available at www.tibet.net/en/diir/enviro.

p. 212   *famed Kongpo forest*   According to the Tibetan government-in-exile's Environment and Development Office, indiscriminate logging in eastern Tibet from 1960 to 1990 caused large-scale environmental destruction. Tibet's forests covered 25.2 million hectares. They were located mostly on steep, isolated slopes in southeastern Tibet's river valleys. Besides tropical montane and subtropical montane coniferous forest, Tibet had evergreen spruce, fir, pine larch, cypress, bamboo, rhododendron, birch, and oak trees. Tibet's forests were primarily old growth; U-Tsang's old growth areas reached 1,000 cubic yards per acre (average is 120), the world's highest stock density for conifers. www.tibet.net/en/diir/enviro.

p. 212 *China had earned billions . . . from mining* Tibet holds a significant share of the world's reserves of gold, chromite, copper, borax, iron, oil, and natural gas. Its output of chromite, for instance, makes up 80 percent of China's total.

Beijing's Tenth Five Year Plan for the TAR lists mining as one of the key industries. Beijing offers preferential policies, such as tax exemptions, to foreign investors in order to entice them into investing in mining in Tibet. China's Eleventh Five Year Plan for the TAR outlines further exploitation of Tibet's resources, including oil and natural gas on a large scale. A vast oil deposit in Qiangtan, a remote part of northern Tibet, may hold as much as one hundred million tons of oil, according to the official Xinhua news agency. Meng Xianlai, director of China's Geological Survey, revealed that sixteen major new deposits of copper, lead, zinc, iron, and crude oil have been found along the railroad line, worth an estimated $128 billion.

Months after the railroad began operation, the government-run portal China Tibet Information Center published official announcements that the monumental discoveries had been made during a secret, seven-year, $44 million geological survey project, involving more than one thousand researchers across the Qinghai-Tibet Plateau, which began in 1999 and preceded railroad construction. The reserves are expected to yield forty million tons of copper (one-third of China's total), forty million tons of lead and zinc, and more than one billion tons of high-grade iron, shifting China's three-decades-long dependency on foreign imports of copper and iron altogether. The railroad plays a major role in facilitating the exploitation of these resources by providing a means for shipping them out of Tibet. Fresh sets of satellite images from Google show a large increase in road construction branching off the new railroad route. Abraham Lustgarten, "China Mines Tibet's Rich Resources," *Fortune Magazine*, February 21, 2007.

The gold mine Tashi had mentioned was the Shethongmon gold and copper reserves, 150 miles southwest of Lhasa, a project of Continental Minerals Corporation of Canada. Operation is scheduled to begin in 2010, when the railroad extension from Lhasa to Shigatse is completed, allowing for large-scale extraction. The Western Development Program gives little priority to investment in local agriculture and livestock even though the majority of China's western populations, especially the ethnic, non-Chinese populations who experience the most acute poverty, fall into these two sectors. www.tibet.net/en/diir/enviro.

p. 224 *scattered all over the world like ants*   The progressive thirteenth Dalai Lama predicted: "When the iron bird flies and horses run on wheels, Tibetans will be scattered all over the world like ants." Based on past experience with the Communists in Outer Mongolia in 1905 and the Chinese invasion of Tibet in 1910, the thirteenth Dalai Lama warned prophetically in his last testament in 1932 of the threat that Chinese Communists posed for Tibet. Glenn Mullin, *Fourteen Dalai Lamas: Sacred Legacy of Reincarnations* (Santa Fe, N.M.: Clear Light Publishers, 2001), 506.

p. 231 *fourteen Tibetans whom the Chinese had recently arrested*   As I heard it, the background on the arrests was that Chinese authorities had ordered Tibetans to stop wearing fur for some time, but their orders were ignored. Then the Dalai Lama called for an end to the killing of endangered species whose fur was used to trim *chubas*, and the Tibetans immediately complied. In March 2006, thousands of Tibetans publicly burned animal furs. During Losar a year later, in March, some Tibetans turned on other Tibetans who were wearing fur accessories in the Barkhor. I was told that the next day, Chinese security forces set up some people wearing fur to deliberately provoke the Tibetans and arrested fourteen people.

p. 233 *the aunt who had saved the robes*   The Dalai Lama wrote that he had left Lhasa so quickly in the near panic after PLA troops started shelling his residence that "all I could take was one or two changes of lama robes." *Autobiography of His Holiness the Dalai Lama of Tibet* (London: Panther Book, 1964), 177.

p. 237 *In Hurricane Katrina, 75–80 percent of the survivors were women*   "Women Worse Hit by Katrina," *File: York's Daily Bulletin*, York in the Media, September 16, 2005. The article quotes Joni Deager, dean of York University's Faculty of Environmental Studies, in her article "Natural Disasters Expose Gender Divides," in the *Chicago Tribune*, Women in the News, September 14, 2005. www.yorku.ca/yfile/archive/index.asp? Article=5099.

According to the International Committee of the Red Cross report "Women and War," based on two years of research, between 1998 and 1999, approximately 80 percent of war victims are women and children. In World War I, casualties were limited largely to soldiers on battlefields; by World War II, nations had learned to fight deep in enemy territory in order to disrupt war industries and factories. In our modern age, civilian casualties are high because "military conflict now commonly engulfs towns and cities." Lubna Jerar Naqvi, "Rape Earns Dubious Distinction as a Weapon of War," *Japan Times*, June 25, 2005, http://search.japantimes.co.jp/member/member.html?fl20050625a1.html.

p. 237   *Of the approximately seventy thousand who fled Tibet for India*   Donald Lopez, *Prisoners of Shangrila* (Chicago: University of Chicago Press, 1999), 151.

Author's phone conversation with Tenzin Tethong, Palo Alto, California, October 5, 2005. Tethong is a former representative of the Dalai Lama in Washington, D.C., a visiting scholar at Stanford University, and former chair of the Tibetan Cabinet. He stated that in the period 1959–60, those who escaped from central Tibet to India were "almost all men," because only men were government officials and monks.

p. 238   *disproportionate number of women seen plowing*   Jamyang Norbu, "The Tibetan Resistance Movement and the Role of the CIA," *Resistance and Reform*, ed. Robert Barnett (Bloomington: Indiana University Press, 1994), 189.

EPILOGUE

p. 244   *203 Tibetans were shot dead*   Robert Barnett, "Thunder from Tibet," *New York Review of Books*, May 29, 2008.

p. 244   *Tibetan Communist Party chief Zhang Qingli was quoted*   "Harmony Retort to Games Rebuke," *Hong Kong Standard*, June 27, 2008.

p. 244   *Beijing suspended all foreign tourism in Tibet*   "Lack of Tourists Takes Toll in Riot-bruised Lhasa," *Hong Kong Standard*, June 23, 2008. www.tangula-luxurytrains.com. Tourism resumed later that summer, but the total in 2008 was 2.25 million tourists, off 44 percent from the previous year. The record 4 million tourists in 2007 was a 60 percent increase from 2006. "Tibet Tourism Warms As Spring Comes," Embassy of the PRC in the United States of America, February 13, 2009, www.china-embassy.org/eng/xw/t537083.htm.

GLOSSARY

Amala. Mother

Amdo. The northeastern region of Tibet, bordering on China. It has now been mostly incorporated into the Chinese provinces of Qinghai and Gansu. Amdo was semi-independent from the central government in Lhasa.

ani or **anila.** A nun

Barkhor. The holy pilgrim circuit encompassing the Jokhang Temple in the center of Lhasa. Also the site of political protests. Literally, "the Middle Circuit."

bodhicitta. Altruism, a good heart, loving kindness. Also the aspiration to achieve buddhahood for the benefit of all sentient beings.

bodhisattva. A being who, having developed the awakened mind, devotes her life to the well-being of all living creatures. Embodiment of compassion and insight.

Bonpo. A follower of the Bon religion, the animist pre-Buddhist religion of Tibet

CCP. Chinese Communist Party

chang. Traditional alcoholic beverage, a beer made from the fermentation of barley or other grains

Chamdo. Capital of Kham, eastern Tibet

Changtang. Literally, "Northern Plain." A vast, frozen, windblown expanse in north central Tibet traditionally inhabited only by nomads. Averaging 16,400 feet in elevation, with sparse vegetation and low precipitation, it is the world's largest and highest plateau and one of the least populated parts of the Tibetan Plateau. Also **Jhang thang**

choe. Honorific term for the invitation to eat or drink

Chon Joog. Classic text popularly known as *Guide to the Bodhisattva's Way of Life*, by the eighth-century Buddhist master Shantideva

chorten. Buddhist monument, similar to a stupa. Often conical or bell-shaped.

chuba. Traditional dress, worn in various forms by both men and women. Traditionally made of wool or sheepskin and worn cinched up and tied at the waist with a belt, forming a pouch in front of the chest in which one carries personal possessions.

Chushi Gangruk. Tibetan resistance forces in Kham. Literally, "Four Rivers and Six Ranges," the ancient term for eastern Tibet.

dharma. Buddhist religion, truth, Buddhist teachings

Dalai Lama. Spiritual and temporal leader of Tibet. Believed by the Tibetans to be the reincarnation of each of the previous Dalai Lamas, who are considered to be manifestations of Avalokiteshvara, or Chenrezig, Bodhisattva of Compassion. The current, fourteenth Dalai Lama is Tenzin Gyatso, born 1935.

Dharamsala. Seat of the Tibetan government-in-exile and residence of the Dalai Lama in the foothills of the Indian Himalayas, since 1960. Home to thousands of Tibetan refugees, schools, monasteries, and cultural centers.

Gansu. Chinese province containing eastern portions of Tibet

Geshe. Title awarded to a person who has completed the highest degree of religious training in the Gelugpa sect of Tibetan Buddhism, broadly comparable to a Doctor of Divinity degree.

Hui. Chinese Muslims

inji. A foreigner, usually Caucasian

Jokhang Temple. The most sacred temple in Tibet, located in the Tibetan quarter or Old City of Lhasa. In Tibetan, Tsuglakhang.

Kashag. The chief executive council of the Tibetan government, composed of four ministers, or *kalons*.

khata or **kata.** A long, white, ceremonial scarf used to greet a person upon arrival or upon departure, or to show friendship or respect. Made of fine muslin, cotton, or, for special occasions, silk, it is draped around the receiver's neck.

Khache. A term used generally for a Muslim. Khaches, originally from Kashmir, are one of the two long-standing communities of Tibetans Muslims, the other being the Horpaling, of Chinese origin. Islam in Tibet dates to the eighteenth century. In recent years, "Khache" refers to a Chinese Muslim from Xinjiang.

Kham. Eastern province of Tibet

kora. The circumambulation (clockwise) of a religious site

Kyichu River. Also called the Lhasa River where it runs through Lhasa. A tributary of the Yarlong Tsangpo, its name in Tibetan means "River of Happiness." Nestled in a belt of glades and woodlands in the capital, it was a popular picnic site in pre-1950 Tibet.

la. Honorific tag added to the end of a name or word. For example, Amala for Mother, *anila* for a nun.

lama. A spiritual master or Buddhist teacher, not necessarily a monk

lingkor. The traditional outer pilgrimage circuit around the holy city of Lhasa. It runs around the Potala Palace, along the banks of the Kyichu River, past the bridge to Thieves Island, to the now destroyed medical college, Chagpo Ri.

Losar. Tibetan New Year, around February or March. Considered the most important and happiest of the Tibetan holidays, with celebrations that lasted a month in traditional times.

mala. A string of 108 beads used by Tibetan Buddhists for counting prayers and mantras

mantra. A short sacred phrase repeated continuously, bringing protection and helping to center the mind

mola. Grandmother

Monlam. The Great Prayer Festival for world peace, the greatest religious festival in Tibet. Traditionally, this three-week festival in Lhasa, held at the Jokhang Temple shortly after New Year, saw about twenty-five thousand monks praying for the well-being of the state, the Buddhist religion, the people, and all sentient beings.

mu (Chinese). A unit of measure of land area, approximately an acre

pala. Father

Panchen Lama. The second-most important figure in Tibet after the Dalai Lama, traditionally based in Shigatse at Tashilungpo Monastery. The modern-day Panchen Lama was held by the Chinese for decades and then died mysteriously in 1989. His reincarnation is considered the youngest political prisoner in the world and has been kept by the Chinese government at an unknown location since 1995, when he was six years old.

PAP. People's Armed Police, a paramilitary unit formed in 1983

pola or **bola.** Grandfather

Potala Palace. The Dalai Lama's winter palace on a hill west of Lhasa, built by the fifth Dalai Lama. It contains more than a thousand rooms and the tombs of previous Dalai Lamas.

prostration. A series of purification sequences in which a person, with hands in prayer position, stretches out fully on the ground after touching the hands to forehead, lips, and heart (symbolically, mind, speech, and body). The sequence is repeated either in place or while moving forward a distance equal to the length of the body. Also a gesture of reverence, performed, for example, to greet an esteemed person.

PSB. Public Security Bureau

rinpoche. A title of respect for lamas who are recognized as reincarnations of previous adepts. Literally, "precious one."

sang. A traditional purification ritual of burning juniper, performed daily on the roof terrace of homes, usually early in the morning. Also performed at temples and other sacred places. The fragrant juniper smoke is considered an offering to the gods.

Sera. One of the three great, capital-based monasteries in Tibet, formerly residence of five thousand to seven thousand monks, located north of Lhasa

Seven-Limb Path. A practice to purify oneself and to accumulate positive potential—consisting of prayer, visualization, confession, prostration, and other practices

sky burial. A method of disposing of the dead in central Tibet. Due to the scarcity of wood for cremation and the frozen ground, which prevents burial, corpses are taken to a designated overlook where they are cut up and offered to the vultures.

stupa. A Buddhist monument containing sacred objects, such as texts and bone fragment of great masters. Constructed of five parts: a square base symbolizing earth; a dome shape representing water, upon which sits a triangular tongue representing fire; a smaller crescent moon representing air; and then a spherical pinnacle on top for the sun.

TAR. Tibet Autonomous Region. The area designated as Tibet by China and officially made an autonomous region in 1965. The TAR is roughly half the area of cultural Tibet. The other parts of Tibet are contained in four other Chinese provinces: Yunnan, Sichuan, Qinghai, and Gansu.

TCV. Tibetan Children's Village. A residential school for Tibetan children in Dharamsala, established in 1961, now with branches throughout India, providing preschool through high school education.

thamzig. Known as "struggle sessions," the Chinese Communist Party's violent and abusive political denunciation meetings pitting the "masses" or "peasants" against enemies of the state, those associated with religion, landholding, or political dissent. People in the target sectors were forced to submit to these sessions, often daily, for years.

thangka. A religious scroll made of silk or cotton and finely painted with sacred images, often Buddhist deities. Used for meditative and devotional purposes.

tsampa. Roasted barley flour, a traditional staple of the Tibetan diet. Commonly served as a porridge or formed into soft balls and eaten with yogurt, cheese, dried meat, and the like.

tsepon. A minister in the tax/finance office of the Tibetan government before 1959

tulku. Reincarnated lama

U Tsang. Traditional Tibetan name for central Tibet

Zhou Enlai (1898–1976). Foreign minister of the People's Republic of China (1949–58), premier (1949–76). Prevented the Red Guards from attacking the Potala Palace.

ACKNOWLEDGMENTS

I AM INDEBTED to the Tibetan women who allowed me to interview them for this project, and especially those who appear in this book: Sonam Choedron, Choekyi Namseling, the late Rinchen Dolma Taring, and the late Mrs. Paljorkhyimsar. I owe much to the many Tibetans in Tibet, whom I must decline to name, whose lives inspire me and whose enduring friendship and generosity of spirit have enriched my life.

I thank those in Dharamsala who aided me in my work, most notably my dear and longtime friend Ani Lobsang Dachen, for her calm demeanor and perfect reliability, and, for translation help, Sonam Morad, Nyaljor Samten, Tenzin Chunzom, and Tsepal Yuthok.

I want to acknowledge Tenzin Wangmo Dhongshar of Geneva, for many years of faith and assistance, and the family members of my interviewees, Dolkar Phuntsog Gyltag and N. J. in Switzerland, Yangchen Tregung in Seattle, and Tsering Chokteng in Denver.

Thanks go to my fiscal sponsors, Kearny Street Workshop (especially Ellen Oh) and Tibet Justice Center (formerly International Committee of Lawyers for Tibet), and to the organizations and individuals who funded this project: Sister Fund of New York (especially Helen Hunt, who made an exception to support the project in its early stages); the San Francisco Art Commission, for an Individual Arts Grant in Literature; Madeline Houston; Sharon Bacon; the San Francisco Foundation; Phyllis and Dean Addison; and especially Nancy Kittle and the Nu Lambda Fund.

My deep appreciation goes to the artists' residency programs that gave me time and shelter: the Djerassi Resident Artists Program, the Mesa Writers Refuge, and most of all, the grand Virginia Center for the Creative Arts and all its wonderful staff, who offered invaluable weeks of residence at a crucial point in the drafting of the manuscript.

Friends Gayle Alexander and Wanda Swenson, Patricia Yenawine, Margo Cooper, and Jill Lippit opened up their homes in rural northern California to offer me writing time.

For editorial help, I am grateful to Catherine Knepper, Shoshana Alexander, Nicole Harwood, and Martha Tod Dudman, and for transcription help to Pema Dachen. Kate Reber offered incomparable coaching at many levels and much personal generosity. I thank Sharlynn Mar for her ever patient technology support through the years, and, also in the IT realm, Bob Hsiang. I owe heartfelt appreciation to my dear friend Jeanne Hauser for her skillful eye and photographic expertise in patiently helping prepare the photographs and for her unflagging encouragement and enthusiasm throughout the long process of bringing this book to real form. Abby Zimberg also cheerfully helped with the photo preparation.

Many people gave stalwart support to this project in its early stages, in the 1990s, but I especially want to acknowledge Mona Oikawa, Peggy Bennington, Elise Ficarra, Emily Jarosz, Marilyn McKenna, Kathryn Mudie, Eddie Waller, Mushim Ikeda Nash, Sheridan Adams and Jeff Kitzes, Margery Farrer, Bhuchung Tsering, Mary Felstiner, and, in Dharamsala, Cassandra Purdy, Pema Yeshi, Sandy Benson, Christabelle Baranay, Yangchen Lakar, and Sherab Gyatso at Tibetan Children's Village.

For faith and support in the early years of this project, I thank Barbara Collier, Bob Gee, Edward and Josephine Sam, Carol Liu, Edward and Marjorie Dodge, Daniel Cumings, and Marc Lieberman.

The following people gave generously of their expertise or offered logistical support: Caroline Pincus, Philippa Russell, Jeremy Russell, Dorsh de Voe, Cathy Cockrell, Brad Bunin, William Wong, Alice Y. Hom, Lucy Bledsoe, Calvin Roberts, Melinda Mazzetti, and, most especially, the ever wise Judy Yung. I want to acknowledge Katie Boyle for her effort related to an early version of this book, Anna Ghosh for her gift of counsel, and the brilliant Jane Wattenberg for pitching me the concept for *Sky Train*.

Also my gratitude to the following people: for scouring this manuscript with academic scrutiny and prompt assistance with historical details, Elliot Sperling; for gracious help with Tibetan-language issues, Karma Thinley Ngodup of the University of California, Berkeley, and with the Chinese language, See See Lo; for coming to my photographic rescue in Dharamsala, Tashi Norbu and Shannon Thompson; for a lifeline when I most needed it, Judy Rubin and Annie Lamott; for spiritual support on the road, Marjorie Hilsenrad and Tony Lambe; for her companionship on the path of both the art and the business of producing one's first book and for always setting the bar high, Minal Hajratwala; and for their sustained support, Winnie Chu, Shizue Seigel, Minko Nishimura, Wendy Etsuko Siu, Tomi Arai, Virginia Bowen, Amanda Kim, and especially Gwyn Kirk, who never ceased to offer her friendship and experienced guidance to me at every stage of the writing and production.

I would not have lasted all these years without help from Nancy Hom on so many levels, from funding to editing to networking. Thanks to my support group, for their unshakeable faith in this project and for showing up: Louisa Stone, Joanne Connelly, Lisa Korwin, Kip Walsh, Melinda Stone, and Marta Friedman.

I will always be indebted to my closest colleague in the budding Tibet support movement in the late 1980s, the peerless Doc O'Connor.

I thank Lorri Hagman at the University of Washington Press, who immediately grasped the uniqueness of this book and pursued its publication, and Laura Iwasaki, Marilyn Trueblood, Rachael Levay, Alice Herbig, and the rest of the staff at the University of Washington Press, as well as at Silkworm Books, for lending their talent, resources, and ardent support to bringing this book into being.

My gratitude to my root teachers, Venerable Thich Nhat Hanh and His Holiness Tenzin Gyatso, and to all my dharma teachers for their gifts to me and to the development of a peaceful human culture in the world today. May they thrive in happiness and security.

For her complete faith and for always going the distance, my thanks to Lucy Estella Lim, whose help on so many levels was indispensable. And everlasting appreciation to my mother and late father for everything else.

Dedicated to the memory and the legacy of
Mrs. Rinchen Dolma Taring

And to the memory of my grandparents,
Quai Seen and Horn Yuen Jing

Photo by Jeanne Hauser

CANYON SAM is a writer, performance artist, and activist from San Francisco. She has published articles, plays, and stories in *Shambhala Sun, Seattle Review,* and *San Jose Mercury News,* for Agence France Presse, and in numerous feminist and Buddhist anthologies. Ms. Sam is also the writer/performer of nationally acclaimed solo theater pieces that explore contemporary issues through the lens of Buddhist practice. *The Dissident,* her show about doing human rights work with a Buddhist nun in Tibet, which toured the United States and Canada, prompted *The Village Voice* to call her "a master storyteller . . . whose work is universally relevant."

In 1986, in her late twenties, Ms. Sam, a third-generation Chinese American, left the United States to live in China for a year but instead became drawn to Tibet—where she traveled and lived—and eventually to Dharamsala, India, the Tibetan capital-in-exile. She was a grassroots activist for Tibetan independence in the mid-1980s through early 1990s and funded the Tibetan Nuns Project in its first years through slide shows of images from her year away. In 1989, at the request of Congressman Tom Lantos, she addressed a congressional subcommittee hearing on Tiananmen Square, linking the event with human rights abuses in Tibet.

Ms. Sam earned a Master of Fine Arts degree in creative writing from San Francisco State University and has taught at colleges and universities throughout the Bay Area. A DVD of *The Dissident* is available for purchase at www.canyonsam.com.